Scouse: A Social and Cultural

Scouse

A Social and Cultural History

Tony Crowley

Liverpool University Press

First published 2012 by
Liverpool University Press
4 Cambridge Street
Liverpool
L69 7ZU

British Library Cataloguing-in-Publication data
A British Library CIP record is available

ISBN 978-1-84631-839-9 cased
        978-1-84631-840-5 limp

Typeset in Minion by R. J. Footring Ltd, Derby
Printed and bound by CPI Group (UK) Ltd, Croydon CR0 4YY

For
Emily
Joseph and Louise

Contents

Acknowledgements

I would like to express my gratitude to a number of institutions, particularly their librarians and archivists, for their generosity, professionalism and commitment to scholarship. First and foremost, I need to thank the wonderfully helpful and informative staff at the Liverpool Record Office, together with those at the Bodleian Library, the British Library and the Huntington Library. I also wish to recognize the material support provided over the past six years or so by the Dean's Office at Scripps College (under Deans Michael Lamkin, Cecilia Conrad and Amy Marcus-Newhall), and I would like to express general thanks to my colleagues at Scripps. In addition I wish to thank the staff at Liverpool University Press, in particular Anthony Cond, Jenny Howard and Helen Tookey, and my readers, Professor John Belchem and Professor Michael O'Neill, for their comments and criticism. I also acknowledge Carcanet Press for their permission to reproduce an excerpt from Donald Davie's 'Winter's Talents', from his *Collected Poems*.

My personal debts are numerous and deep. I am grateful for the influence and support of many friends and colleagues: Judith Aissen, Nancy Bekavac, Frank and Joan Boyce, Deborah Cameron (who probably forgets that she told me to write this book a very long time ago), Jane and David Chin-Davidson, James Clifford, Chris Connery, Frank and Denny Cottrell Boyce, Sam Cronke, David Denison, Frank Downes, Terry Eagleton, Sue Forber, Rachael Gilmour, Paul Hamilton, Roy Harris, Gail Hershatter, the late and much missed Richard Hogg, Hao Huang, Rachel Vetter Huang, Cándida Jáquez, John Joseph, John Kerrigan, Steve and Kirsten Koblik, Grace Laurencin, Ronald Macaulay, Andrew McNeillie, Deborah Mulhearn, Rachel Mulhearn, Tom and Susan Mulhearn, Bernard and Heather O'Donoghue, Mark Ord, Tom Paulin, John Peacock, Angela Poingdestre, Bruce Robbins, Rita Roberts, Cathy Rosario, Mary Scott, Dion Scott-Kakures, Alan Shelston, Helen Small, Stephen Sheedy, Liane Tanguay, Tolly Taylor, Frances Timlin, Nigel Vincent, Cheryl Walker, Sheila Walker, Nicole Weickgenannt, Bernard and Mary Weston, Zhu Xiaomei and Paul Young. Needless to say, I have relied once again on the support of my family: Jacky, Terry, Colette, Nicky and the nephews and nieces – Jack,

Ellie, Rory, Erin, Roisín, Tom, Matt and Helen – as well as Teddy and Ann Crowley (Teddy for his Dingle recollections and Ann for her accomplished work in genealogy), Bob Fyldes (to whom I'm grateful for information on Garston), and Geneviève and Michael Cuming (for their unstinting kindness and hospitality). Finally, and most important of all, I am delighted to be able to say thank you to the ever-present non-Scousers in my life: to Emily (best friend as well as best reader) and the kids, Joseph and Louise. I am grateful to the three of them – for everything, of course, but particularly for their inspiration, for the happiness they bring and for their love. Though they aren't Liverpudlians, I hope Joe and Louise enjoy reading (well, after they have learned to read) about the city in which their dad grew up and to which he remains attached.

Liverpool: language, culture and history

> If we can truthfully say of a man that he has a Scotch accent, or a Liverpool accent, or a Welsh accent, or a London accent, or a Gloucestershire accent, then he does not speak 'good English' with perfect purity. (Henry Wyld, *The Growth of English*, 1907)[1]

In *Heathcliff and the Great Hunger: Studies in Irish Culture*, Terry Eagleton makes an interesting observation on the figure of Heathcliff in Emily Brontë's *Wuthering Heights*. He begins by recalling that Brontë started her novel in 1848 a few months after her brother Branwell had visited Liverpool, and that the city at that time would have had a large number of Irish immigrants (as a consequence of the Great Famine).[2] Eagleton goes on to remind us that Heathcliff, who is picked up starving and homeless from the Liverpool streets by Mr Earnshaw, is described as a 'dirty, ragged, black-haired child', 'as good as dumb', who, when he does speak, utters only 'some gibberish that nobody could understand' (Brontë 1995: 35). Eagleton's conclusion from this collection of historico-literary facts is that Heathcliff, the quayside waif, is Irish. In fact he suggests a variety of potential identities: 'Heathcliff may be a gypsy, or (like Bertha Mason in *Jane Eyre*) a Creole, or any kind of alien.' But his judgement, which is central to his argument, is that Heathcliff is the archetypal figure of the 'beast, savage, lunatic and demon' best known to the English as an Irishman (Eagleton 1995: 3). This is an interesting and typically provocative claim, and one that fits Eagleton's reading well. It is also, of course, nonsense. For Heathcliff, a dirty little lad wandering about the Liverpool docks talking a language/dialect that no one could understand (or at least that no Yorkshireman could understand), is clearly not Irish. He is in fact the embodiment of that charming and repellant, funny and violent, sentimental and ruthless figure known as the Scouser. Or at least he might have been if there had been any such term as 'Scouser' in the early to mid nineteenth century, or if there had been any such linguistic form as 'Scouse' at the time. But unfortunately for the Heathcliff as Scouser thesis, this book will demonstrate that neither of the categories of 'Scouser' nor 'Scouse' existed at that period; they were later developments (much later in the case of 'Scouse').[3]

The central aim of this work is to consider the question of language in Liverpool from a historical and theoretical perspective. The project began not with a desire to restore Heathcliff to his proper status as Liverpool street urchin (*Wuthering Heights* as a sort of *Her Benny* gone wrong), but with a sense of surprise and piqued intellectual curiosity as a result of two observations on language in Liverpool that I came across.[4] One was articulated by Gladys Mary Coles, editor of *Both Sides of the River: Merseyside in Poetry and Prose* (the 'Bible' of Liverpool literature as it has been called). Commenting on Alun Owen's *No Trams to Lime Street* (1959), an early television drama, she noted that it was 'significant in the author's use of the Liverpool accent and idiom, which he had to defend at the time and which can now be seen as a milestone in the growth of Merseyside's sense of identity' (Coles 1993: xii). This seemed innocuous enough, although it raised a series of questions about representations of language in Liverpool. For example, if Owen's text, written at the end of the 1950s, was a milestone, particularly in terms of its use of 'accent and idiom', then how had the language of Liverpool been represented previously? Why was Owen's work 'significant' and why (and against what) had he been forced to defend it? And what exactly was the link between this form of language and the 'sense of identity' with which it was associated, and when had that connection been established? Once I had started to research these issues, over and against an established and popular version of the history of language in Liverpool (one with which I had become familiar as I grew up in the city), I increasingly had a nagging sense that there was something not quite right, that there were other questions that needed to be addressed, that something was missing. This feeling was exacerbated as a result of conversations with people from Liverpool (some with older members of my own family), and by reading in the history of the place. It culminated when I came across an almost throwaway comment in John Belchem's important essay, '"An accent exceedingly rare": Scouse and the inflexion of class', in his *Merseypride: Essays in Liverpool Exceptionalism*. Referring to historians Tony Lane and Jim Dillon, Belchem reported that 'some oral historians attest that many working-class Liverpudlians failed to exhibit any "scouse" characteristics (Irish or otherwise) in their speech until well into the twentieth century' (Belchem 2000b: 44). This claim seemed surprising: there were working-class Liverpudlians who didn't speak Scouse? There were 'many' working-class Liverpudlians who started speaking Scouse only well into the twentieth century? Needless to say, my interest was stimulated and I looked for a reference to underpin what was being claimed, but intriguingly, and frustratingly, there was no evidence to support the assertion – just the allusion to Lane and Dillon. At which point my professional training began to kick in. What if...? Well, what if the popular and indeed the received histories of language in Liverpool were not right? More to the point, what were these histories exactly and on what basis were they constructed? What evidence was there in relation to the use of language in the city, what was its nature, and how far back did it go? And again, when people referred to language in Liverpool, what were they alluding to: an accent, a dialect, a 'variety', a language per se? And so the project started, though, as will become clear, it expanded to take in other issues as well – not least the purported relationship between language and cultural identity in representations of Liverpool made not only by people from elsewhere, but by the inhabitants of the place itself.

To return to that wannabe Liverpudlian Heathcliff for a moment, it is import-ant to note that although there were no Scousers in the 1840s, there were 'Dicky Sams'. And if he had spent any time in the Liverpool workhouse, Heathcliff might well have eaten the dish called Scouse, since the first use of the term that I discovered (one that pre-dates the *Oxford English Dictionary* citation by forty-odd years) is found in a report on scran (food) in the Liverpool poorhouse in 1797. Heathcliff as a Dicky Sam then? But since when were Scousers known as Dicky Sams? Since the early nineteenth century is the answer: Dicky Sam was one of the names that has been used for the inhabitants of the city over the past couple of centuries. But why did the Dicky Sam become the 'Whacker', and later the Scouser? And at a more basic level, why did the 'Liverpolitan' become the 'Liverpudlian'? Such questions might be taken as mere curiosities, local philological tittle-tattle in effect. But one of the arguments of this book will be that such questions are significant because they open up a linguistic route into history, which in turn raises important issues related to the theoretical con-sideration of culture. This is not to claim that the study of words and phrases can provide direct access to an established and undisputable past; but it is to assert that it may facilitate insight into a contested history and into modes of cultural understanding. The emergence and disappearance of linguistic forms, the ways in which they change over time, their semantic transfer, expansion and narrowing, all indicate the shifting patterns of demarcation, evaluation and contestation that take place in the formation of a culture in history. For language does not simply reflect history in some passive sense, as though it were just an inert record of changes going on elsewhere; rather it has a crucial role in the shaping of history and it is central to the process of change and development. Thus another of the goals of this book will be to analyse how specific terms and phrases appeared, were used and developed over time, in order to gain an insight into the ways in which Liverpool has been represented and understood historically.

The book is divided into a number of chapters that are concerned with ques-tions of history and linguistic and cultural theory, and it ends with an account of how the project grew and developed in a life that began in the Dingle, just off Park Road, and continued a long way away in southern California. It is a journey that has taken in all sorts of exotic locations and contexts – a move to Allerton/Garston, education at St Edwards College (Liverpool's leading Catholic grammar school at the time) and then Oxford University, and academic posts in Southampton, Manchester and now Los Angeles. In all of these places, of course, my language, my voice, came with me, a constant reminder both of where I 'come from' and of the relationship between language use and patterns of cultural and social evaluation. In that respect, I have been professionally blessed in having been born in a place whose language – as I found in the course of this work – has been the subject of so much narration, confusion, inaccuracy, antipathy, pride, romanticizing and imagination. That wasn't the only benefit of 'being from' Liverpool, but it was, I came to realize, an important one. Not the least of its advantages was that it enabled me to understand that linguistic prejudice is not just an enduring phenomenon in Britain, it is also one of the last to be socially respectable. If there is any doubt about this point, consider the epigraph at the head of this introduction and compare it to Charles Nevin's account of the response of the contemporary 'metropolitan middle classes' to any mention of the Scouser: 'depending on articulacy, intelligence, the time of day and the ingestion of artificial stimulants, they will be off, flat out, in top sneer, on a tour de Scouse that will take in the dreadful accent, the awful tracksuits, how they all think they're so bloody funny and how you can call one in a tie the defendant, how they're always whinging and never working...' (Nevin 2006: 57). Plus ça change... and yet this is not to claim that prejudices against forms of speech (Liverpool speech in particular) are always and everywhere the same; if they were they wouldn't be so difficult to challenge. For in fact, as the book demonstrates, perceptions of Liverpool speech have varied historically, even though its representation as a sort of inferior sub-form has persisted in specific contexts over an extended period.

The story of language in Liverpool, then, is complex, and although this book focuses on the modern development of Scouse, its historical analysis begins almost two centuries before the first use of that term in its linguistic (as opposed to culinary) sense. Thus chapter one of this study considers what early observers of Liverpool made of its rapid economic, social and cultural development in the eighteenth and early nineteenth centuries. Given space and other constraints, the aim here is not to present the historical details of Liverpool's growth from a small town on the Mersey to a major port of international importance, but rather to see what commentators ranging from Daniel Defoe to the first historians proper of Liverpool made of the cultural consequences of its change in status. Chapter two then moves from general analysis to a consideration of one aspect of the cultural transformation of Liverpool: the appearance of a form of language that became identified with the town. As the argument demonstrates, this is a development that is usually understood to have taken place after the large-scale influx of Irish immigrants provoked by the Irish Famine. Yet this point, which constitutes the foundation of the received version of Liverpool's linguistic history, is challenged in this chapter in two ways. First, this touchstone of the standard account is deconstructed through an examination of its dubious origins in popular journalism and its later (equally questionable) development in modern linguistic theorizing. And second, evidence is considered that suggests that a distinctive form of Liverpool speech existed before 1830 (the date that the dominant account cites – on the basis of a mis-reading – as marking the last known point at which Liverpool speech and South Lancashire speech were one and the same). Having disputed the received history and provided an alternative, the argument turns to the beginnings of the process by which the language and culture of Liverpool came to be seen as distinctive. Chapter three then focuses on the first signs of self-reflexivity about Liverpool as a site of linguistic and cultural practice, ranging from the earliest use of the phrase 'Liverpudlian English' in 1891, to popular concern with words taken to be 'unique' to the city (often mistakenly), and through to the investigation of 'the half-secret tongue' of Liverpool in the early 1950s that marks in effect the beginning of an interest in Scouse (a term that, in this sense, dates from this period). Extending this analysis, chapter four considers the appearance and consolidation of Scouse as a linguistic term by focusing on the role played by Frank Shaw and others in a relatively small group of culturally motivated men (there were few if any women involved) in the construction of the 'Scouse industry'. And yet despite the fact that the Scouse industry undoubtedly flourished, its success was based in part on a productive confusion about the nature of Scouse itself. Chapter five considers this issue from two perspectives, historical and theoretical. First, the account demonstrates how both the language of Liverpool (pre-Scouse) and Scouse itself have been classified in any number of different ways. And second, the argument considers how the problematic categorization of Scouse itself reveals difficulties with dominant modes of thinking about language and languages. The chapter then proposes, using theoretical tools taken from recent work in linguistic anthropology, a different way of conceptualizing Scouse altogether, one that avoids linguistic essentialism by concentrating instead on its status as the central component of a specific mode of cultural identity that often stands metonymically for the city of Liverpool and its inhabitants. This theme is taken up in the final chapter of the main body of the text, in which the analysis takes the form of a somewhat personal account of the research journey that is recorded, at least in part, in this book. In this chapter, then, I attempt to question the reductive equation of Scouse with Liverpool by addressing the differences (spatial, historical, cultural and linguistic) within the city. I do this not to reject the category of 'Scouse', nor its correlative 'Scouser' (though I do draw attention to some of the ways in which both have been used to denigrate the people of Liverpool), but to try to highlight the proper complexity of the history that underpins not just the use of these terms, but any significant understanding of the city itself.

The appendix to the main argument is a historic-linguistic study of a number of terms: 'Liverpool', 'Liverpolitan', 'Liverpudlian', 'Dicky Sam', 'Whacker', 'Scouse' and 'Scouser' (in other words, the name of the city and the names that have been used to refer to its inhabitants over the past couple of centuries). While I contend that the research that supports the investigation of these terms is original and illuminating, it is nonetheless important to note that this chapter does not deliver the 'truth' of these words, in the sense of an account that explains definitively their origin and development. Rather, what it demonstrates is the way in which these terms have been the source of inquiry and narration for a long time (for more than four hundred years in the case of 'Liverpool'). As a matter of fact, the beginnings of many of these terms are obscure, and their history – in terms of transfer and extension of meaning – is often unclear. But perhaps that isn't the point. It may be that the most significant thing about these words is precisely that they have been made the subject of story-telling, since the telling of stories about a particular subject bespeaks a certain confidence in it. An emphasis on confidence and stories – what better way could there be to start (and end) a book on the language of Liverpool.

Notes

1   Henry Wyld, *The Growth of English* (1907), 48.
2   For an account of the impact of Irish immigration on Liverpool in this period see Frank Neal, *Black '47: Britain and the Famine Irish* (Neal 1998: chs. 4, 5).
3   As will become clear, the argument of this book is that 'Scouse', in the sense of a form of language, is a relatively recent term and category. For this reason I use inverted commas in the first instances of its use (and indeed the correlative term and concept, the 'Scouser') to draw attention to its historically constructed status. However, both for ease of reading, and because the term is well-established in contemporary usage, I do not continue to use the inverted commas except in specific cases.
4   Silas Hocking's *Her Benny* (1879) is the moralistic rags-to-riches tale of Benny, a Liverpool street kid who survives various forms of abuse and ignominy to emerge as a wealthy Christian gentleman.

The sea, slavery and strangers: observations on the making of early modern Liverpool and its culture

To which is Liverpool most indebted for its present commercial importance, the salt trade, the African trade or the admission of strangers? (Title of one of Thomas Banner's Great Room Debates, late eighteenth century)[1]

The aim of this chapter will be to lay the groundwork for the analysis of various aspects of language in Liverpool that will be the central concern of this book. To do this, it will be helpful to begin by outlining how early observers made sense of the enormous economic, social and cultural changes that took place in Liverpool in the eighteenth and early nineteenth centuries. Needless to say, the intention is not to render an exhaustive account of the history itself (an impossibility given the space constraints), but to present a sketch of responses to the alterations brought about by the development of the town as a major site of national and global trade and commerce.[2] Of course certain aspects of Liverpool's history are familiar; even the most rudimentary account will draw attention to the town's role in the slave trade and its function as one of the most important centres of immigration and emigration. Less well-known, however, are the ways in which contemporary historians and commentators interpreted and evaluated the results of the change in the town's long-standing status from relatively minor backwater (except in times of war) to its role as a international port that trafficked the oceans.[3] Thus the focus in this first chapter will be on the critical narratives produced by early commentators on the emergence of modern Liverpool. Of particular interest in these first historical accounts is the apparent sense of the town as not just an economic force within the Atlantic and indeed world systems of commerce, but as a location that was both typical and distinctive in relation to the political and cultural effects that the developments of mercantile capitalism and industrialization brought about. For in many respects Liverpool was a place like many others in Britain at this time: it was subject to the consequences of changes in patterns of capital accumulation and distribution, technological developments and their uses, and demographic shifts of an extent previously unknown. Like a number of British towns, Liverpool in the 1830s would have been unrecognizable to a person growing up in the late seventeenth and early eighteenth centuries. And yet Liverpool was also in many ways a place apart in relation to political and cultural developments. Politically the specific nature of the local history produced major difficulties and tensions as the different groups of monied interest battled for control over this rapidly emerging international citadel. Yet culturally too it is clear that Liverpool was unusual in several aspects of its development (a fact that has led John Belchem to argue the case for 'Liverpool exceptionalism').[4] This odd feature of Liverpool's history – its typicality in some respects and yet the anomalous nature of the place in others – is an important element in understanding how Liverpool's culture (including its language) has been framed. But before moving to consider that topic, it is necessary to turn first to a brief account of the ways in which the making of modern Liverpool was recorded.

The emergence of Liverpool: the early commentators

In his *Tour Through the Whole Island of Great Britain* (1724–26), the novelist Daniel Defoe, an early eighteenth-century observer of Liverpool, described the town as 'one of the wonders of Britain', noted its expansion and potential by declaring 'what it may grow to in time, I know not', and took account of its threat to the status of the major port of Bristol on the basis of its 'increasing every way in wealth and shipping'. Specifying the importance of 'the trade to Virginia, and the English island colonies in America', he also noted that Liverpool merchants 'send ships to Norway, to Hamburg, and to the Baltick, as also to Holland and Flanders', as well as engaging in 'a great inland trade, and a great correspondence with Ireland and with Scotland' (Defoe 2005: 541). As Defoe remarked, the town's advantage in terms of domestic trade depended on its geographic location; it was well situated for commerce with the east and north coasts of Ireland, North Wales, the 'northern inland counties of England' and, by means of water navigation, with places 'quite through the kingdom'. Significantly, his report articulated clearly the emerging role of Liverpool as a locus of both international *and* national trade. It was this combination that drew his laudatory assessment that the traders of Liverpool 'are almost become like the Londoners, universal merchants' (Defoe 2005: 541).

Defoe's observations were in many respects remarkably accurate and prescient. By the early eighteenth century, Liverpool had already started to capitalize on the opportunities for trade in tobacco and sugar with the West Indies and North America (the town's merchants had first imported these commodities in the mid seventeenth century). But unlike its main provincial rivals (Bristol and Whitehaven), Liverpool had the distinct advantage of the local availability of desirable raw materials; Cheshire salt and Lancashire coal were the central components of its coastal trade with the rest of Britain and Ireland and underpinned its commerce with northern Europe. In addition, its proximity to the textile manufacturing base of Manchester and its environs, together with the pottery makers of the north Midlands, gave further impetus to the expansion of the town and to its eventual emergence as the second port of the Empire. Key enterprises that established the infrastructure necessary to sustain such status included the ambitious and financially speculative construction of the dock system (beginning with the completion of the world's first commercial wet dock in 1715), and a number of schemes to improve the navigability of rivers or to open canals (from the Mersey and Irwell Act of 1720 to the opening of the first section of the Leeds–Liverpool canal to Wigan in 1774). Yet if Defoe's account managed to identify many of the factors that contributed to Liverpool's eighteenth-century growth, it was silent on one crucial element in the process: slavery. Defoe had nothing to say on the subject for the simple reason that it hardly featured at the time of composition of the *Tour*. For although Liverpool Corporation had joined other British ports in challenging the monopolistic practices of the Royal African Company in 1709, the town's involvement in the slave trade became economically significant only after parliamentary de-regulation in the 1730s led to the effective decline of that company in the 1740s and the passing of the African Trade Act of 1750 (Picton 1875: I, 193; Longmore 2006: 132). Yet once they had gained a foothold in a business described in James Picton's detailed *Memorials of Liverpool* (1875) as 'a traffic in human flesh and blood', based on a 'perversion of the instincts of humanity' that 'polluted our own country by its hateful presence' (Picton 1875: I, 194–95), Liverpool traders proved themselves second to none in the pursuit of profit. Between 1741 and 1810 Liverpool ships transported 979,647 slaves, and in the period 1750–1807, 'African coastal merchants sold two of every three enslaved Africans loaded directly on British slavers to Liverpool master mariners' (Morgan 2007: 25; Behrendt 2007: 86). It is hardly surprising then, given the enormity of the trade, the wealth it stole and produced and its global effects, that the complex political and cultural legacy of slavery has dominated the narrative of Liverpool's rise, even if this has often been at the expense of an acknowledgement of other significant factors.

Forty years or so after Defoe's work, Samuel Derrick's *Letters Written From Leverpoole, Chester, Corke, The Lake of Killarney, Tunbridge-Wells, and Bath* (1767) gave a more expansive view of mid-century Liverpool. Derrick, Master of the Ceremonies at Bath, minor acquaintance of Johnson and Boswell, and author of the best-selling *Harris's List of Covent-Garden Ladies* (a directory of London prostitutes), made a number of observations on the 'very opulent town' after a visit en route to Ireland in 1760. In the style of the travel literature of the period, the description began with topography: 'Leverpoole stands upon the decline of a hill, about six miles from the sea. It is washed by a broad stream called the Mersee, where ships lying at anchor are quite exposed to the sudden squalls of wind, that often sweep the surface from the flat Cheshire shore on the west, or the highlands of Lancashire that overlook the town on the east' (Derrick 1767: 9). But the more interesting aspects of his commentary were social and historical. Observing that the three docks, which 'have been built with vast labour and expence', are 'flanked with broad commodious quays surrounded by handsome brick houses inhabited for the most part by sea-faring people', he noted that the town 'is populous, though inferior in this respect to Bristol', consisting of a population of 'near forty thousand', a figure that had increased by 25 per cent over the previous fifteen years (Derrick 1767: 10–11, 16). The pace of the transformation clearly caught Derrick's attention:

> Although the lively aspect which Commerce has lately assumed here, in every quarter, bespeaks vigour, and inspires chearfulness; yet, a hundred years ago, there belonged to this place only one pitiful dock, seventy-two rated seamen, and eight vessels, none of them above twenty tons burthen. The change for the better has been amazingly rapid. They now rival the great mart of Bristol, and have, it is confidently said, for two years last past, paid more duty to the crown: they even carry on a greater trade with the coast of Guinea and the West–India islands than London itself. (Derrick 1767: 14)

As Derrick remarked, by the 1760s Liverpool's burgeoning prosperity was in part built on the triangular trade that was to make it what an early nine-teenth-century commentator was to call 'the metropolis of slavery' (Morgan 2007: 15):

> The principal exports of Leverpoole are all kinds of woollen and worsted goods, with other manufactures of Manchester and Yorkshire; Sheffield and Birmingham wares, &c. These they barter, on the coast of Guinea, for slaves, gold-dust, and elephants teeth. The slaves they dispose of at Jamaica, Barbadoes, and the other West-India islands, for rum and sugars, for which they are sure of a quick sale at home. (Derrick 1767: 15–16)

The disposable bodies of Africans constituted one of the foundations on which Liverpool's economic expansion was constructed. Yet if they (along with cloth and sugar) were the means by which mercantile Liverpool flourished, Derrick maintained that its wealth-production was also based in part on an-other form of human resource:

> This great increase of commerce is owing to the spirit and indefatigable industry of the inhabitants, the majority of whom are either native Irish, or of Irish des-cent: a fresh proof, my lord, that Hibernians thrive best when transplanted. They engage in trade as in battle, with little or no spirit at home, but with unparalleled gallantry abroad. (Derrick 1767: 14)

The claim that the majority of Liverpool's inhabitants at this point were either Irish or of Irish descent is dubious, even though there were long-standing connections with Ireland that stretched back to the use of the town as a port of embarkation for the Anglo-Norman Conquest. Nonetheless, the Irish were evidently among those who flocked to Liverpool in search of work and opportunity in the eighteenth century (Derrick himself was an Irish exile). And it may have been the complex mix of people produced by the influx of workers, traders and investors that created the particular cultural characteristics that Derrick ascribed to the townspeople, or at least those of the mercantile class:

> Though few of the merchants have had more education than befits a count-ing-house, they are genteel in their address. They are hospitable, nay friendly, to strangers, even those of whom they have the least knowledge: their tables are

plenteously furnished, and their viands well served up: their rum is excellent […]
But they pique themselves greatly upon their ale, of which almost every house
brews a sufficiency for its own use. (Derrick 1767: 15)

The richness of the hospitality (as well as its national and international flavour)
is revealed by the quality of the ale served by Mr Mears, a merchant-trader with
Portugal, who bought his malt in Derby, his hops in Kent and had his water
brought express from Lisbon (Derrick 1767: 15).

Derrick's account of Liverpool is interesting in that it catches the town at
a transitional moment between the early eighteenth-century development of
the port and the late eighteenth- and early nineteenth-century expansion of
the town as a major centre of imperial trade and commerce. In fact many of
Derrick's observations had been anticipated by Defoe, but there are two aspects
of the descriptions of these commentators that are worthy of note. The first is
the depiction of the town as already, by the early to mid eighteenth century,
an important site of both national and international commerce. The second
is the relatively limited comment on the impact of this economic activity on
the cultural texture of Liverpool life. This is not to say that it is not possible to
trace the development of a distinctive civic culture in Liverpool, since it is clear
that 'a combination of ebullient commercial confidence, humanitarianism and
wealth' produced a number of political, institutional and architectural legacies
(Longmore 2006: 154). But beneath the level of official culture, the tracing of
the emerging practices and patterns of daily life is a more complex issue, a fact
demonstrated by Liverpool's treatment in the developing field of English historiography. The anonymous but influential *Geography and History of England*
(1765), for example, described 'Leverpoole (vulgarly *Lirpole*)' as 'a convincing
instance of what trade ought to be in the eye of every *Englishman*' but it lacked
descriptive detail as far as the inhabitants were concerned, contenting itself
with the claims that there were three times as many as there used to be and
that they showed their gratitude to the 'family of *More* of *Blackhall*' (Anon 1765:
84).[5] The pattern was repeated even in the first texts that took Liverpool itself as
their focus (accounts written for a variety of purposes, and for different audiences, by people who carefully distinguished themselves as either natives of the
place or outsiders).[6] Thus despite the fact that William Enfield's *Essay Towards
the History of Leverpool* (1773) attacked antiquarianism in favour of 'modern
history', and ridiculed the outdatedness of the representation of Liverpool
given in the 1765 *Geography* (not to mention the seventh edition of Defoe's *Tour*
printed in 1769), the author managed to say remarkably little about the culture
of the people who inhabited 'a place which has lately emerged from obscurity'
(Enfield 1773: 8). Instead the *Essay* addressed itself primarily to the history
and progress of the town in a narrative consisting mainly of a presentation of
natural, institutional and statistical facts in support of a number of significant
conclusions. One of the most important of these was the observation that,
given the birth and death rates in Liverpool and the 'perpetual demand' for
sailors, the explanation for the rapid increase in the population figures over
the century could only lie in 'a continual influx of strangers' (Enfield 1773: 28).

Commerce and culture(s) in late eighteenth- and early nineteenth-century Liverpool

Two texts that did manifest a concern with the cultural aspects of Liverpool life in the late eighteenth century, though they differed in their judgements, were William Moss's *Familiar Medical Survey of Liverpool* (1784) and James Wallace's *General and Descriptive History of the Ancient and Present State of the Town of Liverpool* (1795). Moss, a local medic, was principally interested in addressing the charge that Liverpool was an unhealthy place marked by insanitary living conditions, and a large part of his work is devoted to issues such as topography, pollution, sewers and drainage, housing, employment, brewing and alcohol consumption, disease and the relative healthiness of the townspeople.[7] Noting that 'the annals of English history do not furnish a circumstance similar to that of the rapid progress which the town has made in extent and importance', Moss hailed the social and cultural effects of 'COMMERCE' on Liverpool. Thus confessing not to know whether the docks conveyed 'more of the sublime or the beautiful', he outlined the way trade had created a population that had international concerns and affections:

> There is not, perhaps, a place within the confines of the globe, where scenes, so interesting to human nature, are more frequently exhibited, than on the arrival of ships from our connections and possessions abroad; as scarcely a vessel can arrive from those parts, in which a majority of the inhabitants are not nearly interested, or immediately affected; some, by ties of nature; some, by friendship; and others by interest – all remotely. (Moss 1784: 11)

From a cultural perspective, one interesting aspect of Moss's text is his account of the 'urbanity' (in the emerging eighteenth-century sense of 'civility and manners') of 'the third and upper order of *Merchants* and *Principal Inhabitants*' of Liverpool. His claim was that their lack of social pretension, an effect of 'general commercial intercourse', meant that 'distinctions are much levelled' and that members of the middle and upper class shared in 'that happy medium which separates an untutored familiarity from the extreme of ceremony, wherein good sense is rarely offended by the rude freedoms of unrestrained vulgarity, or insulted by the grimace of modern refined manners' (Moss 1784: 61). What Moss was describing may well have been the negotiation at the level of social comportment of the economic changes that were taking place in the relations between the bearers of the older and newer forms of wealth.[8] Be that as it may, in comments whose gist was repeated in his *Liverpool Guide* (1796), Moss's Liverpool was an 'invariably cheerful, lively and animated' place, which wore 'a perpetual air of satisfaction, freedom and complacency' as a mark of its distinctive 'social intercourse, unclouded by those affectations of precedence among equals in general endowments, so prevalent in all smaller and less employed and attached societies' (Moss 1784: 61–62). In short, Liverpool was an ideal, egalitarian sort of place; big, busy and properly at ease with its bourgeois self (an interesting self-representation given the dominance of slavery in Liverpool's affairs). And yet of course not all of the inhabitants conformed to the terms of this idyllic state. The failure of the authorities to be as assiduous in encouraging virtue as in 'discovering the resources, and securing the revenues, of the kingdom' had brought about 'the profligacy of manners, so distinguishable in the inferior orders of the age; who, from the errors of education, are uninformed of, and less governed and restrained by, those laws of decorum which regulate and direct their superiors in knowledge and information of the world and its social refinements' (Moss 1784: 60). Significantly, Moss was one of the first to hint at the appearance of an urban working-class culture in Liverpool, though he also articulated the social anxieties that accompanied this new phenomenon.

The dominant encomiastic tone of Moss's accounts was not replicated in Wallace's *General and Descriptive History of the Ancient and Present State of the Town of Liverpool* (1795). Describing himself as 'neither a native nor regular inhabitant of the town', Wallace stressed his aim of impartiality and criticized previous histories on the grounds that they were 'written with a view to please' and 'replete with eulogy and partial panegyric', with the result that 'the manners and customs of the inhabitants, and real constitutional state, is seldom truly represented' (Wallace 1795: 2). Indeed the difficulty of establishing a factual rather than speculative account of Liverpool life was exemplified in Wallace's exasperation with the means by which death was treated in the town, since that caused problems for the accurate calculation of population figures. Wallace's point was that the method used by parish clerks failed to make a distinction between 'stranger or inhabitant' in the death records, with evident consequences for the ascertainment of the number of 'settled inhabitants' of the place. Significantly, his reporting of this issue gave an important insight into the shifting nature of the populace, since although the problem was common to all cities and towns, Liverpool's maritime character brought specific difficulties. For an improving Scot such as Wallace, such inconveniences added to his evident sense of annoyance at the hyperbolic praise that had been heaped upon Liverpool, an attitude that led him to scorn its recent and rapid rise in fortune (taken by others to be a sign of its eminence) and to frame that process as 'the precipitate start of an obscure town, from the vale of necessity to the brow of national commerce' (Wallace 1795: 279–80). Noting that 'there is perhaps no town in England that has so small pretensions to historic description [...] or that has attracted the pen of less writers, ancient and modern' (Wallace 1795: 4), he evinced scepticism towards the benefits of business success per se, and notably failed to confirm Moss's observation of an emergent bourgeois public sphere in Liverpool. In Wallace's view, 'the only pursuit of the inhabitants is COMMERCE', with the result that 'Liverpool is the only town in England of any pre-eminence that has not one single erection or endowment, for the advancement of science, the cultivation of the arts, or promotion of useful knowledge' (Wallace 1795: 283). For the people of Liverpool, he added contemptuously, 'the liberal arts are a species of merchandize in which few of the inhabitants are desirous to deal, unless for exportation' (Wallace 1795: 284). Somewhat begrudgingly, Wallace declared himself impressed by a town which had 'arisen like another Venice from the waters':

> We are animated by a view of her numerous ships, the capaciousness of her docks, the avidity of her traders, the solicitude of her people, and the busy face of traffic, which in one continued rotation, appears on all her wharfs and quays; we see the capacious cornucopia constantly yielding its successful tribute, while the industrious labourers in the vineyard are constantly employed in its repletion. (Wallace 1795: 284)

But 'the important question' that all of this activity raised, and one that Wallace used to end the narrative part of his history, was 'whether a vigilant pursuit of commerce, or an unwearied application to the promotion of the arts, is most conducive to the happiness and welfare of a people, and to the honour and renown of a kingdom?' (Wallace 1795: 284–85).

If the scale of achievement of Liverpool's economic success led Wallace to pose a general – if rhetorical – aesthetic and political question to the prevailing social order (one that tapped into wider debates in late eighteenth-century England), his response to the effects of the development of the town at another level of cultural practice was more explicit. Noting the general orderliness of the town, he nonetheless drew a distinction between the activities of different elements of the population. Sunday best behaviour, for example, was analysed in terms of class and gender divisions:

> Order and dominical propriety, seems limited to the streets and residences of the principal inhabitants only! It is no unusual thing to see a great number of girls, and many of the inferior inhabitants of the town, assembled in the evenings at various diversions, in the narrow streets and outlets of the town, to the great annoyance of such of the inhabitants as are disposed to a peaceable and quiet residence, even the squares are not exempt from this nuisance, where it is common to see boys and girls playing at ball, and other diversions, every Sunday afternoon. (Wallace 1795: 272)

Despite this, Wallace's conclusion was that Liverpool's problem with disorder was minimal (disturbances to the Sabbath excepted), and that this was a remarkable fact given 'the number of people which must be supposed to be constantly fluctuating in a seaport town' (Wallace 1795: 275). Such social propriety may have been produced by the tight grip on public order exercised by the puritanical magistracy, a fact that might also have brought about the decline of a set of cultural practices that had been maintained until the very recent past (though Wallace considered that the cause may simply have been 'the improving hand of time'). Bear-baiting, bull-baiting and the sacrifice of cocks on Shrove Tuesday had fallen into disuse, though there was one cultural tradition, or 'ridiculous ceremony', that had endured. On Easter Monday groups of men tossed all the women they met in the air a number of times, 'without regard to distinction or order' (women did the same to men on Easter Tuesday). If later reports are accurate, 'Easter lifting' persisted in the late eighteenth century through to the early decades of the nineteenth (Wallace 1795: 278–79).[9]

Wallace's narrative was niggardly at best, but a more sympathetic account of Liverpool's rise, progress and contemporary status was rendered in Thomas Troughton's illustrated *History of Liverpool. From the Earliest Authenticated*

Period Down to the Present Time (1810). One interesting aspect of this commentary is the focus on the growth of the population and its causes. Thus, remarking that Liverpool 'must have experienced many fluctuations in its population, according to the failure or success of its different branches of commerce', Troughton identified the increase in population from 4,240 in 1700 to more than 12,000 in 1730 as a direct result of the inhabitants' 'improvements in manufactures, and the increase of their foreign commerce' (Troughton 1810: 78). And he attributed the expansion to 35,000 in 1770 to 'the advancement of its trade to Africa and the West Indies' (Troughton 1810: 82). In effect Troughton's attention to the material and political issues that affected demographic change is an indication of his perception of the importance of immigration to the growth and success of Liverpool. He noted, for example, the flight from Ireland of a substantial number of Irish Protestants in the 1640s as a consequence of the violence of the Great Rebellion and the Confederate Wars, and the effects of the arrival of another wave of immigrants after the 1798 Rebellion:

> In the summer of 1798, so great was the influx of persons of every description into this town from Ireland, that house rent and the price of lodgings were greatly advanced [...] Many respectable families, who came over to Liverpool, as a place of refuge from the horrors of rebellion and martial law, have settled here and contributed to the wealth and population of the place. At the same time it must be acknowledged, that many very immoral characters of the lower class have also emigrated from Ireland hither; but the vigilance of a well-regulated police will, doubtless, repress the operations of criminality in this town, whether native or foreign. (Troughton 1810: 198)

It was Wallace's charge of cultural backwardness, however, that particularly took Troughton's attention and his text can be read as an implicit response to the earlier account. He argued, for example, that as a consequence of its 'progressive prosperity', Liverpool 'ranks next to the Metropolis: but not merely so in political importance; it also has a claim to superiority over the other provincial towns in the cultivation of the fine arts' (Troughton 1810: vi). Even so, he did admit that there had been a lag between commercial success and the cultivation of high cultural pursuits in mid-eighteenth-century Liverpool. Describing the 'slow advances in civilisation' of the inhabitants, for example, he confirmed Wallace's judgement that their amusements evinced 'the vulgarity of the rustic', and agreed that they were 'ignorant and incurious respecting those elegants arts and scientific attainments' necessary for civilized life (Troughton 1810: 92). And, like Wallace, he mentioned the hugely popular activity of bull-baiting (on the occasion of the election of the mayor in October), as well as city dinners to mark the beginning of the Liverpool Fairs (in July and November), the celebration of the Derby Wakes (again featuring bull- and dog-fighting, with the bull brought back from West Derby to Liverpool 'in triumph' on the last day of the Wakes), and the annual Liverpool races, held on Crosby marsh. Yet despite sharing Wallace's apparent disdain for many of these traditional practices, some of which in all likelihood reflected the rural cultural predilections of members of the migrant labour force, Troughton insisted that the situation had changed by the end of the eighteenth century as a result of the town's commercial success and consequent opulence. His argument was somewhat undermined by the fact that, as he noted, several of the institutions that were inaugurated failed after a few years; he specified a circulating library in the 1760s, an art academy in the early 1780s, a literary debating society in 1796 (closed because of a controversy surrounding the admission of women), a literary society in 1803, and a society for the dissemination of religious and moral truth in the early nineteenth century. Nonetheless, other institutions found more success, including the establishment of a theatre (in Drury Lane in 1759, and then as the Theatre Royal in Williamson Square in 1772), the Athenaeum (1798), the Lyceum (1802), the Botanic Gardens (1802) and the Liverpool Royal Institution (1814), while the Infirmary, the Dispensary, the Blue Coat Hospital and School, the Blind Asylum and the Marine Society were all funded by charitable support.

Rather than a place barren of culture, then, Troughton's claim was that Liverpool's material prosperity had brought with it demonstrations of a 'taste for literature and the fine arts'. A poem written for the occasion of the opening of the Theatre Royal (the first play was a performance of the anti-Islamic *Mahomet the Impostor*, an English translation of the Voltaire piece *Le Fanatisme, ou Mahomet le Prophète*) reinforced the link between profit and patronage: 'Wherever commerce spreads her swelling sail, / Letters and arts attend the prosperous gale' (Troughton 1810: 148). Yet significantly, Troughton depicted the economic growth of Liverpool as somewhat double edged: 'commercial prosperity has, invariably, been attended with improvements in the polished arts of life, while it contributed to habits of dissipation' (Troughton 1810: 205). While claiming that capitalist success encouraged high cultural activity, he was also aware of the more wide-ranging effects of the new social order on the everyday activities of the emergent working class. Traditional pastimes such as bear-baiting and bull- and dog-fighting may have been grounded in the 'rusticity of the pastoral state', and 'young people of the lower class' may have played 'rustic games' on Minden's Green (Leeds Street) in the 1760s, but these had clearly been superseded by the new urban way of life with its attendant problems. Some difficulties were clearly related to the impact of a growing population and its needs; in 1768 the *Liverpool Chronice* reported the public health nuisance of the practice of emptying privies into the streets, while fines were imposed in order to stop draymen and carters ('that brutal, though necessary, part of the community') from riding in the main thoroughfares (Troughton 1810: 144). Other problems were evidently caused by 'the influx of poor families into this town' for work and their exploitation by the unscrupulous. Troughton mentions, by way of example, a scheme whereby landlords transferred responsibility for paying the taxes liable on their property to their poor tenants, a ploy that had the effect of further impoverishing the needy, decreasing the tax revenues, increasing the pressures on the magistracy and encouraging officers of local towns to give incentives to their own poor to move to Liverpool. When a mayoral remonstrance failed to halt this practice in 1769, the town raised £8,000 to build a 'commodious workhouse' (completed in 1771) to deal with the 'begging women, children, whores and thieves' who were 'filling our streets' and behaving as 'a disgusting and dangerous nuisance' (Troughton 1810: 145–47). The activities of the new immigrants (a word which in the eighteenth and nineteenth centuries referred to people from other areas of the country as well as non-nationals) were clearly a source of anxiety and Troughton observed that 'a disgusting vulgarity of manners prevailed among the lower class of society' in the 1770s. Boys and young men snatching nose-gays from respectable women revealed 'the tardy progress of civilization among the laborious class of this community', but there were more serious problems, as Troughton demonstrated with reference to a commentary on the social scene that had been published in 1773:

> There is nothing, perhaps, more alarming to the welfare of society, and to the preservation of the morals of youth, than that some regulation should be taken with those public nurseries of vice, the infamous brothels of this populous town, which are grown to such a height of refined wantonness unknown to any former period [...] Common prostitutes, parading the public streets, in all the fashionable elegancies of dress, or conveyed in carriages and chairs to the public amusements, is too sure a sign of corruption amongst us. (Troughton 1810: 153)

War with America and France also produced difficulties, at least indirectly, as evinced by Troughton's reflection on a report in 1778 (the year of the Treaty of Alliance between Britain's enemies) on the behaviour of the crews of privateers and vessels authorized by letters of marque: 'The manners of the common people, at this period, made a retrogression towards barbarism [...] This was the natural consequence of that spirit of enterprize cherished by the proprietors of privateers; for successful adventurers, upon their return to report, spent in excess what they had obtained with danger' (Troughton 1810: 168). Though this was hardly the last time in Liverpool's history that note was taken of the propensity of sailors to blow their money on drink and prostitution, Troughton's main point was that such behaviour served by way of a contrast between past and present. Following a Royal Proclamation in 1787, the Liverpool magistracy had taken steps to regulate 'excessive drinking, blasphemy, profane swearing and cursing, lewdness, profanation of the Lord's day, or other dissolute, immoral, or disorderly practice'. The measures included the curtailment of drinking hours, the forbidding of 'that pernicious practice of paying wages at public-houses, whereby the morals of the lower ranks of people are greatly depraved', and the organization of the police into four districts to cover the 'rapid increase in extent and population' of the town (Troughton 1810: 173–75). Again, however, Troughton's assertion that the power of 'the magistracy has been successfully exerted for the preservation of order and tranquility amongst all ranks of people', thus ensuring 'that refinement of manners, which has ever been considered the best proof of civilisation', was somewhat undermined by his account of the behaviour of 'the common people' during the 1790s.

> It was a common practice for witlings, in the public houses, to make some irritable individual the object of ridicule for the amusement of the rest of the company. Nocturnal riots were in the streets were not unfrequent. A number of

> hot-headed young men, who were distinguished by the appellation of bloods, were often engaged in those disgraceful frays [...] Another scandalous practice of these young men was, the circulation of hand-bills, in which young ladies were offered for sale. (Troughton 1810: 192)

As is clear from this and other comments, Troughton's report details the emergence of at least one mode of urban popular culture in Liverpool. Marked by laughter and violence, it was, like the civic culture in general, predominantly male (the street presence of prostitutes excepted), and manifested itself in the drinking houses and public spaces of the town.

Further commentary on the cultural specifics of Liverpool appeared in other works of the same period such as the anonymous *The Stranger in Liverpool; Or, An Historical and Descriptive View of the Town of Liverpool and Its Environs* (1812), a text that set out a curious contradiction. For the inhabitants of the town were described as possessing 'no characteristic particularly striking' in that they had 'but too largely participated in a national dereliction of morals'. And yet the work also reiterated Moss's no doubt exaggerated claims about the socially transformative effects of trade in Liverpool – 'as in all other places wholly commercial, the intercourse between the different ranks of society is free and open' – a contention that is again best read in terms of the shifting social and cultural negotiations between the 'pride and nobility' of the aristocracy and the 'supposed inferiority' of the emergent bourgeoisie. Not for the last time, there was mention of opposing tendencies at work in the formation of the culture of a town that was highly regarded, at least by some:

> Hospitality, social intercourse, civility to strangers, and that freedom from local prejudice which is produced by the residence of so great a proportion of strangers, may likewise be adduced as very favourable features in the general portrait; and though great refinement of manners should not generally be met with, they will have spent but a little time in the town [...] who do not discover what to every man of reflection is far more estimable, – very considerable remains of the frankness and warmth of the old English character. (Anon 1812: 43)

Liverpool, it was clear, was a fast-developing place in which elements of both cosmopolitanism and tradition combined to produce new and often disturbing cultural practices and patterns.

Conclusion

This chapter has attempted to show how a number of the first historians of eighteenth- and early nineteenth-century Liverpool made sense of the changes involved in its tremendously rapid transformation from backwater to global port. But the more specific aim has been to demonstrate the ways in which such observers noted and represented not simply the economic and political developments, but also the evolving forms of cultural activity that were beginning to appear in the town. No doubt many cultural practices built upon the residual forms used by the inhabitants of a small, isolated port on the Mersey.

Others must have combined traditional modes with the customs brought to the town by the 'strangers' whose influential presence is so marked in the early accounts. And others were surely engendered by the new social formations created by the operations of capital on a large scale as Liverpool became a focus of global exchange and movement (of people as well as things). The effects of such changes were evidently felt across the social order: from the behavioural relations between social classes, to the production of an identifiable civic culture; from the social investment in 'high' culture, to the appearance of new and, at least to some, worrying forms of culture identified with the urban working class. The net result was the emergence of a town of notable social and cultural complexity; it is with one, central, aspect of the culture of this singular place that the rest of this book will be concerned.

Notes

1   Title of one of Thomas Banner's Great Room Debates held at the Golden Fleece, Dale Street, in the late eighteenth century, cited in Longmore, 'Civic Liverpool: 1680-1800' (Longmore 2006: 143).
2   For older accounts of the development of eighteenth- and early nineteenth-century Liverpool, see Thomas Baines, *The History of the Commerce and Town of Liverpool and of the Rise of Manufacturing Industry in the Adjoining Counties* (1852); Sir James Picton, *Memorials of Liverpool. Historical and Topographical* (1875); Ramsay Muir and Edith Platt, *A History of Municipal Government in Liverpool From the Earliest Times to the Municipal Reform Act of 1835* (1906); and J. Touzeau, *The Rise and Progress of Liverpool from 1551 to 1835* (1910). The most interesting and persuasive recent studies are Jane Longmore, 'Civic Liverpool: 1680–1800', in *Liverpool 800. Culture, Character and History*, ed. John Belchem (2006); Sheryllynne Haggerty, *The British-Atlantic Trading Community, 1760–1810: Men, Women, and the Distribution of Goods* (2006); and Diana Ascott et al., *Liverpool 1660–1750: People, Prosperity and Power* (2006).
3   Liverpool's global traffic is indicated in Troughton's account of the number of ships entering (1,744) and clearing (1,839) the port in 1788. They included vessels bound for and returning from Africa (non-specific), British colonial possessions in North America, Denmark, Flanders, France, Germany, Greenland, Guernsey, Holland, Honduras, Ireland, the Isle of Man, Italy, Jersey, Norway, Poland, Portugal, Prussia, Russia, Spain, Sweden, Turkey, the United States and the West Indies (Troughton 1810: 262). Troughton's figures do not include vessels engaged in the extensive coastal trade within the British Isles.
4   See John Belchem, *Merseypride: Essays in Liverpool Exceptionalism* (2000).
5   The More family played a significant civic role in medieval and early modern Liverpool.
6   For a discussion of the emerging historiography of Liverpool in its wider context, see Rosemary Sweet, *The Writing of Urban Histories in Eighteenth Century England* (1997).
7   In *The Liverpool Guide* (1796), Moss presented figures that purported to show that in terms of 'proportionate annual mortality', Liverpool performed better than (in order) Vienna, Edinburgh, London, Amsterdam, Rome, Breslaw, Berlin, Manchester and Chester (Moss 1796: 112).
8   For a discussion of the way in which considerations of language were affected by

the shifting relations of class and gender in the eighteenth century, see John Barrell, *English Literature in History 1730–80: An Equal Wide Survey* (1983); Tony Crowley, *Language in History: Theories and Texts* (1996); Janet Sorensen, *The Grammar of Empire in Eighteenth Century British Writing* (2000); and Linda Mitchell, *Grammar Wars: Language as Cultural Battlefield in 17th and 18th Century England* (2001).

9   In his later history, Picton also referred to 'lifting': 'within living memory of many persons now living, it was impossible for a female to pass through any of the lower streets of Liverpool on Easter Monday without being laid hold of by a set of good-natured ruffians, who asked for "*backsheesh*," and if it was not granted, she was taken by the head and heels and heaved three times into the air. On Easter Tuesday, the females retaliated, and many a "grave and reverend signior" has had to run for it; to pay toll, or to be seized by a posse of stalwart women, who were not over particular in handling him' (Picton 1875: II, 302–03). This may be the origin of the 'lifting' that takes place at some weddings in Liverpool.

2

Language in Liverpool: the received history and an alternative thesis

The origins of our speech still await a Darwin. (Frank Shaw, 'The Origins of Liverpoolese', 1962)[1]

It was argued in the first chapter that as a result of its particular history, Liverpool emerged as a place influenced by not only national and international developments but by very specific local features. With this context in mind, the aim of this chapter is to start upon a consideration of one aspect of Liverpool's cultural past – its language. To begin with, this will take the form of an analysis of the dominant narrative of the history of language in Liverpool, a story, as will become clear later, that was constructed through various media – from the work of folklorists, journalists and practitioners of specific types of popular culture to the research of professional linguists. This is a necessary step towards understanding a phenomenon that is otherwise somewhat peculiar: the fact that in Britain and Ireland at least, Liverpool and Liverpudlians are most widely recognized by their association with a distinct form of spoken language.[2] Or as John Belchem puts it in '"An accent exceedingly rare": Scouse and the Inflexion of Class' (one of the few sustained historiographical accounts of the topic), the identity of Liverpudlians 'is constructed, indeed it is immediately established, by how they speak rather than what they say. Instantly recognizable, the accent is the essential medium for the projection and representation of the local micro-culture' (Belchem 2000b: 33). Of course this is not to claim that Liverpool and its inhabitants are not connected, often metonymically, with other cultural modes – comedy, football and popular music for example. But it is the link with language that predominates and it will be argued in this chapter that this connection is based on a particular understanding of Liverpool's linguistic history that needs to be challenged and revised. In order to do this it will be useful to start by examining a variety of issues from a number of historical, textual and theoretical perspectives. The material that will be considered ranges from eighteenth-century histories of Liverpool to the most accomplished recent historical accounts; from a slavery-based comedy of the 1760s to Dickens' representation of the language of dockside Liverpool; and from eighteenth-century dialect texts to contemporary linguistic theorizing. The analysis will commence with an outline of the received version of the history of language in Liverpool and a preliminary sketch of how this was produced, before moving to the postulation of an alternative thesis that proposes a more nuanced understanding of the history in question. This chapter then will form a necessary prolegomenon to the investigation of the appearance and consolidation of 'Scouse', as the language of Liverpool has been termed since the mid twentieth century.[3]

The history of language in Liverpool: the official account

The spoken language that was used as the everyday medium of discourse by the members of the different social groupings who lived, worked and played in Liverpool appears to have attracted little or no comment in the eighteenth and nineteenth centuries. Indeed according to the established record, there are only a few scattered remarks, in a variety of sources, that offer tantalizing insights into this sphere of social and cultural life. As noted earlier, Derrick judged that the merchants of Liverpool, though relatively uneducated, were 'genteel in their address', while in an entry in his *Journal*, John Wesley asserted in 1755 that Liverpool was 'one of the neatest, best-built towns I have seen in England', and that its 'people in general are the most mild and courteous I ever saw in a seaport town'. As evidence of the character of the town's cultural propensities, Wesley remarked upon the inhabitants' 'friendly behaviour, not only to the Jews and Papists who live among them, but even to the Methodists (so called)' – a comment that is interesting given the religious divisions that so marked Liverpool's later history (Wesley 1768: 7–8). But like Derrick's assessment, Wesley's passing observation is a somewhat vague reflection on manners rather than a detailed insight into the linguistic forms used in the changing urban space of Liverpool. And despite a small number of comments on either gentility, courtesy and civility, or vulgarity and improper decorum (depending on the section of the town's population under consideration), the evidence regarding the actual language of Liverpool in the period appears to be relatively thin. Moss's *Liverpool Guide* (1796) described a fishmarket near George's dock in which 'the Sisterhood [of fishwives] will be found to enjoy as great a privilege and refinement of the tongue, as most other similar seminaries' (Moss 1796: 54–55). He also noted specific pronunciations of local place names: Wavertree, 'pronounced Wa'tree'; Childwall, 'pronounced Childa'; Woolton 'pronounced Wooton' (Moss 1796: 129–30). A little later, Thomas De Quincey, the Manchester-born Romantic, recorded a sketchy memory of taking 'just, subtle and all-conquering opium' while staying in the 'gentle eminence of Everton' and looking down on 'the many-languaged town of Liverpool' (De Quincey 2000–03: II, 228). On a similar note, and later again, in Elizabeth Gaskell's *Mary Barton* the eponymous heroine walks along the Liverpool quayside hearing 'the cries of the sailors, the variety of languages used by the passers-by' (interestingly she describes sailors as a 'new race of men') (Gaskell 1996: 290). But apart from these intriguing remarks, there is little else of any detail until the report of a conversation given by Robert Syers in *The History of Everton* (1830).

In view of the significance attached to this account, it is important to note that Syers made clear that his example was 'a specimen of the manners, and of the mental attainments, of the highest class of society at Everton, *some eighty years ago*' (emphasis added), as represented in a reconstruction of a meeting at a pub near Everton beacon between 'the nobles of the township' and 'some of their boon companions of Liverpool' (Syers 1830: 118). Set circa 1750, the fictional description presented a boozy altercation between 'Thomas o'th H------'s' (a noble of Everton), William Ripley ('an eminent grocer of Liverpool') and 'Wm. R' ('a legitimate legislator' of Everton). Noting that 'in the days here alluded to, the English language was generally spoken at Everton in a plain and unadorned manner', Syers represented a speech in which Thomas o'th H------'s made an assertion deemed by some to be 'a sin against veracity'. To which William Ripley, after steadying himself on his feet, responded 'Thou liest!' Wm. R then joined the debate:

> 'Dus ta' ca' Tummus o'th H------'s a liar? 'Aye,' replied the valiant Ripley. Then, foaming with fury, and almost choked with the *posse* of angry words which his angry brain thrust, pell-mell, into his throat, the doughty adversary of the still undaunted Ripley in 'terrific silence stood:' at length, a few emphatic hems disentangled the sentences which had most unceremoniously jostled together in his windpipe, and one of them escaped, embodied in a roar of which a bull would not have been ashamed, bellowing in the ears of the now half-frightened Ripley, 'Then thou'rt a bear!' (Syers 1830: 120)

In order to understand the context for this piece of anecdotal humour, it is important to recall that throughout his *History*, Syers distinguished between the historic village of Everton (he imagined its possession by the 'ancient Britons' before its entry in the Domesday book) and the modern town of Liverpool. He did so by figuring Everton as an idyllic contrast to its near-neighbour: 'in picturesque, beautiful and interesting scenery, it has scarcely a rival in Britain. On its western side, it rises with gentle acclivity, until its crest, or the summit of its brow, acquires a commanding eminence, which overlooks the modern Tyre' (Syers 1830: 2). This became a key trope for Syers as he insisted on the distinction, despite their proximity, between the rural delights of Everton and the urban cacophony of Liverpool:

> A short walk, of only a few minutes' duration, takes a pedestrian from Liverpool's busy and bustling scenes into a modern Arcadia, where, gradually, the hum of human toil is lost, and is exchanged for that of the busy bee, and the sparrow's merry chirp; then it is, that, having escaped the hoarse, croaking cries of venders of wares, the vehicles of trade, and the converse-killing rattle and noise of the carts of commerce, as he journeys into Everton, his ears are greeted and delighted at every step, with sweet notes, gratuitously offered, by the 'cheerful songsters of the grove' – songsters, which can charm and delight the natural ear much more than can the artificial capabilities of a Sontag, or a Catalani. To people proceeding from Liverpool into Everton, the suddenness of this change of scene, and the exhilarating effects of meliorated air, seem almost the effect of magic. (Syers 1830: 92)

It was in fact the very propinquity of the rapacious city that threatened the arcadian purity of the village since, as Syers noted, 'so magical is now the builder's power' that 'the western parts of Everton are rapidly assimilating and connecting themselves with Liverpool'. Such changes were evidently a danger to the status of Everton as a place apart, but in a passage that at once confirmed Everton's former alterity and indicated the source of the contemporary intrusion, Syers commented:

> It was only at a comparatively late period that Everton emerged out of a state of rudeness; much less than a hundred years ago, with perhaps one or two solitary exceptions, the township was inhabited by persons of the plainest rural manners, and of truly rustic habits. In the latter part of the last century, a few settlers from the neighbouring town of Liverpool were the first to introduce genteel manners and a polish into Everton society : a few eminent, and some humble merchants of that great commercial town, desirous of relaxation from business, settled themselves on Everton-hill; where, with every advantage of a rural residence, they were still not too far removed from the town's conveniences, and at hand and ready, when required, to aid or conduct their commercial enterprises. (Syers 1830: 339)

By the 1820s the landscape was altering in new and unwelcome ways. Among the 'numberless dwellings' being built were 'beautiful villas and elegant mansions, where the wealthy children of the commerce of Liverpool, and the retired gentry' lived. There were, however, other forces at work: 'small domiciles, and chiefly intended for the occupation of the humble' had started to appear along the western edges of Arcadia (Syers 1830: 3). The human toilers, croaking venders and commercial cart drivers had begun to inhabit the houses that were being constructed in the space between Tyre and its near-neighbour; no doubt they spoiled the view.

It is necessary to consider Syers' text in detail because his imagined dialogue between a Liverpool grocer and Evertonian nobles in 1750 has played a central role in the construction of what stands as the official version of the history of language in Liverpool. Postulated by the professional linguist Gerry Knowles in an unpublished doctoral dissertation ('Scouse: The Urban Dialect of Liverpool') in 1973, this narrative provided academic respectability for already existing popular-cultural accounts and played a role in forging the standard history.[4] Yet despite its later significance, it is important to note the putative nature of Knowles' account of the development of a distinctive form of language in Liverpool. Admitting, for example, that 'there is no direct evidence for the development of Scouse' and that the best that can be done is 'to draw a broad outline on the basis of the few scraps of circumstantial evidence available' (Knowles 1973: 18), he nonetheless asserted that 'the rise of modern Scouse' can be dated 'possibly after 1830 but certainly well before 1889' (the date of an important survey by one of the founders of British dialectology, A.J. Ellis). He took 1830 as the starting point on the basis of what he called 'the slenderest shred of negative evidence': none other than Syers' account of the imaginary mid-eighteenth-century exchange between the Liverpudlian grocer and the Evertonian gentry.[5] In fact, as he made clear, Knowles did not take the dialogue itself as evidential. Instead he drew a conclusion (a type of negative deduction) from the absence of any remark by Syers on the use of linguistic forms that appear to belong to South Lancashire dialect by both characters in the exchange. Thus on the basis of Syers' failure to comment, Knowles proposed the hypothesis that 'it is just possible that as late as 1830 [...] the speech of the city was still similar to that of surrounding districts of Lancashire' (1973: 17).[6] The significance of this observation is that if it were true, then the emergence of a distinct form of speech in Liverpool would be historically specifiable. As he puts it: 'it is not really surprising that when the port of Liverpool was just a little town on the Lancashire coast, its inhabitants spoke with a Lancashire accent. The growth of Scouse follows the growth of the port' (1973: 16). In truth, Knowles' identification of the origins of Scouse lay not so much with the increase in the size of Liverpool as a port per se (Liverpool stopped being a 'little town on the Lancashire coast' a long time before 1830), but with one of the causes and consequences of that expansion: 'massive immigration from Ireland, which reached its peak in the 1840s' and which established 'the Anglo-Irish character of Liverpool' before 1889 (1973: 18). His story was essentially that successive waves of Irish immigrants changed the linguistic situation in Liverpool to the extent that there developed a non-prestige 'Anglo-Irish' vernacular that was confined to the slum areas, together with 'traditional North-Western English – presumably modified by other immigrants – which was the local standard' (1973: 23–24). What happened, Knowles' argument continued, was that over the next century or so the prestige forms of 'standard' grammar, vocabulary and phonological structure shifted downwards to pro-duce a uniform type of working-class speech (otherwise known as Scouse), whereas the phonetic forms of 'Anglo-Irish' moved upwards. For Knowles, such changes explain the historical development of Scouse and indeed its spatial distribution within the city.

Problems with the received version

Though he does not acknowledge it, Knowles' argument about the history of language in Liverpool is derived from a text which he otherwise describes as 'pretentious', based on 'pseudo-expertise' and, when it lapses into the aes-thetic judgement of linguistic forms, not worthy of comment (despite the fact that Knowles himself uses the phrase 'poor and ugly' to refer to Scouse 'voice quality') (Knowles 1973: 52).[7] For in Richard Whittington-Egan's essay 'Liverpool Dialect is Dying Out', originally published in the *Daily Post* on 14 April 1955,[8] he makes the observation that

> it seems fairly certain that Liverpoolese is of comparatively recent origin. According to Syers's *History of Everton*, as late as 1830 Evertonians were speaking with a broad Lancashire accent, and there is no reason to suppose that the other inhabitants of Liverpool were any different. The change doubtless dates to the great influx of poor Irish emigrants at the time of the terrible famine of 1846. (Whittington-Egan 1955a: 6; 1955c: 216; 1972: 10)

The pertinent point is that not only does Knowles use Whittington-Egan's citation of Syers (which Whittington-Egan himself plagiarized from Frank Shaw, one of the founders of the 'Scouse industry' as we will see), he also borrows Whittington-Egan's/Shaw's account of the linguistic situation in Liverpool before the arrival of the large numbers of Irish emigrants in the 1840s and after.[9] This is not to say that these authors agree in their interpretation. Whittington-Egan (following Shaw) appears to think that Syers' dialogue represents the language of the 1830s (missing its hypothetical setting eighty years earlier), whereas Knowles emphasizes Syers' lack of comment on the use of Lancastrian dialect as evidence. Nonetheless, Knowles accepts Whittington-Egan's/Shaw's idea that before the influx of Irish refugees, the inhabitants of Liverpool spoke a form of language whose pronunciation was largely that of the surrounding county of Lancashire. Whittington-Egan specifies that they spoke with 'a broad Lancashire accent', while Knowles argues that they pronounced with 'a Lancashire accent' until the development of 'Scouse', whereupon there were two varieties – 'Scouse' and a 'local standard', modified 'traditional North-Western English' (Knowles 1973: 23–24).

The basis of this interpretation of Liverpool's linguistic history will be challenged below, but in terms of the development of a local form of speech, Knowles' version appears to have some plausibility. It is possible, for example, to find some evidence for the spatial distribution of at least one form of language as described by Knowles. In Dixon Scott's *Liverpool* (1907), the author comments on the two main slum areas of the city as 'two dirty smears, one on either side of the clean-swept central spaces'. In the northern slum area, Scott notes the predominance of Irish immigrants, from which, he says,

> it follows, therefore, that here alone in Liverpool do you get a specific dialect. They speak a bastard brogue: a shambling, degenerate speech of slip-shod vowels and muddied consonants, more debased even than the Whitechapel Cockney, because so much more sluggish, so much less positive and acute. (Scott 1907: 144)[10]

And in '"An accent exceedingly rare": Scouse and the inflexion of class', John Belchem quibbles with Knowles' claim as to the post-Famine origins of Scouse (on the basis that the Irish contribution may have been more complicated and prolonged), but agrees that Knowles' version 'accords well with Liverpool's distinctive socio-economic and topographical structure' (Belchem 2000b: 45).

Yet the key point of Knowles' account, derived by negative deduction, is the assertion that before the influx of Irish refugees in the early to mid nineteenth century, the inhabitants of Liverpool spoke a form of language whose pronunciation was largely that of the surrounding county of Lancashire. But although this claim is now central to what has become the received version of the history of language in Liverpool, its veracity is open to serious doubt on a number of grounds. For example, Knowles sets great store by the fact that the 1841 census records state that 17.3 per cent of the population of the city of Liverpool (49,562/286,487) were Irish, and that by 1861 the figure had shifted to 24.5 per cent (66,086/269,742). He takes this as evidence that the 'Anglo-Irish' influence must have been, so to speak, pronounced. But the census figures also tell us that, in 1841, a total of 44.9 per cent of the population were immigrants (in the technical sense of the term noted in chapter one – that is, those born elsewhere than the county in which they were counted); thus 27.6 per cent of the population was from outside Liverpool but not from Ireland (79,070/286,487). In 1861 the total immigrant figure was 49 per cent, meaning that the number of non-Irish immigrants was precisely the same as the number of Irish inhabitants. These figures alone might give a historian of culture and language pause for thought since, given the mix of population in Liverpool, both from within Britain and elsewhere, and the percentages involved, it seems unlikely that Irish immigrants alone would have had the sort of influence that Knowles claims. In addition, a further factor that complicates Knowles' account is his use of the vague term 'Anglo-Irish' to refer to the language of Irish immigrants. For although they were predominantly from the south and west of Ireland, the Irish who arrived and stayed in Liverpool would have originated in different parts of the country, bringing with them distinct forms of pronunciation, syntax and vocabulary (to say nothing of the fact that some of them would have had very little English at all).[11] It seems somewhat problematic therefore to lump them all together as though they all used the same 'Anglo-Irish' form, which then impacted on the language of the inhabitants of Liverpool.

A further problem with the dominant Irish thesis, as an analysis of the statistics indicates, is that it tends to elide the existence of other linguistic communities and their influence, which produces in turn a type of blindness to the multicultural history of the city. This is not an unusual feature of accounts of Liverpool history (despite the recent appearance of somewhat dubious claims about Liverpool being 'the world in one city').[12] Indeed an interesting early example of precisely this process is produced in Charles Dickens' report of an evening with the Liverpool police in the dock areas of Liverpool in *The Uncommercial Traveller* (1860). At first sight it seems as though Dickens is introducing the reader to various linguistic communities in Liverpool: the Irish, 'Ah, sure, thin, you're right, surr'; the black, 'Ah, la'ads… gib the jebblem a darnse. Tak' yah pardlers, jebblem'; and the Latino – 'Me Spanish' (Dickens 1987: 43–48). But in fact what Dickens does by this type of linguistic stereotyping is to mark these characters off as not properly belonging to Liverpool at all since the dialogue with 'non-exotic' Liverpool working-class characters is represented in standard English orthography. In Dickens' account it is the Irish, the blacks and the Latinos who don't quite count as Liverpudlian; in Knowles' version it is the Irish alone who were the principal contributors to the creation of Scouse. Though the emphasis is different in each case, they both have the unfortunate consequence of contributing to what Belchem has called in a slightly different context an 'ahistorical ethno-cultural stereotype' of the 'proper' Liverpudlian (Belchem 2000b: 56).

There are other difficulties with Knowles' story of the development of Scouse. One significant and problematic issue, for example, relates to the claim that the impact of 'Anglo-Irish' was so influential in Liverpool and yet not in Manchester, despite the fact that they had comparable patterns of

Irish immigration at around the same period and that the fate of the Irish in both towns was similar. Even more puzzling is the question of how it is exactly that a non-prestige form, spoken by the very poorest, often by people stigmatized for their religious beliefs within a city divided on sectarian lines, should become so influential in terms of the common language? To put it bluntly, how does a 'bastard brogue' become a city-speech? As Belchem notes, Knowles' account is somewhat opaque on this point – his claim being simply that prestige forms 'percolated downwards' and 'phonetic forms of Anglo-Irish have spread upwards' (Knowles 1973: 24). Yet Belchem's own explanation also raises more questions than it answers. His claim is that 'once established as the vernacular of the central areas, "slummy" scouse flourished in a nodal position at the heart of the Merseyside communications network and the main labour market' (Belchem 2000b: 45). But leaving to one side the question of how and over what period '"slummy" scouse' was 'established' as the form spoken in the poorest working-class areas (Knowles' account appears to envisage this as a process that took one or perhaps two generations), Belchem's narrative leaves the central question unanswered. It may be, as he asserts, that what became known as Scouse was used as 'the vernacular of the Liverpool waterfront, as a lingua franca' and 'a form of linguistic bonding' (Belchem 2000b: 46). But this does not explain why such a form would be adopted by speakers of what Knowles calls the 'prestige' form. In fact it seems more likely to be a reason why 'prestige' speakers would shun Scouse, given its clear identification with a very specific spatial location, a particular social function and a certain social class.

Belchem's history of Scouse, largely based as it is on Knowles' truncated account, opens up a larger and more significant issue. For Belchem confidently reiterates Knowles' claim that 'until the late 1880s, indeed, serious phonetic studies made no distinction between the town and the surrounding country-side: apparently Liverpool spoke like the rest of South Lancashire' (Belchem 2000b: 33–34). This is a curious claim on two counts. First, there were no 'serious phonetic studies' (if by that is meant analysis of speech using the methods of modern phonetics) before the last quarter of the nineteenth century in Britain.[13] And second, by corollary, there were certainly no serious phonetic studies of Liverpool that showed that its inhabitants spoke like those of the rest of South Lancashire. As has been shown above, there is one piece of anecdotal textual evidence that could be interpreted as suggesting this – the passage cited by Shaw, Whittington-Egan and Knowles from Syers' *History of Everton*. But there are other possible interpretations of this evidence. It may be, for example, that Syers was attempting a reconstruction of the language of the past through the use of archaism. Or he might have been drawing on the stylized accounts of Lancashire speech that had been popularized in the humorous, not to say satirical, Tim Bobbin dialect texts originally published in 1746 (anonymously by John Collier of Urmston) and reproduced in more than one hundred editions over the next century or so. Indeed it is possible that a later edition of Collier's *View of the Lancashire Dialect; by way of Dialogue, between Tummus o'Williams, o'f Margit o'Roafs, an Meary o'Dicks, o'Tummy o'Peggy's.*

Containing the Adventures & Misfortunes of a Lancashire Clown, may have been a direct influence on Syers since there are stylistic commonalities between his depiction of Lancashire speech and features included in the Bobbin text. For example, the rendering of 'dus[t]' for 'dost', 'ta' for 'thou' (more often 'teaw') and 'Tummus' for Thomas are all found either in the Bobbin text or the expanded glossary that accompanied it from the second edition of 1748 onwards – as is the explanation of the form 'Tummus o'th H------'s' ('used in some Parts of Lancashire to distinguish Persons, where there are many of the same Name, in the Neighbourhood') (Bobbin 1748: n.p.). Another possible explanation for the form of Syers' dialogue is that it is a combination of an attempt to represent an archaic form of Liverpool speech, again as a way of setting the exchange in the past ('Thou liest!', 'Aye'), with a representation of Evertonian speech as Lancastrian, with the purpose of demarcating Everton linguistically as a rural place apart – a goal that, as noted earlier, would conform to one of Syers' principal purposes in his *History*. And finally there is the possibility that Syers was rendering an accurate representation of the speech of Liverpool and the speech of Everton and that they were in fact distinct from each other, since there is nothing in the dialogue that makes clear that the Liverpool grocer and the Evertonian noble are using the *same* linguistic form (use of specific terms such as 'thee' in both forms does not mean that the forms themselves are identical).[14] In short, there are various possibilities that are suggested by Syers' dialogue. But it is a long way from any of them to the suggestion that by failing to comment on the linguistic usage of the fictional characters in the dialogue, Syers thereby intended to aver or even imply that 'as late as 1830 [...] the speech of the city was still similar to that of surrounding districts of Lancashire' (Knowles 1973: 17).

Belchem's acceptance of Knowles' account (albeit in slightly modified form) leads him to pose a significant but revealingly misleading question: why, 'given its provincial pre-eminence' and concern with image and identity, 'did nineteenth century Liverpool not acquire a distinctive linguistic identity?' (Belchem 2000b: 36–37). There are two difficulties with this question. First, given the politics of language in Britain in the late eighteenth and nineteenth centuries, it is highly unlikely that Liverpool's new bourgeoisie would have wanted to cultivate a distinctive form of Liverpool speech. Unlike other areas of culture, in which city-based competition was fostered – architecture, public events, social and artistic life – speech was one sphere in Britain in which local pride was heavily regulated and tended to operate only at the level of popular culture. In terms of what Pierre Bourdieu describes as the 'legitimate language' (though legitimated would be a better term for it), a specific mode of pronunciation was constructed as the dominant form in mid to late eighteenth century Britain from which all others were construed to be deviant and hence either 'provincial', or, in later terms, 'non-standard' (Bourdieu 1991: 43–65; Crowley 1996: 73–97; Mugglestone 2003: 7–49). The justification for this development was often couched in nationalist terms. Britishness was to be cemented linguistically as well as politically, as Thomas Sheridan noted in his massively popular *Course of Lectures on Elocution*:

> Uniformity of pronunciation throughout Scotland, Wales and Ireland, as well as
> through the several counties of England, would be a point much to be wished; as
> it might in great measure destroy those odious distinctions between subjects of
> the same King, and members of the same community, which are ever attended
> with ill consequences, and which are chiefly kept alive by difference of pronun-
> ciation, and dialects. (Sheridan 1762: 206)

National unity was only one aspect of this emphasis on language, however,
since pronunciation or the use of specific linguistic forms were socially significant in that they revealed 'the place of a man's birth, whenever he speaks,
which otherwise could not be known by any other marks in mixed societies'
(Sheridan 1762: 206). Being able to 'place' someone geographically also meant
being able to locate them in terms of social space. As William Enfield, tutor at
the Warrington Academy, author of the best-selling elocution text *The Speaker*
and early historian of Liverpool, pointed out, proper attention to models of
pronunciation and 'free intercourse with the polite world, are the best guards
against the peculiarities and vulgarisms of provincial dialects'. Speech errors,
he warned 'must be corrected in the pronunciation of a gentleman, who is
supposed to have seen too much of the world, to retain the peculiarities of the
district in which he was born' (Enfield 1774: xiv). Pronunciation was a form
of social capital desired by those whose aim was the acquisition of capital of
another sort, and so, as Philip Withers observed:

> The importance of a correct Mode of Expression in BUSINESS is sufficiently
> obvious. SHOPMEN, CLERKS, APPRENTICES, and all who are engaged in the
> Transactions of commercial Life, may be assured that the acquisition will procure
> them Respect, and be highly conducive to their Advancement in Life. (Withers
> 1789: 30)

None of this was lost on the newly rich Liverpool merchants; like their bourgeois counterparts all over the country in the early to mid nineteenth century,
they sent their children, particularly their sons, to schools in which this form
of pronunciation (later called Received Pronunciation, sometimes Public
School Pronunciation) was taught.[15] In any case, the last thing the Liverpool
middle class would have fostered was a 'distinctive linguistic identity' for itself.
Institutions, buildings, clubs and societies were all ways in which this new
social group made its civic mark, but it would have been extraordinary if it
had sought to cultivate its own speech as a mark of social distinction. And yet
this, paradoxically, raises the second problem with Belchem's question, which
is that it is grounded in a more basic misconception. For while the Liverpool
mercantile class did not seek a linguistic form of its own in order to forge a
particular type of cultural identity, it appears that it nonetheless used a mode
of speech that was specific to the city and that identified the speaker as being
from Liverpool. As will be demonstrated below, despite the fact that Knowles'
account suggests that a characteristic Liverpool vernacular emerges only after
1830 and sometime before 1889, there is circumstantial, theoretical and textual
evidence that such a form existed long before Scouse was created.

The persistence of the model

Before examining the evidence for an alternative account of the history of language in Liverpool, it is worth considering the way in which the established version has been updated in line with recent developments in historical linguistics and dialectology (without any serious questioning of the premise upon which it was built). Perhaps the best example is the narrative of Liverpool English furnished in the work of the contemporary phonologist Patrick Honeybone in 'New Dialect Formation in Nineteenth-Century Liverpool: A Brief History of Scouse', in the recent collection *The Mersey Sound. Liverpool's Language, People and Places* (2007). Honeybone's research relies for the most part on a theoretical model set out by Peter Trudgill, sociolinguist and field expert in dialectology, in his *Dialects in Contact* (1986) and *New-Dialect Formation. The Inevitability of Colonial Englishes* (2004). As Honeybone notes, there are problems with Trudgill's somewhat deterministic attempt to predict which dialect features will survive in specific dialect contact situations (based largely on an account of the development of 'New Zealand English'), but it nonetheless offers a way of interpreting 'new-dialect formation'. Honeybone outlines the salient features of Trudgill's model and adopts his tripartite analysis. In stage one,

> Adult speakers of established varieties come together, thanks to substantial population movements, in one place. These adults start to accommodate to each other linguistically, to rub off the most extreme differences between their varieties, or to lose features which clearly stand out as minority forms, or which might diminish intelligibility. (Honeybone 2007: 112)

Such contact, however, does not in itself produce a new dialect, since this requires the praxis of children either born to parents in the new location, or children who moved there at an early age. This leads to stage two, which depends on the fact that this first generation

> have to come to terms with the various different dialect forms that they hear and are themselves subject to considerable variation because they do not have clear linguistic role models in their peers. They pick up a number of features from their parents and from others around them, in line with the different proportions of the features in the dialects of the speakers who formed the new community, and start the process of koineisation. (2007: 112)

These speakers can produce creative 'interdialect' features that are not found in any of the formative dialects and, in stage three of the process, act as the means of transmission of the new dialect to the second generation. At this point a 'stabilised, focused koine or new-dialect' is formed.

There are difficulties with such a paradigm since the emphasis is focused more on the formal explanation of linguistic change than on the social and historical details by which such change takes place. In this case, for example, while the generational framework is useful and draws attention to the family as an important locus of linguistic transmission, there are many other factors that are simply elided. Honeybone himself notes the failure of Trudgill's model to take account of the role of prestige in linguistic change (an element that has un-doubtedly increased through the development of the technologies of the mass media), though stigmatization is surely just as important. But there are many other complex features that could affect the type of linguistic development under consideration. They might include, to name but a few: patterns of liter-acy among parents and children; the effects of particular types of schooling; the fact that migration can often be a to-and-fro process rather than a static fact; connections with the parental (or grandparental) place of origin; the spatial stratification of a population in a specific location; the nature, regularity and place of work; the distinctiveness of gender-related experience and the cultural formations that surround it; marriage patterns; the function of various types of institution in the formation of identity and difference; the modalities of local (sometimes very local) pride and allegiance; and the symbolic imagination of community in macro- and micro- social and cultural forms. It may be that the elision of such features is simply a function of the difficulty of explaining causation within sociolinguistic analysis (a problem that results in a preference for the relatively simpler field of formal analysis). Yet despite the problems, the important point for present purposes is that Honeybone adopts Trudgill's model in his account of Scouse, taking from it the essential claim that 'dialect contact inevitably results in dialect mixture' (2007: 112).

It is worth considering in detail Honeybone's version of 'the emergences [*sic*] of an identifiably distinct Liverpool English', or,

> What most people, and present-day work in Perceptual Dialectology, would call 'Scouse' [...] a variety which is closely associated with the urban area in and around Liverpool and which is clearly not simply part of the Lancashire-to-Cheshire dialect traditional dialect continuum. In some sense before there was this new-dialect, although English was spoken in Liverpool, there was no perceptually real 'Liverpool English'. (2007: 117–18)

As he makes clear, and like Belchem before him, Honeybone bases his analysis on the assumption that Knowles' account of Liverpool's linguistic history is correct. Indeed, referring directly to Knowles' study, he notes that 'having conducted a long search for contemporary commentaries or direct evidence for the formation of a distinct and recognisable dialect in Liverpool', Knowles 'found only very little such evidence'. Nonetheless, Honeybone adds, Knowles did 'cunningly interpret some of the few sources that he finds to set the dates for the development of Liverpool English as between 1830 and 1889, based on direct comments from contemporary observers on the variety of English spoken in Liverpool, and on the *absence* of such comments' (emphasis in the original) (2007: 117). This is a somewhat peculiar analysis. The 'long search' is presumably the research for Knowles' PhD (a small part of which – eight from a project of 347 pages – is devoted to the history of language in Liverpool), while the claim that Knowles' conclusions are based on 'direct comments from contemporary observers' is slightly misleading. As pointed out earlier, Knowles makes clear that there is in fact 'no direct evidence' to support his interpreta-tion, while the contemporary sources he cites – Syers (1830), Hume (1878),

Ellis (1889) and Lloyd (1899) – are interpreted as supplying what can only be termed negative evidence on the basis of comments that they do *not* make about 'Liverpool English'. Nonetheless, having accepted Knowles' account, Honeybone produces what he calls 'a brief history of Scouse', a description of 'the formation of a completely new dialect' that is 'among the many cultural achievements of the people of Liverpool' (2007: 134). Using Trudgill's schema, he presents a sketch of the development of 'the perceptually distinct Liverpool English that now exists', placing it within 'the Late Modern English period':

- Stage 1: broadly pre-19th century
- Stage 2 (especially mid) 19th century
- Stage 3: broadly post-19th century

Crucially, during stage one, 'there was no "distinct" Liverpool English' since although English was spoken in Liverpool, 'it would essentially have "simply" been part of the Lancashire-Cheshire dialect continuum, and would likely have been essentially the same as (or, rather, part of) South Lancashire English' (2007: 119). In stage two, to which 'most attention needs be directed', since this is the point at which 'Liverpool English' emerges, there are three further sub-stages:

- Stage 2i: dialect mixture and accommodation among adult speakers
- Stage 2ii: koineisation: levelling and development of inter-dialect forms in the early generations of children of in-migrants
- Stage 2iii: focusing of the dialect mixture the emergence of a stable koine [*sic*] (2007: 119)

Stage 2iii is dated as occurring towards the end of the nineteenth century (producing 'the basis of Liverpool English as we recognise it today'), while 'stage 3 is ongoing'.

Honeybone's analysis is noteworthy and his assertion that Scouse is the result of a hybrid mix of dialect influences certainly serves as a useful corrective to the idea that 'Liverpool English can be simply assumed to involve South Lancashire English and the varieties of language/languages that the Irish brought to Liverpool' (a notion that is epitomized in the claim purportedly made by Knowles: 'Scouse: a Lancashire dialect with an Irish accent') (2007: 119, 120). Thus despite the fact that this conception has seeped into popular consciousness (Scouse = Lancashire dialect + Irish-English), Honeybone is correct to say that it is implausible.[16] The question remains, however, as to whether Honeybone's account is any more plausible – or whether indeed it makes sense even on its own terms. The most significant point at stake is this: Honeybone argues that in his historical analysis of new-dialect formation in Liverpool, 'a study of population movements will be crucial, so population statistics (such as census returns) will be very important' (2007: 111). In other words, the movement of people to Liverpool in great numbers is central to his account since it is that which produces dialect mixture and thus a new linguistic form. But if this is the case, then it is somewhat puzzling that Honeybone argues that 'most attention' should be paid to stage 2 of his schema – '(especially mid) 19th century', on the grounds that this is when 'recognisable "Liverpool English" emerges'. In fact, given the population statistics, and the constant refrain of the early cultural commentators about the influxes of 'strangers' (as noted in the previous chapter), it would make more sense to argue that if a new linguistic form was created in Liverpool, then its development surely began (and the form may have even been established) in the eighteenth century. The figures show, for example, that between 1700 and 1801 the population of the town increased fifteen-fold from some 5,145 to 77,653, and that the eighteenth century witnessed 'percentage growth rates greater than for most decades in the nine-teenth century' (Pooley 2006: 175). Before the eighteenth century, Liverpool appears to have been largely self-sustaining in terms of population. But 'by the early decades of the eighteenth century, the town's migratory pull was significantly greater. With the diversification of the economic base, especially the dock developments of the early eighteenth century, labour was increasingly required from elsewhere to maintain and satisfy Liverpool's demand' (Ascott et al. 2006: 57). Moreover, in terms of the location of origin of these workers, population modelling and parish registers suggest that although the majority probably arrived from the Lancashire hinterland, the various ports of Cheshire, North Wales and Wirral also contributed, to say nothing of those who migrated from Ireland, Scotland, America and the West Indies (Ascott et al. 2006: 55–58). Given these facts, why then does it make sense to assert that a 'recognisable' form of 'Liverpool English' dates only from the mid nineteenth century when all of the factors that are central to Trudgill's model, and Honeybone's adapta-tion of it, were in place earlier? Various answers suggest themselves. First, Honeybone, along with many others, may simply have made the mistake of accepting as given Knowles' dubious hypothesis (largely based on Syers' failure to comment on the language of a fictionalized dialogue set in 1750) about the lack of distinction between forms of English used in Lancashire and Liverpool. Second, if Knowles' speculative account were rejected, it would mean that the established history would have to be revised, which is always a difficult proposition. And third, given the problems with eighteenth-century sources, the gathering of evidence for an earlier form of 'recognisable' Liverpool English would present genuine difficulties for the precise elucidation of the history of language in Liverpool. Of course difficulties related to a lack of material can be overcome in various ways. Honeybone notes, for example, that given that 'clear records of the phonology of Liverpool English do not start until the mid twentieth century', it is evident that 'we cannot assume that all of the current features of Liverpool English were present in the late nineteenth century' (Honeybone 2007: 119). This is, however, precisely what he does in his analysis of 'the formation of four Liverpool linguistic features', even though he acknowledges 'the risk of incautiously projecting the present onto the past' and the dangers of relying on the 'little or certainly not enough work on the history of many of the varieties' of English that would suffice to underpin his account (2007: 122–23). Such a procedure appears methodologically peculiar, as is the fact that such an accomplished linguist has been led to stray so far from applying the theoretical tenets of his model to the available historical evidence. Perhaps the explanation is simply that the received version of the history of language in Liverpool has such a hold that it prevents even the best scholars from seeing past it.

Historical and textual evidence for an alternative account

If the authorized version of Liverpool's linguistic history is open to doubt, is there an alternative? In fact both historical and textual evidence suggests that there may well be. Thus, referring to a debate in *Notes and Queries* in 1888 as to whether Gladstone spoke with a 'provincial accent', Belchem correctly notes that some correspondents thought that the prime minister spoke with a Lancashire accent (Skeat, editor of the Oxford *Etymological Dictionary of the English Language*, simply says 'North'), but that one, James Picton, the famous Liverpool architect, historian and local luminary, argued that his voice was distinctively Liverpudlian. Given that Picton claimed that he had, over many years, 'frequent opportunities of conversing with and listening to Mr. Gladstone both in private and in public' and was 'therefore entitled to speak with some confidence' (Picton 1888: 210), it is surprising that Belchem makes little of his remarks because they are worth considering in detail. In his note, Picton observed that along with other details of his life, Gladstone's public profile meant that his 'dialect and manner of speech are brought under review' and that 'there is no man, however educated and refined he may be, who has not contracted in early life some peculiarity or mannerism of accent, tone, or dialect, derived from his surroundings, of which he can never entirely rid himself' (1888: 210). Arguing that 'dialect and tones' are not derived from parents (Gladstone's were Scottish), but from 'daily intercourse with those about us whose language, intonation and peculiarities are insensibly imitated', Picton concluded that the fact that Gladstone was born (in 1809) and brought up in Liverpool meant that 'the current language of the locality would tend to mould his outward expression and form of speech; and so it has' (1888: 210). The 'current language of the locality' presumably refers to at least one mode of Liverpool speech in the early nineteenth century that Gladstone would have learned as a child.[17] It was evidently a form that he continued to use, possibly with modification (given his education and career), throughout his life. As Picton noted: 'his tones and mode of utterance are decidedly of Liverpool origin. We bring our words out "ore rotundo," without the mincing word-clipping of the cockney and equally distant from the rough Tim Bobbin Lancashire dialect' (1888: 210).

Picton's distinction is historically significant. Neither London nor Lancashire, Liverpool had a speech of its own that functioned as a mark of identity. 'Liverpool gentlemen' sounded different from 'Manchester men':

> The cities of Liverpool and Manchester, only thirty miles apart, differ materially in their dialect. The Manchester cotton-spinner, magnate though he may be, on his appearance on the Liverpool 'flags' is instantly recognised, and the Liverpool merchant is soon 'spotted' on the Manchester Exchange. (1888: 210)

Interestingly, however, though asserting that 'Liverpool has no reason to be ashamed of the dialect or tones of her distinguished son', Picton nonetheless cited a linguistic change that had evidently taken place in the recent past (1888: 211). Noting that Liverpool's population in 1809 was only a fifth of that in 1888, he asserted that 'the vast majority of this increase must of necessity be immigrants, not natives, which has had a powerful influence in breaking down the distinctions of dialect' (1888: 211). In one sense this confirms Knowles' general, if not specific, argument that Liverpool speech was affected by the large numbers of 'immigrants' who flooded the town. Yet there is a more important implication in Picton's words. For his narrative suggests that there was, before the large influxes of the mid-century, a specific Liverpool vernacular, perhaps with different class-based modes of 'accent, tone or dialect', that distinguished the inhabitants of the city. This was not, however, *pace* Belchem, a type of speech that the Liverpool middle classes cultivated as a marker of cultural identity and regional belonging. As noted earlier, given the politics of language that have held in Britain for much of the past two centuries, this would have been extraordinary. But the evidence implies that a form of language did exist that had the function of identifying speakers as Liverpolitans (to use the most popular nineteenth-century term for the inhabitants of the city).

The idea that a specific and localized spoken language developed in Liverpool as it expanded in the eighteenth and early nineteenth centuries goes against the grain of the dominant historical narrative. But it is a much more plausible notion than that which presumes that the inhabitants of Liverpool spoke the same dialect as that found in Lancashire (whose rural hinterland stretched from Hawkshead in what is now Cumbria to the north, to the southernmost tip of Manchester, and from Liverpool in the west to the Pennines in the east). Moreover there are various forms of support for this alternative hypothesis. For example, a number of historians and cultural observers comment on the distinctiveness of Liverpool before the post-Famine Irish influx. Thus in a passage that argues for a much earlier Irish influence on the town, Troughton's identification of the importance of trade with Ireland in the early development of Liverpool as a port led him to assert that once the Mersey surpassed the Dee during the seventeenth century (as a result of silting), the Irish presence in Liverpool not only grew, it also contributed to the formation of a distinctive local culture:

> Several natives of Ireland settled in Liverpool, and laid the foundation of some of the principal mercantile houses, while they contributed to form the local manners of the town, which have always been distinguished from those of the other towns of Lancashire, by a peculiar hospitality, activity and sprightliness. (Troughton 1810: 104)

And contemporary evidence for pre-Famine immigration suggests that there was a sizeable Irish component in Liverpool's population in the late eighteenth and early nineteenth centuries. The Royal Commission on the Condition of the Poorer Classes in Ireland, which reported in 1836, estimated that there were 4,950 'Irish Catholics' in 1800 (cited in Belchem 2007a: 7) against a total population of 75,270 in the 1801 census (Laxton 1981: 80) – a proportion of 6.57%. It is more than likely, however, that this figure is a serious under-estimate given the uncertainty of the census itself and the lack of clarity concerning the methods used for calculating the numbers of Irish people (did the numbers include only those who had been born in Ireland rather than those whose parents were Irish? Did people of Irish Protestant descent classify themselves as Irish? Did the Irish poor co-operate willingly with parish overseers in the politically fraught year of 1801?)[18] Be that as it may, Troughton's claim that an early Irish presence was a factor in the development of 'local manners' that were notably different from those of surrounding towns is significant. But as noted earlier, it is evident from the overall population figures that the Irish were not the only immigrants who settled in Liverpool, since the sheer rate of expansion can only be explained by what the first historian of the town called the 'continual influx of strangers' (Enfield 1773: 28). As early as 1753 Williamson's *Liverpool Memorandum Book* recorded that the town's geographic advantages had served to stimulate trade during the wars of the 1740s, with a consequent impact upon the composition of the populace:

> The Harbour being situated so near the Mouth of the North Channel between *Ireland* and *Scotland*, (a Passage so little known to, or frequented by the Enemy) afforded many conveniences to the Merchants here, so untasted by other Ports, which invited Numbers of Strangers from different Parts to begin Trade and settle here, finding it so advantagious a Mart. (Williamson 1753: n.p.)

Likewise, towards the end of the century, Wallace noted the difficulties of calculating the number of people in Liverpool given that 'strangers at sea ports [are] perpetually arriving, inhabitants constantly emigrating, and the routine of people in perpetual circulation' (Wallace 1795: 66–67). Confirmation of such observations can be drawn from recent research. Rawling's study of parish registers indicates that only something in the region of 20 per cent of the expansion in Liverpool's populace between 1660 and 1760 was attributable to 'natural' increase (cited in Longmore 2006: 119). And Langton and Laxton point out that of the rise in population of 45,000 between 1773 and 1801, only 8,800 appears to result from 'natural' growth, 'leaving over 36,000 to be accounted for by net immigration – an astonishingly high 80 per cent' (Langton and Laxton 1978: 76). Given such figures, it is possible to concur with Lawton that in 1801 'the population of Liverpool was a hybrid one' (Lawton 1953: 122), a point reinforced by another study of late eighteenth-century parish registers that demonstrates that 'Liverpool had already gained a cosmopolitan population' by this time (Pooley 2006: 175). And yet, as Longmore has argued, it is important to note that early patterns of migration were distinct from those which followed later in the nineteenth century. Unlike the dominant mid-nineteenth-century influx from Ireland, which was driven by the desperate need to escape severe poverty and death, earlier flows were determined by the different possibilities that Liverpool offered for profit and labour. Most of those who arrived in Liverpool would evidently have been looking for work in transport (as sailors), in the major maritime crafts and related industries (shipbuilding and sailmaking), in the manufacturing base of the town (textiles, food and brewing, pottery, minerals), or as general labourers (Langton and Laxton 1978: 80). But there were others who came to exploit the opportunities for the entrepreneurial investment of capital of the most speculative kind – from investment in new docks to the commodification of human beings in the industry of slavery. Liverpool in this period, then, was not just a socially and culturally complex place, it had an amalgamated population; composed of many diverse elements, the town provided just the sort of conditions in which 'new-dialect formation' would have taken place.

But is there any evidence that this did in fact occur? As noted earlier, this is difficult to establish. Yet it is worth considering in this regard a text that has not previously been analysed in any detail. Published in Liverpool in 1768 (and performed at Drury Lane theatre), Thomas Boulton's comedy *The Sailor's Farewell; Or, the Guinea Outfit* provides an interesting indication of the complexity of the linguistic situation in the city.[19] The main plot of the piece deals with the recruitment of sailors to crew an African slave-trader (a perennial problem for commercial operators, especially in times of war), while the sub-plot concerns Kitty, daughter of Squire Hard, who has been betrothed by her father to Squire Catesby, but who is in love with Thomas Free, a penniless though educated naval surgeon. In terms of the main plot the play is interesting for its account of the means by which seamen were persuaded, cajoled or simply tricked into joining a vessel whose voyage would be long, unpleasant and dangerous (several of the characters express serious reservations about signing on). The sub-plot, on the other hand, is a relatively predictable story of a father desiring to marry his daughter to a gentleman with capital rather than a poor lover, the daughter's rebellion and elopement, and the final reconciliation of father, daughter and suitor. Yet the play's main significance, for this study at least, lies not so much at the level of plot as in its depiction of the heteroglot nature of mid-eighteenth-century Liverpool.

Several of the play's characters embody distinct aspects of Liverpool life and their language reflects their identity in terms of occupation or social class. Will Whistle, for example, a sailor just returned from a voyage through the Straits of Gibraltar, speaks to his wife in parodic maritime discourse (aspects of which run through the play):

> Wife, aye, dam'mee, Nell, thou'rt my wife, my life, my sheet anchor, my buoy and buoy rope, my sheet cable. Why, if thou didst not bring me up, I should founder on the rocks of New-street, or run aboard some of the vessels in Populary-wient. (Boulton 1768: 5)

The Irish immigrant presence meanwhile is represented by Dr Murphy O'Fegan, a character whose first and last lines signal Irish and British unity ('Huzzah for potatoes and beef' […] 'He'll talk to me in Irish, which I won't understand,/ But I'll give him a kick with the back of my hand'). Born in Ballatague and 'brought up in the shitty of Dublin', O'Fegan 'travelled by water to Liverpool' and articulates his Irish-Englishness in his pronunciation.[20]

I'm pretty well accustom'd to go to sea. It is only five days ago I left Limerick; there was nineteen of us on board, and every shoul shick of the shea, but myself and Daniel O'Dempsey, the shoe-builder's son in Youghall. (1768: 5)

The language of working-class women in the play is likewise clearly delineated. Mrs Cobweb, a landlady, welcomes the opportunity for a song as a way of resolving conflict, 'for as Mr. Shickspur says, music has charms to sooth the savage bear' (1768: 12), while Nelly, a sailor's wife, rebuffs a kiss with the admonition 'stand off you calf you; or I'll slap your chops for you' (1768: 32).[21] The addressee in this case is Bob Bluff, a clown, whose speech reveals his social status as he takes up the offer of a drink (made as part of the attempt to entice him to join the Guinea ship):

Hartily, eye, by'th'blud will I --- why I had ne'er such a taist i'this ward ----- londs youre hat, maister, and I'll look at my sel i' th glass ----*Mate gives him his hat* ------ *Bob looks in the glass*; Ads flesh I'm no more like Bob Bluff, than I'm like my fether's mastiff dog Towser. (1768: 31)

At the other end of the social and perhaps geographic scale, by contrast, is Squire Catesby. On one level, the would-be relationship between Catesby and Kitty, Squire Hard's daughter, conforms to a typical comic scenario based on a mis-match between parental and filial desires. Yet it is also possible to see a deeper level of social significance in their interaction. Given that Squire Hard is described in the dramatis personae as 'a Citizen' and Squire Catesby as 'a Country Gentleman', the fact that they fail in their attempt to achieve a common goal might be read as signifying the complex and often unhappy relations, not to say power-struggles, between the Liverpool mercantile elite and the traditional Lancastrian landowning class.[22] Such conflicts were exacerbated by religious differences. Eighteenth-century Liverpool has been described as 'an inward-looking community of Protestants in a county with continuing Catholic sympathies' (Longmore 2006: 154), and there may be an allusion to this in the play since there is more than a whiff of Catholicism in Catesby's question to Kitty – 'You've learn'd your catechis, ain't you? (Boulton 1768: 25).[23] But in addition to these historical allusions, there is also an undercurrent of ridicule in the comic discrepancy between the interests of the city woman and the country gentleman, represented by Catesby's depiction of rural delights:

... in the country you see, we've an opportunity of many sights, as she can't have in town: there'll be hay-making coming on, in a short time ----- now there'll be a rare sport at hay-making ---- zounds to see all the lads and wenches about the town, rowling and tumbling. (1768: 25–26)

The clearest instance of this mode of social distinction, manifested in the form of linguistic difference, is set out in an exchange between Kitty and Catesby:

Enter 'Squire with a whip and a pair of dirty boots on.
'Squire. Aye, by the mass am I, miss, and have been up to'th knees i'th' slutch...
Kitty. I'm very sorry that 'Squire Catesby should put himself in any trouble on my account.

'Squire. Nay, miss, as to that it's no trouble at all; but you'll give us a kiss, waint yo, miss Kitty? (1768: 24)

The point is reinforced in the squire's response to the begrudged kiss: 'God bless her little heart, hoo has a breath as sweet as a honey-suckle.' The form 'hoo' (from Old English 'heo') for the feminine pronoun, which the *OED* records as still current in Lancashire usage at the time, serves in this context to 'place' both Kitty and Catesby precisely.[24]

The most interesting feature of the play from a linguistic point of view, however, occurs when Kitty persuades Dr Free to impersonate a cousin of the rural squire in order to deceive her father into letting him into the house in order that they can run away together. Kitty's written instructions to the doctor include the stipulation that when pretending to be Catesby's cousin, he should '*Mind and forget not the Lancashire dialect*' (1768: 24) Thus when the doctor enters in disguise, in a scene that involves Squire Hard, Kitty, a servant Betty and the doctor, the comedy rests on his linguistic performance (including, presumably, a recognizably non-Liverpool pronunciation to match the 'Lancashire dialect'):

Hard. This is she [Kitty], sir; come this way my dear, this is 'Squire Catesby's cousin.
Doctor. Ads flesh; but well done James; come hither, my pipin: by the awns but cousin Catesby has none such a bad notion of things, neither.
Betty. [*To Kitty aside*] Lord bless him how rarely he acts it.
Doctor. Come, my little merry-gold, with 'Squire Catesby's leave, and let's have a buss (O ambrosial nectar) [*aside*]. (1768: 28)

The comic irony continues:

Doctor. Why I suppose that was Miss's sweetheart, that doctor, eh, sur?
Hard. He would have been I believe, had he met with encouragement, but I never saw him since I set Jowler at him the other night.
Doctor. Did the cur bite him, sur, or did it but freeten him? (1768: 28)

There is a good deal of linguistic play in this dialogue. 'Pipin', a word now marked by the *OED* as regional English, chiefly from the north, was originally used of persons in a derogatory sense, but came to be deployed as a term of endearment, especially for women; it may function in both senses here as a form of teasing.[25] 'Awn', meaning the hair that protrudes from the grain-sheath of barley or oats, helps with the representation of the rural cousin. But it is in terms of specific items of lexis and pronunciation that the doctor's speech is marked as specifically Lancastrian. 'Buss' is recorded in Joseph Wright's *English Dialect Dictionary* as widely used in the north, but a citation is given to a work of the Lancashire dialect writer Benjamin Brierley. And both 'sur', for 'sir' and 'freet'(en) for 'fright'(en) are included in the expanded glossary in Samuel Bamford's revision of Collier's *Dialect of South Lancashire, Or Tim Bobbin's Tummus and Meary* (1850).

If it were simply for its representation of heteroglossia in the language of Liverpool in the mid eighteenth century – the discourse of sailors, working-class men and women, an Irishman and a Lancashire squire – *The Sailor's Farewell* would be an important text. But its real significance lies in the fact that it suggests that the standard account of language in Liverpool is in need of revision. Because what Kitty's order to the doctor not to forget the 'Lancashire dialect' implies is that the speech of at least some of the inhabitants of Liverpool was not the same as that of Lancastrians (even those who lived, as Catesby does, only fourteen miles away). In fact forms of Liverpool speech were apparently sufficiently distinct to require representation as dialectal (in the case of the working-class Bluff), or in need of disguise in order not to reveal the speaker's Liverpudlian identity (in the case of Dr Free). Such a conclusion contradicts the use that Shaw, Whittington-Egan, Knowles, and by default Belchem, make of Syers in order to demonstrate that Liverpudlians were speaking with 'a broad Lancashire accent' as late as the 1830s. For as the analysis above demonstrates, Boulton's text indicates that the linguistic situation of Liverpool was much more complex than has previously been thought. Of course it will no doubt be noted that, like Whittington-Egan's argument, this account is based on relatively thin textual evidence, and it is important not to pretend otherwise (even though the evidence in this case is taken from a text written in the period rather than a fictionalized reconstruction). But even from the abstract viewpoint of the linguistic theory examined earlier, it makes sense to ask which is the more plausible account: that Liverpool, as a major port and trading centre with an ever-expanding, hybrid population (and consequently the site of significant linguistic difference over a long period), should have evolved a distinctive vernacular mode in the eighteenth century? Or that it managed to retain the same linguistic form as the surrounding area until the mid nineteenth century?

Conclusion

The argument of this chapter has been that there is sufficient cumulative evidence, from textual, historical and theoretical sources, to cast doubt on the standard history of the language of Liverpool and to revise that account accordingly. The point has not been to question the integrity of the work of linguists such as Knowles or Honeybone, or indeed historians of the stature of Belchem, but to suggest how a particular narrative of history, once accepted, can lead to the production of research that simply produces further support for the premise upon which the initial account was based. The aim then has been to look at the established story and to question it – to ask whether it is plausible, to challenge its assumptions, to consider evidence that contradicts it. It is possible that further research – for example corpus-based linguistic analysis – may be able to provide more evidence for the contention that is set out here (although as the argument of this chapter suggests, there are always inherent complexities in the use of textual sources for arguments about vernacular speech). But the central claim stands: that the narrative that asserts that Liverpool vernacular could have been the same as that used in Lancashire as late as the 1830s, and that a distinctive Liverpool vernacular appeared only in the mid nineteenth century, is not tenable.

Notes

1   Frank Shaw, 'The Origins of Liverpoolese. Evolution of a Lingo', *Liverpool & Merseyside Illustrated*, January 1962, 9.
2   The association of Liverpool and Liverpudlians with a form of language is largely restricted to Britain and Ireland. Linguistic sensitivities elsewhere in the world are not quite so sharp, and in any case the predominant motif connected with Liverpool globally is that it was the birthplace of the Beatles.
3   The use of 'Scouse' as a term to refer to the language of Liverpool will be discussed in chapters 3–6.
4   The popular, not to say populist, accounts will form the subject matter of chapters 4 and 5.
5   There is in fact evidence that at least some Liverpudlians spoke 'Lancashire dialect' in the early nineteenth century. Maria Edgeworth noted in a letter dated 6 April 1813 that Liverpool was a town full of 'money making faces, every creature full drive after their own interest, elbowing, jostling, headlong after money! money! money!' She commented sardonically that 'if you ask a question you must *buy* an answer and then it is given in the Lancashire dialect which you can't understand'. It appeared to be a welcome relief to meet the historian, poet, politician, botanist, philanthropist and anti-slavery abolitionist William Roscoe at Allerton Hall, 'about seven miles from Liverpool'. Yet the generally favourable impression Edgeworth had of Roscoe was apparently undermined by the fact that he 'speaks excellent language but with a strong provincial accent which at once destroys all idea of elegance'. Mrs Roscoe (a native of Liverpool) was 'an honest-faced, fat, *hearty*, good natured hospitable body, without the least pretensions to polish, but with a downright plain good understanding and uncommonly warm heart which throws out all her thoughts and feelings in broad Lancashire dialect – Almost as broad as Tummus and Meary' (Colvin 1971: 10–11). There are two notes of caution with regard to this account. First, as Chandler notes, 'it is difficult for the modern Liverpolitan to realise that any native of Mount Pleasant (now in the inner heart of Liverpool) could be born a countryman. Yet Roscoe was a countryman' (in his upbringing and early work in the market-garden of the house) (Chandler 1953: 6). Second, Edgeworth had very pronounced opinions on the provincial speech of England (which she compared very unfavourably to the Elizabethan purity of the Irish peasantry), as articu-lated in the *Essay on Irish Bulls* (1802) (co-written with her father). She noted for example, that 'in England, almost all of our fifty-two counties have peculiar vulgar-isms, dialects and brogues, unintelligible to their neighbours'; she also referred to local English idioms as 'a jargon unlike to any language under heaven' (Edgeworth 1802: 200). For a discussion of Edgeworth on language in Ireland and England, see Crowley 2005: 84ff. It may be that Edgeworth's poor estimation of local English speech led her to hear Lancashire dialect rather than Liverpool English, though it is also possible that the influence of Lancashire, even if affected by the factors out-lined in this chapter, was still strong in certain classes or in particular areas of the town or its outskirts.
6   The durability of this account is notable. In *Citizen Soldiers: The Liverpool Territorials in the First World War* (2005), Helen McCartney claims that 'the Liverpolitan accent

had more in common with that spoken in surrounding parts of Lancashire in 1914 than it does today' (McCartney 2005: 86). McCartney cites Belchem in support of this claim, although this is not in fact what he says. As noted in the introduction, Belchem states that 'oral historians attest that many working-class Liverpudlians failed to exhibit any "scouse" characteristics (Irish or otherwise) in their speech until well into the twentieth century' (Belchem 2000b: 44). This isn't the same as saying that people from Liverpool spoke like their Lancastrian counterparts in 1914.

7   Knowles asserts that dialectologists are prone to defending their dialect against charges of linguistic 'debasement', 'laziness', or 'ugliness', but in the second half of the same sentence he declares: 'Scouse has a voice quality – whether inherited or developed natively – which is undeniably poor and ugly, as these terms are normally understood' (Knowles 1973: 116). He doesn't specify how these terms are 'normally understood' when referring to language.

8   The essay was published under this title in the *Daily Post* on 14 April 1955, reprinted under the more open title 'Is Liverpool Dialect Dying Out?' in Whittington-Egan's *Liverpool Colonnade* (1955), and printed again (in slightly shortened form under the title 'Scouse Isn't What It Used To Be') in the *Liverpool Echo* on 20 July 1972.

9   Like Knowles, Whittington-Egan failed to record that he had borrowed the Syers reference; it was first mentioned in an article by Frank Shaw in the *Liverpool Echo*, 8 December 1950, 'Scouse Lingo – How It All Began': 'Probably until about one hundred years ago Liverpolitans spoke as they do in Bolton, or even in nearby Prescot. Certainly in 1830, according to Syers' *History of Everton* (which was where the Liverpool "nobles" lived) a broad Lancashire dialect was spoken by all.' Shaw described himself as a member of 'the Scouse industry' in *My Liverpool* (1971: 237). Shaw's contribution to the formation of Scouse will be discussed in detail in chapter four.

10   He also calls the speech of the area 'hideous jargon' and 'dull bleared speech'.

11   An indication of the looseness of the term 'Anglo-Irish' can be derived from a consideration of the situation in contemporary Ireland. Despite the impact of various standardizing forces in the twentieth century, the vocabulary and pronunciation of Ulster English are markedly different from the forms used in rural Cork; the variation was likely to have been greater in the nineteenth century. Honeybone makes the same point in his 'New Dialect Formation in Nineteenth-Century Liverpool: A Brief History of Scouse' (2007: 120).

12   In its day as one of Britain's major ports, Liverpool was undoubtedly a multicultural place – the existence of long-established black, Chinese, Irish, Scottish, Welsh and Jewish communities attests to the fact. But recent claims about Liverpool's multi-culturalism are more to do with civic 'boosterism' than demographic and social reality. Though population statistics do not measure cultural diversity in any direct or simple way, the 2001 census reported that 3.3% of the Liverpool population was born outside the European Union (14,371), while 1.5% (6,449) were non-British EU nationals; 94.3% of the Liverpool population was classified as 'white'. For an important anthropological account of race and cultural identity in Liverpool, see Jacqueline Nassy Brown, *Dropping Anchor, Setting Sail: Geographies of Race in Black Liverpool* (2005). And for useful discussions of Liverpool's cosmopolitan past, see John Belchem and Donald MacRaild, 'Cosmopolitan Liverpool' (2006) and John Belchem, 'Liverpool: World City' (2007b). As Belchem and MacRaild note, despite its cosmopolitan heritage, Liverpool was 'neither role model nor front-runner for the multicultural Britain of the twenty-first century' (2006: 388).

13   The study of language in Britain lagged behind the pioneering Germans in this respect; many of the most important British linguists such as Henry Sweet and Joseph Wright were trained in Germany.

14 Evidence that 'thee' may have been used in Liverpool in the mid-eighteenth century is given in Thomas Boulton's *The Sailor's Farewell; Or, the Guinea Outfit* (1768), a text that will be discussed below.

15 For a discussion of the role of the public schools in the formation and dissemination of a particular form of pronunciation as a mode of social and cultural distinction, see Mugglestone 2003: 212–57.

16 There is a cultural and political issue at stake in the use of the terms 'Anglo-Irish', the later 'Hiberno-English', and the contemporary usage 'Irish-English' (see Hickey 2007: 3–5). In this work the term 'Irish-English' will be used.

17 Gladstone's father was a wealthy merchant in Liverpool and a major figure in the establishment of the Liverpool Corn Exchange; he was worth £333,000 in 1820, mostly derived from investments in Demerara (Shannon 1982: 1). Born in Rodney Street, where he spent his early years, Gladstone was educated locally at St Thomas's prep school in Seaforth before he was sent to Eton at the age of twelve.

18 For a discussion of the many complexities of interpreting the extant manuscript record of the 1801 Liverpool census, see Laxton 1981.

19 Thomas Boulton was a sea surgeon who authored this play and *The Voyage* (1773), a long poem that takes as its topic a voyage on a slave ship; the play was published in a second edition under a slightly different title: *The Guinea Outfit; or, the Sailor's Farewell. A Comedy, in Three Acts* (London: 1800). In 1769 Boulton had served on *The Delight*, a Liverpool slaver, on which there was a slave revolt. For a brief discussion of Boulton's career and work, see Rediker 2008: 19–21.

20 'Ballatague', a mis-rendering of the Irish *baile Tadhg* – Tadhg's home. Tadhg was an earlier nickname for an Irishman (from the late sixteenth century); it started to be replaced by 'Paddy' in the eighteenth century.

21 As the *OED* indicates, 'chops' here means mouth or jaw, a usage relatively common from the late sixteenth century on as a variant of 'chap'; both probably derive from the northern usage 'chaft', from an Old Norse source. A modern rendering would be 'a smack in the chops'. *Oxford English Dictionary*, 2nd edn (Oxford, 1989), *s.v. chop n²*.

22 In this respect the comic resolution in which Squire Hard is reconciled to the match between his daughter and the naval doctor is significant; he settles £200 a year on the couple, the same sum that he had quoted when attempting to persuade his daughter of the benefits of marriage to Catesby – 'two hundred a year, Kitt, in land' (Boulton 1768: 22). For a discussion of the relations between the dominant class forces in Liverpool, see Ascott et al. 2006: 162–84.

23 The religious conflicts that were being played out at the international level are also alluded to at several points in the play. The Prologue, 'spoken in the character of a sailor', ends: 'O happy theatre, happy Drury Lane,/In you there's charms to conquer [Catholic] France and Spain' (Boulton 1768: 46).

24 *Oxford English Dictionary*, 2nd edn (Oxford, 1989), *s.v. heo* pron.

25 'Pippin' is cited in the *English Dialect Dictionary* as a northern dialect form that was used in Lancashire and Cheshire. 'Pippins' – the pips of apple, pear or orange – were squeezed between finger and thumb until they flew; their direction indicated the path to a future wife or husband. *English Dialect Dictionary* (Oxford 1898–1905), *s.v. pippin* sb. 1.

3

Language and a sense of place:
the beginnings of 'Scouse'

Liverpool people can be recognised as soon as they open their mouth. Why Liverpool should be ashamed of this or touchy about it I cannot imagine. The intonation is the label of a citizenship which has no reason to hang its head. They should let London have its joke. All capital cities (not hearing themselves speak) think that provincial talk is funny. Marseille sends Paris into stitches, but a fat lot Marseille cares. (H.R. Shaw, 'Liverpool Accent', 1950)[1]

The previous chapter attempted to challenge and revise the standard history of language in Liverpool by arguing that a distinctive form of language must have appeared in the eighteenth and early nineteenth centuries and thus that the claim that the inhabitants of Liverpool used the same speech form as their Lancastrian neighbours as late as the 1830s is false. Notwithstanding this important revision, however, it is clear that the language of Liverpool must have been affected by the patterns of immigration to Liverpool (predominantly Irish but including other significant elements) in the mid to late nineteenth century. Evidence of the form itself is scant, though there are possible glimpses in literary accounts (always remembering, as noted earlier, the problems with textual material). *Her Benny* (1879), for example, the one book with which all Liverpool children used to be familiar, provides representations of the speech of Liverpool street kids that seem to confirm that there was indeed a distinct form in that environment at least. Thus on the opening page Nelly declares: 'I'm glad as how they're lighting the lamps, anyhow. It'll make it feel a bit warmer, I reckon... for it's terrible cold.' And later Benny, her brother, exclaims, 'Be jabbers, it's a thripny... Oh, glory! ... if't ain't haaf a bob [...] If he'd a-catched me, I'd got a walloping, an no mistake' (Hocking 1966: 1, 14).[2] It is also clear that there was some sense of the appearance of a distinctive local form in the late nineteenth and early twentieth centuries. In William Tirebuck's dreadful melodramatic Liverpool novel *Dorrie* (1891), for example, reference is made to 'Liverpudlian English' (probably the first use of the phrase) (Tirebuck 1891: 290),[3] while, as noted previously, in Scott's *Liverpool* (1907), the author describes the northern and southern slum areas and asserts that 'here alone in Liverpool do you get a specific dialect' (Scott 1907: 144). And yet despite this support for the thesis of an emerging local form, what is particularly noteworthy is the absence of any sustained reference to this form – and none at all to Scouse. In this chapter then the focus will turn to the beginnings of the process by which 'Scouse' became established as a linguistic and cultural category. As will become clear, this was a complex development in which local interest in the use of words and cultural practices in a specific urban space – the philology and folklore of the back street so to speak – became the foundation for what was later called 'the Scouse industry'. It was a development that began in the early to mid twentieth century, a point at which Liverpool's prominence as a global port had passed and the first signs of decline, which was later to become wholescale blight, had started to become evident. The story is convoluted, strange and unpredictable; it is also central to the understanding of representations of Liverpool as a social and cultural space.

Words and culture: letters to the papers

In letters and a number of feature articles in Liverpool newspapers between the early 1930s and the 1950s, contributors compiled evidence for what was claimed to be a specifically Liverpudlian lexicon (and engaged in a running comment- ary on the items included in the putative glossary). Setting the tone, 'Postman', the feature writer of the 'Day to Day in Liverpool' column in the *Liverpool Post and Mercury*, reported a letter from a correspondent regarding the local terms 'nix', 'jowl' and 'ek, ek'.[4] 'Nix', as in 'nix, the bobby', was a warning – 'look out, here's the bobby', though in verbal form ('to keep nix') it could also mean 'to keep watch'; 'ek, ek', as in 'ek, ek, here's the bobby', was likewise admonitory – 'watch out, here's the bobby'; and 'jowl', as in 'the boy did a jowl', meant 'the boy ran off hurriedly' (though 'jowler' was given in this particular letter as 'not known') ('Postman' 1931a: 5). As with many 'Liverpudlian' words, the origins of these terms are obscure. J.C. Hotten's *Dictionary of Modern Slang, Cant and Vulgar Words Used at the Present Day in the Streets of London* (1860) defines 'nix' as 'the signal word of school boys to each other that the master, or other person in authority, is approaching', while 'keeping nix' was evidently also used in Dublin, as attested by James Joyce's short story 'Eveline' (1914): 'Her father used often to hunt them in out of the field with his blackthorn stick; but usually little Keogh used to keep *nix* and call out when he saw her father coming' (Joyce 1992a: 29). But the etymological root of the term is unclear, as is that of 'ek, ek', a phrase attested in slightly altered form in J.L. Haigh's neglected Liverpool novel set in the Scotland Road area, *Sir Galahad of the Slums* (1907): 'Tim Sharkey, the bruiser, and Pat Nolan, a lad of very promising talent, were having a boxing-match, in which poor Pat was getting the worst of it, when a sudden cry of "Heck, heck!" outside, and the quick appearance of Longfellow [a policeman] inside, upset the whole proceedings' (Haigh 1907: 20).[5] The origin of 'jowl' is also opaque. 'To do a jowl', in the sense of 'to run off', probably derives from 'jowler', which was later defined as an alternative to 'jigger'; hence 'to do a jowl' may have meant 'to run down a back entry' ('Postman' 1947b: 6).[6]

In fact both 'jowler' and 'jigger' featured repeatedly in these early reports of Liverpool words, though again the roots ascribed to them were often dubious.[7] On the basis of a reader's note, 'Postman' gave the etymological explanation of 'jowler' as 'to dash one's head against something' (on the basis of 'jowl' in the sense of 'head'), an account that was clearly derived from the *OED* ('Postman' 1947b: 6). A more plausible explanation was the derivation from the common phrase 'cheek by jowl', in the sense of 'side by side, very close' (Griffith 1950: 2).[8] For 'jigger' a variety of etymological possibilities were presented. Again citing a correspondent, 'Postman' asserted that it was 'an old word used in the south end of the town to denote a back-passage or entry between two rows of houses', whose derivation was the 'jigger-mast', meaning the aft mast of a sailing ship, an account that prompted the comment: 'what more applicable term could so briefly express the phrase "back-entry" in such a sea-going community as South Liverpool was in the latter days of the tall ships?' ('Postman' 1945e: 5). But two years later, 'Postman' reported two further letters, the first suggesting that the word came from a practice in the Liverpool (later Martin's) Bank – 'jigger' being the name of 'the short flexible vellum markers inserted in the pages of the ledgers to facilitate reference' ('Postman' 1947a: 4).[9] The next day brought a counter-claim that asserted that the word belonged to the north end of the city (Everton); the etymology was given as the term used to describe 'a series of rapid jerks' (as with a fish on a line) ('Postman' 1947b: 6). But as *Green's Dictionary of Slang* (Green 2010) notes, a more likely origin than any of the above is a link to a Lancashire dialect form, with the sense of 'a narrow entry between houses', possibly originating in the cant term 'jigger, a door', dating from the eighteenth century. The ultimate origin of the canting sense may have been 'gigger', first recorded in the sixteenth century and possibly derived from the Welsh 'gwddor', 'a gate'.[10]

The accounts of terms such as 'nix', 'ek, ek', 'jowl(er)' and 'jigger' are interesting in that they illustrate not simply local use, but also the tendency to assert (often inaccurately) the uniqueness of specific terms to the Liverpool area.[11] Another example was 'butty', which was discussed in a 'Postman' column in the *Liverpool Post and Mercury* in 1931. Described as an 'age-old' Liverpool term, it was, it was asserted, the elliptical form of 'sugar-butty', a phrase that referred to 'an attractive mixture of bread, butter and sugar. A slice of bread was buttered in the ordinary way and then sprinkled with granulated sugar. This taste was pleasing, and often made it easier for the parent of an intransigent child to persuade it to school' ('Postman' 1931b: 5). Again, however, the claim for the unique provenance of this phrase was without substance. The *OED* records 'butty' as northern dialectal and gives a reference to Mrs Gaskell's *North and South* (1855); while the *English Dialect Dictionary* (1898–1905) notes that the usage was common in Yorkshire, Lancashire, Cheshire and Staffordshire and defines it as 'a slice of bread and butter; also bread spread with treacle, sugar &c'. 'Give me a sugar-butty' is furnished as an example from Cheshire.[12] As other examples demonstrate, the inaccurate though culturally significant propensity to assert the local specificity of terms persisted. George Price listed 'many strange "slang" words which I dare venture are not heard in any part of the country', some of which 'must be as old as Liverpool itself!' (His collection included 'nix', 'douse', 'jigger', 'jowler', 'slop' – a policeman – 'scuffer', 'decko', 'meg', and 'Aye, aye' – 'a salutation'.) He also reported causing 'great consternation in these parts' (he lived in Staffordshire) 'by asking for a panmug'; sad to say the locals hadn't heard of 'muggen jug' either (Price 1950: 4). Such sentiments in a whole series of letters and articles in the local newspapers evinced an attitude towards words used in Liverpool that managed to combine philological curiosity with a range of often clearly felt responses (ranging from deep local pride to complete contempt). If nothing else, the prolonged correspondence indicated that there was a developed sense that Liverpool as a place had a vocabulary (and a mode of pronunciation) that was part of its cultural distinctiveness within Britain.[13]

A few examples can illustrate both the fascination and the different per-spectives articulated in the newspaper coverage. One interesting item discussed in the 'Day to Day in Liverpool' column was the term 'the Artful Dodger', though not in the sense first recorded in the sixteenth century – a haggler or trickster (immortalized in the Dickens character in *Oliver Twist* in 1838). In Liverpool it referred instead to 'a workman who would rather do without a beer than have a half pint' and derived from a 'dodger', 'a glass of beer containing less than half a pint and more than a "pony" or quarter pint' (both of which were generally treated 'with contempt') ('Postman' 1931b: 5).[14] There was, however, an alternate form – 'a Peter Hudson', whose derivation (thought to be unknown by the original correspondent) was clarified the next day. It derived from the name of 'a Liverpool worthy forty or fifty years ago', a brewer by trade, who was 'strict in limiting his morning consumption to about two-thirds of one half pint glass' ('Postman' 1931d: 5). In a different vein, 'tatting' was declared confidently by 'Postman' to be 'applied to collecting rags and bones'; it derived, 'residents in Scotland Road would doubtless be surprised to know', from the Icelandic word 'tötturr' (though in fact the etymology is uncertain and contested) ('Postman' 1932a: 5).[15] 'Wet Neller' (or 'Wet Nellie'), another term that was cited repeatedly, was the name for a Nelson cake, described by 'Postman' as consisting of 'a bunloaf soaked in treacle' and identified as a term coined in the mid Victorian period and 'only sold in the poorer class of confectioners' ('Postman' 1932b: 5).[16] A correspondent in the *Liverpool Post and Mercury*, under the title 'Liverpool Slang', provided other examples of 'Liverpool words commonly used thirty to forty years ago' (writers often commented on the disappearance of the local vernacular – for better or worse), mostly from 'the south-end of the city'.[17] They included 'purely "Liverpool"' items such as 'the Stick' – the Landing Stage; 'a fudge' – a farthing; 'a meg' – half-penny; 'a win' – a penny; 'a joey' – threepenny piece; 'snitch' – tell on someone; 'clat' – tell-tale, gossip; 'scuffer' – policeman; 'jack' – plainclothes policeman; 'sag' – play truant; 'Bully' – Princes Boulevard; 'Monkey Rack' – the boardwalk in Sefton Park; 'Seven Hedges' – the top of Dingle Lane; 'Greasy Fields' – Ullet Road playground; 'Cazzy' – the Cast Iron Shore; 'Cinder Walk' – a walk overlooking the Herculanaeum dock; 'the Spiky' – a short cut between Dingle Lane and the shore (Jones 1935: 5). The topic of monetary terms was revisited in the 'Day to Day in Liverpool' feature in the same paper a couple of years later in a piece entitled 'Liverpool Language'.

A 'spraza', it was reported, 'in the Liverpool gambling world [...] denotes a sixpenny piece', while a half-crown was a 'tusheroon', a ten shilling note was a 'half-bar', a one pound note was a 'bar' or 'nicker', and a five pound note was a 'Royal Liver' ('Postman' 1937a: 6).

The interest in local language also brought other topics to the attention of Liverpool's newspaper readership. Street and place names were frequently discussed – a continuation of a concern typified by James Stonehouse's *The Streets of Liverpool. With Some of their Distinguished Residents, Reminiscences and Curious Information of Bygone Times* (1869).[18] Thus in 'Street Names of Liverpool. Interesting Facts about their Origin', an article in the *Daily Post* reported on a talk given by R. Saunders Jones at the Welsh Calvinistic Methodist Chapel in Garston. Jones, 'an authority on ancient Liverpool, and particularly the Garston district', gave several word-histories. Fazakerley, the name of an area in Liverpool (and a street), was taken from Thomas Fazakerleigh, an important office-holder in fourteenth-century Liverpool, while Hatton Garden, in the heart of the city, was wholly unrelated to its London counterpart (it was coined by two builders to commemorate their birthplace of Hatton, near Warrington). And nearby Cheapside (site of the main bridewell), one of the oldest streets in the city, was formerly known as Dig Lane (and by the nickname 'Dog and Duck Lane') (Anon 1931a: 5). The fascination with the local histories hidden in place and street names later manifested itself in C.M. Daresbury's account of the derivation of Sleeper's Hill in Walton in a letter to the *Liverpool Echo*. The explanation was striking:

> On February 4, 1871, a travelling circus owned by an Irish family named McArdle was proceeding from Preston to the waste ground that is today Liverpool F.C.'s Spion Kop, and owned by a Mr. John Houlding. Halting at Aintree to feed the animals, a lion escaped from his cage. Search parties found the lion asleep in the bushes of the Bodley Estate, hence the subsequent name, Sleeper's Hill. (Daresbury 1950: 5)

Notwithstanding the impressive leonine sense of direction in traversing the five or so miles from Aintree (Bodley Street joins to Sleeper's Hill, which in turn connects to Walton Breck Road – a few hundred yards along which is the Kop end of Anfield), Daresbury recalled a letter from the chief constable to the circus proprietor 'warning him of the dire consequences of bringing lions into the city of Liverpool without being properly caged' (1950: 5). A slightly less bizarre place-name enigma was the puzzle that surrounded 'The Mystery' – properly known as Wavertree playground. Formerly a private estate, the land was bought by an anonymous philanthropist and given to the city of Liverpool as a purpose-built public playground in 1895 (it was one of the first in the country). The mystery, aired by W.H. Carter in the *Daily Post*, was of course the identity of the donor; it was solved by T.J. Bidston in the same paper a few days later when he revealed the mystery man to be Alfred Holt, owner of the Blue Funnel shipping line (Bidston 1955: 4).

As well as local words and the history captured in place or street names, a variety of cultural practices and forms also caught the attention of local social observers – particularly towards the end of the Second World War (a period when a 'return' to former ways of life was evidently a felt imperative). In a letter to 'Postman', a correspondent noted that children had been seen 'pace-egging for the first time in twenty years' in Kirkdale ('pace-egging', properly Paschal-egging, was a ceremony in which eggs were decorated as part of the Easter celebration and distributed by the 'pace-eggers' – groups of garishly dressed mummers who fought mock battles, recited songs and collected money) ('Postman' 1945a: 2). The article suggested that this was more of a Lancastrian than a Liverpudlian custom (which it was – unlike the Dingle tradition of burning Judas on Good Friday), though a few days later a writer to the paper recorded that the practice had taken place at Gateacre Brow earlier that year ('Postman' 1945b: 2).[19] In similar vein a later piece reported the revival of Maypole revels including the dressing of the May Queen (a feature that had been prevented by the rationing of clothing during wartime) ('Postman' 1945c: 2). Liverpool's children, meanwhile, had cultural customs of their own. 'A Southerner' in Liverpool for Christmas was 'puzzled [...] by a nautical carol he heard sung the other night by Liverpool urchins' whose first lines, 'long familiar to Liverpolitans', were:

'Twas a cold, cold night in December,
The wintry winds did blow.
When there came a poor raggedy sailor boy
Knocking at a lady's door...

Querying the origin, he wondered whether it was 'composed or sung at sea years ago by some Dicky Sam [...] whose doggerel seems to have achieved a strange immortality on Merseyside' ('Postman' 1936: 5).[20] The enigma of the 'Mystery Carol' remained unsolved, as did the riddle of the name of the Liverpool bogeyman, 'Daddy Bunchy', though he lent his name to a girls' game of snatch and to a skipping song (Lovgreen 1955: 9; Shaw 1955a: 9; 1969: 31–32).[21] A favourite street game was 'ollies' (marbles), often played with cherrystones (known as 'cherrywobs', 'cherrybobs' and 'cherrywogs') (Bidston 1955: 4),[22] while a variation of pitch and toss was called 'Flemings' in the late nineteenth century and played with metal buttons ('a Fleming was a bright brass button with the name Fleming embossed on it') (J.W. Jones 1955: 4).[23] An alternative name for the game was 'bang off', in which two boys each 'banged off' a button from a wall and then used a special button – a 'Copper Lewie' or 'Deli' (flattened for the purpose on a tram line) to try to cover his opponent's button (H. Jones 1955: 5).

The street was also the location for another aspect of Liverpool life, and in an article entitled 'Oldsters Will Remember Them. Street Characters of a Bygone Day' under the 'Echoes and Gossip of the Day' feature, the *Liverpool Echo* provided the platform for a particular type of cultural nostalgia that was later to become commonplace. Prompted by 'recent articles on Liverpool speech and "slanguage"' [*sic*], the piece recalled various street performers and mendicants: the South End Captain (who wore five coats); the Upper Parliament Blind Bible Reader; the Pudsey Street Legless Beggar who, on the death of his dog, tied the dog to his cart with the plaintive sign 'The Dog is Dead' (often drunk, the man was described as 'not inaptly legless'); Dan the Harpist, whose strings were supplied by the local grocer; Bluebell, the singer with the blind husband accompanist; the Blind Male Quartet; and the Nigger Minstrels (last seen at New Brighton in 1939) of whom only two remained – 'Brudder Bones […] and his small depressed looking partner […] brothers of the burnt cork' (Dawson 1951: 4). Two of the most famous characters were Seth Davy and Tilly Mint. Davy, 'the "old Negro" of Scotland Road', was described as 'the "King" of Scotland Road's entertainers, the "Noel Coward and Ivor Novello" (all in one) of the latter part of the 19th, and early part of the twentieth centuries' (Bailey 1957: 6). West Indian by birth, Davy sang and performed with 'dancing dolls' outside the Bevington Bush hotel, and was later immortalized in the folk song 'Whiskey on a Sunday'. 'Tilly Mint' was the name given to one of the women who sold bunches of herbs – mint, sage and parsley – outside St John's Market on the steps of the fish market on Saturday nights, though she was also identified as a mint, sage and lemon seller on Mill Street in the Dingle (the name itself later became generalized, usually as a way of scolding young women – 'listen Tilly Mint') (Ford 1964: 4; Williams 1964: 6). And yet, notwithstanding the interest in a whole variety of cultural practices and characters that was manifested in the correspondence and feature pages of the local papers, the real concern lay with words used in Liverpool that, it was argued, formed part of the cultural distinctiveness of the place. Thus 'Postman' reported on an actor (the British radio performer Stephan Jack) who was appearing at the Liverpool Playhouse and who was something of a 'Dialect Expert'. Noting that 'Liverpool's accent interested him greatly', 'Postman' reported Jack's opinion that the accent 'was based on Lancashire and Cheshire speech with some Glasgow and London' (in addition to 'the Irish influence' that explained the 'softening of the T and hardening of the TH sounds'). The piece ended with an observation that contained an implicit challenge: 'the whole subject is very mysterious and well worthy of research' ('Postman' 1945d: 2). The same sentiment informed a more direct appeal in the *Liverpool Echo* of 25 June 1947: 'why doesn't somebody at the University write a thesis on Liverpool slang?' ('Postman' 1947b: 6).

'Liverpool speech': postulated origins and influences

A burst of letters in late 1950 and early 1951 evinced the continuing interest in language in Liverpool. Hari O'Hanri explained that 'down the banks' ('to fight, argue or remonstrate') came from the fact that 'years ago if a couple had a few words they went down to the Leeds and Liverpool Canal banks (known as the Lock Fields)' to sort things out (O'Hanri 1950: 2), while Leonard Fleming Prout clarified the meaning of 'Fleming's up the steps', meaning cheap or poor-quality clothing (W.H. Fleming was an established tailor on Scotland Road – 'up the steps' referred to Paddy's Market) (Fleming Prout 1950: 4). And 'maccyowler', thought by one correspondent to indicate a Chinese influence, was ascertained by M. Wright as 'a backyard moggy' or cat, and by extension 'fur coat' (Wright

1951: 4). R. Griffith contributed a note that drew attention to 'brue' – hill or slope; 'dekko' – look ('have a dekko' – have a look); 'keeping douse' – keeping lookout; and 'shaddle' – seesaw (Griffith 1950: 2). Responding to Griffith's list, a letter on 'Liverpool Lingo' added elucidations: 'dekko', it was claimed, was 'Romany' (from 'dik', 'to look, see', though it may have been Hindi – through Anglo-Indian services slang – in origin); 'brue' was described as 'old and little-used standard English' (it derived from Old English *brú*, compare Scots 'brae'); and 'shaddle' was claimed to be 'common across England, including Shropshire' (though the *OED*, *EDD* and the slang dictionaries have no record of this use) (Harvey 1950: 2).[24] A month or so later, another writer registered the Liverpool use of 'parapet' for pavement, a usage that dated back to the eighteenth century (R.H.W. 1951: 2).[25] But it was a more extensive and thoughtful contribution to the features section of the *Liverpool Echo* – 'We All Talk Sailor's Slang' – that set out putative nautical etymologies for common Liverpool terms and phrases. Examples included 'waister', meaning not a person who is 'wasting his life' (hence 'waster', a usage that dates from the mid fourteenth century), but a bungling seaman 'ordered to remain in the waist of a ship' and thus 'less likely to fall overboard or mess up'. 'Hold on', as in 'hold on a moment', derived, it was claimed, from the 'order to stop sailors paying away rope'. And 'at loggerheads' allegedly originated in a description of a 'crew fighting with loggerhead bricks'.[26] 'Take down a peg' (to humble or chasten) has an obscure etymology according to the *OED*, though the author of the *Liverpool Echo* piece proposed that it referred to 'the raising and lowering of a ship's colours'. 'Nipper' (boy) was given as the name of the 'ship boy who dealt with short bits of rope called nips',[27] while 'brace of shakes' (as in 'coming in a brace of shakes' – very quickly) was allegedly based on the quick manner in which 'the canvas shakes when a ship is headed into wind'.[28] 'Bitter end', in an explanation more or less confirmed by the *OED*, derived from the fact that a ship's 'anchor cable was attached to mooring posts called bitts' and 'in a gale sailors paid out cable to what they called the bitter end lest the anchor drag'.[29] And finally, 'to carry on' (to make a fuss, behave badly) was explained as a metaphorical extension of the use of 'carry on' to refer to the action of a sailing vessel when it 'shows too much sail area in a stiff blow of wind', thus losing balance and speed and consequently flopping 'along with her flank slapping the wave and white water slapping the lee wave' (Anon 1954b: 2).[30]

If the nautical influence on Liverpool English was one subject of interest, another was the impact of the city's connections with Ireland (although opinions varied widely). A letter to the *Daily Post* – 'In Liverpool "I felt myself in Dublin"' – noted 'the complex nature of the Liverpool accent' and went on to cite comments from James Phelan, the Irish novelist, in his autobiographical *The Name's Phelan*:

> [I] already felt myself in Dublin as soon as I heard the people speak. No one, so far as I know, has commented on the resemblance between the speech of Dublin and that of Liverpool, or better, of Birkenhead. Somewhere, sometime, the influences must have been the same, for Merseyside speech is as foreign to Lancashire as the Liffeyside accent is to the Ireland around, and the two are almost the same. (Phelan 1948: 201)

As the letter-writer observed, Phelan's remarks related to the pre-First World War period, which provoked the conclusion that 'the Liverpool accent is no recent phenomenon'. Further speculative analysis followed: 'perhaps the slurring of the vowels comes from Ireland and the sing-song lilt from the Welsh and the adenoidal sound from the catarrh which afflicts Liverpolitans'. What's more, the writer continued, 'the accent is tenacious too' (the case of a Liverpool man who had married a Frenchwoman and lived in Normandy for a long period was cited; when heard on the 'wireless' his 'accent was as clear as ever') (Rigby 1950: 4).

The debate on the Irish influence on Liverpool's language was taken up in an important essay by Frank Shaw in 'Scouse Lingo – How It All Began', in which he asserted that it was the Irish who gave more than '200 words used in a way peculiar (almost) to the city, as well as innumerable phrases' and particular linguistic techniques such as 'telescoping' ('marmalize' – to beat someone, possibly from 'pulverize' and 'marmalade'); 'slurring' ('gerrout'); and 'elision' ('isavvy') (Shaw 1950c: 4).[31] Lexical items included 'gob' ('mouth'); 'gom' ('fool' from the Gaelic *gámaí*, 'gamal', 'dolt, simpleton, fool, lout', by way of Irish-English 'gom'); 'mam' (Gaelic *mam*, though a classical root is more likely); 'dug' ('breast' – there seems no evidence for an Irish-English derivation and 'dugge' is used in sixteenth-century English); and 'moider' ('to bother, confuse, upset' – used in Irish-English but more commonly in various forms in northern English dialects – possibly from the Gaelic *modar*, 'dark, murky, cloudy' and by extension *modarthacht*, 'murkiness, gloominess').[32] There were also phrases such as 'backwards the way Molly went to church' and 'strong as a bad egg', both of which Shaw claimed as originating in Ireland (Shaw 1950c: 4). Shaw's article touched a nerve and initiated a testy exchange that lasted for a number of years with Hari O'Hanri ('an scríob'). Thus in 'It's the Irish in Us!', O'Hanri expanded on Shaw's essay by giving 'the Gaelic Irish spelling and pronunciation of many words used by him which are definitely Irish and in common use daily in Liverpool'. Examples included 'gob' for 'mouth' (from the Gaelic *gob* – 'snout, beak, bill', though the usage, marked as northern, dialectal and slang in the *OED*, had been current in English since the sixteenth century); 'puck' for 'hit or strike' – 'a puck in the gob' (from *poc*, 'sharp, sudden blow', 'puck' in Irish-English from the mid nineteenth century); 'lug', for 'ear' (supposedly from *lag*, 'hollow or cavity', though the *OED* gives the etymology as obscure); 'scuffer' – 'policeman' (allegedly from *gab* – pronounced 'guv', 'take hold of, catch', hence *gabhta*, pronounced 'guffter' and thus 'scuffer'); 'kewin' for 'quiet' (from *ciúin*, 'calm, silent, still' on the grounds that if you 'give someone a halfpenny worth of "kewins" and a pin to extract them from their shells, that would keep them "kewin"'); 'cod' from the Gaelic *cad* ('what' – as in 'cod on yer don't know!' – 'wot you don't know is not worth knowing') (O'Hanri 1950: 2).[33]

Others were slightly more sceptical about the influence of Ireland, or more accurately, Gaelic-speaking immigrants, on language in Liverpool. Thus a letter in the *Liverpool Echo* on 3 January 1951 dismissed O'Hanri's argument that Gaelic words had entered the 'Liverpool dialect' – or at least that they had done so exclusively. Apart from the familiar 'galore' (from the Gaelic *go leór* – sufficient, enough), many of O'Hanri's other examples were treated peremptorily as nothing but 'representations in modern Irish orthography of the English slang terms' or as simply mistaken. Thus 'scuird' – 'squirt, splash' (as in 'a scard of tea') was a back-borrowing from the Gaelic *scaird* – 'squirt, jet', while 'slopuck' – 'slovenly woman' – was possibly from the Gaelic *slapóg*, 'slut, untidy woman' (though the 'ock' was an English and Scots dialect ending). 'Scoot' – 'to run off' – had a nautical use and was possibly of Scandinavian origin, perhaps cognate with Old Norse *skiót* – to shoot (hence perhaps the modern 'to shoot off'); 'skelp' – 'to slap, smack' was in all likelihood onomatopoeic; 'slavey' – 'servant, either sex, but usually female' was first noted in Vaux's *New and Comprehensive Vocabulary of the Flash Slang* 1819, but was an Irish-English borrowing (it was deployed by James Joyce in the short story 'Two Gallants' in *Dubliners*).[34] Other than these few dubious items, the correspondent claimed, there were no Gaelic loanwords in Liverpool, although 'some phonetic effect of Irish Gaelic on the local speech cannot be excluded' (D.W.F.H. 1951: 3). Similar scepticism towards the possibility of a direct influence of Gaelic on Liverpool English was expressed a week or so later by Shaw in 'Way of Speech', again in the *Liverpool Echo*.[35] Shaw did, however, argue that the local form 'owed much to the Irish […] way of speaking English, which is, in fact, the way the English spoke English two centuries ago'. As evidence he gave the rhyming of 'creature' with 'nature' (Dryden), 'deserve' with 'starve' (Swift), and 'tea' with 'obey' (Pope). And in an uncharacteristic show of anti-prescriptivism, Shaw noted that 'much of what is thought to be slang and bad English (you was for you were, dropped aitches, slurred final consonants as in huntin, shooting, fishin and the pleonastic double negative – I never saw no one) was once quite good English'. In a final flourish (one that showed some familiarity with the most advanced linguistic thinking of the day), the letter ended with the assertion that like other forms, 'so-called Standard English is merely another dialect' (Shaw 1951: 2).

The lexical and phonological impact of Irish-English on Liverpool English was taken up again by a self-described investigator of the 'Liverpool town dialect', in the *Daily Post* in January 1951. In the piece, 'Liverpool Speech: Some Local Pronunciations', T. Oakes Hirst (a reputable linguist) interestingly confined the effects of language contact to very specific locations within the city.[36] He doubted any 'Irish influence outside its own proper areas – Scotland Road district and Woolton' and made the interesting observation that children of Irish parentage 'retain some Anglo-Irish accent (or brogue)', which formed a contrast with the practice of children of Welsh parents (where the influence was less) and those of 'other nationalities', whose speech forms 'merge into one common type'.[37] With regard to 'Irish areas' such as Scotland Road, however, it was claimed that 'Irish sounds and words' were common (examples included the pronunciation 'say' for 'sea', 'tay' for 'tea' and 'taych' for 'teach'). But like lexical items such as 'skallan' – 'scallion, spring onion' (originally an Anglo-Norman import into Ireland), 'caubeen' – 'hat or cap' (from the Gaelic *cáibín* – 'old hat'), and 'bothered' – 'deaf' (from the Gaelic *bodhar* – 'deaf'), such features were, at least according to this writer, restricted to very particular geographic and social spaces. And again, as with the earlier article in the *Liverpool Echo* discussed in the previous paragraph, the author of this piece noted that a number of words that were considered to be of Irish origin or provenance, such as 'tearing' (as in 'a tearing rage'), 'gab' ('garrulity') and 'scuffer' (policeman'), were not Irish at all (Oakes Hirst 1951: 4).[38] Needless to say, this was hardly the end of the debate. When Shaw published 'Do You Want to Speak Scouse?' in the *Liverpool Echo* a few years later, he cited a philologian's comment on 'Dublinese' – 'an adenoidal delivery with a narrow epiglottal distribution of sounds and a slightly nasal intonation' that was 'almost invariably redeemed by a racy vocabulary and phraseology' – which Shaw glossed by observing that he 'might well be describing Liverpoolese' (Shaw 1955a: 6). Asserting that 'much of our speech came [...] from Ireland', he reported having to teach actors performing his play, *The Scab* (written in 'Liverpoolese'), about aspects of local speech.[39] They included pronunciations such as 'the Anglo-Irish "ow" for "o" in words like "old"', 'me' for 'my' and 'other Gaelicisms': 't'morra', 'minnit', 'cod' (fool), 'on the pig's back' (lucky, wealthy), 'childer' (children). The article appeared to incense Harry O'Henry (Hari O'Hanri as was), who responded in the letters section a couple of weeks later. Arguing that 'the enunciation of English is almost perfect in Dublin', O'Henry rejected the Liverpool plural 'youse' as derived from Irish-English (proposing instead that it was 'introduced into English from the coloured race in South America'), ridiculed Shaw's postulation of 'ow' for 'o' in 'ould fella', and observed that 'the Liverpudlian's grammar leaves a lot to be desired'. He concluded with an unmistakable dig at Shaw: 'if we continue to adopt an attitude of superiority we eventually become a pompous pedant, which in "scouse" is "worse than anything, so it is"' (O'Hanri 1955: 6). There was, evidently, some competition for the role of keeper of the Liverpool-Irish flame.

The half-secret tongue

It is clear from the correspondence and articles in the Liverpool newspapers that there was significant interest in the origins and status of forms of language that were considered to be a unique part of the Liverpudlian cultural scene. Concern with the 'Liverpool accent' (the title of a piece in the *Daily Post*, 4 August 1950) was also beginning to become pronounced (so to speak). Thus, though he denied that there was a Liverpool accent proper, H.R. Shaw (no relation to Frank Shaw) asserted that

> there is a Liverpool intonation. It is highly characteristic, strongly marked and it lasts. Gladstone was said to have retained a trace of it to the end. I hear it distinctly in people of Liverpool birth who have been away from the city for years. They often think they have lost it, but when they are vexed or otherwise off-guard, there it is again. To deny the existence of this lingual label is pointless. (H.R. Shaw 1950: 2)

Adding that 'there is, very definitely, a Liverpool speech habit', his final comment was that it 'can be and is recognized except by Liverpool people themselves. It is probably inbred.' Various commentators opined about the nature and source of the Liverpool accent around this time. J.C. Colman, for example, asserted that 'the authentic Liverpool accent is slightly nasal and often accompanied with a play of the tip of the tongue against the teeth', which made it difficult to imitate (Colman 1950: 4), while C.H. Notan claimed that 'an important element in Liverpool speech seems to be caused by the nasal and bronchial catarrh from which we all suffer more or less' (it wasn't coincidental that Liverpool had a purpose-built Ear, Nose and Throat Infirmary). As a consequence, 'the way Liverpool people produce their voices from their throats – sometimes more harshly – is characteristic and most persistent even in people who would be horrified to think they had a Liverpool accent!' (Notan 1950: 4). Frank Shaw reiterated the claim that language in Liverpool was 'spoken in the distinctive catarrhal manner' (Shaw 1950c: 4), and the observation (origin unknown) that the accent was 'one third Irish, one third Welsh, and a third catarrh' became a commonplace. As far as causes went, there were explanations aplenty. 'Postman' reported the claim that 'the adenoidal thickness' of the accent was attributable to 'the moist and sooty atmosphere' ('Postman' 1945d: 2), whereas Shaw claimed that 'the adenoidal delivery [...] is said to come from the salt in the air' (Harrison 1958: 5). And David Isenberg observed that speakers of 'Scouse' 'are affected for the greater part of their lives by the smoke of industry which has helped a good deal to give them their characteristic nasal tone' (Isenberg 1962: 6).

H.R. Shaw's article drew a response from John Farrell, a local teacher, in the *Daily Post* a few days later.[40] This essay, 'About that Liverpool Accent (or Dialect)', began by recording the irritation felt by 'Liverpolitans or Liverpudlians' when BBC producers 'represent the local speech form as "Lancashire"' and continued to assert that although 'natives often deny the existence of a Liverpool accent', they strongly object when they are 'portrayed as either a countryman or a person suffering from chronic obstruction of the nasal passages'.[41] Such sensitivity, Farrell noted, was hardly surprising, given that in contemporary Britain it was 'difficult to discuss accents objectively. There are as many prejudiced verdicts on speech as there are on politics and religion' (Farrell 1950a: 4). Such prejudice was long-standing and a characteristic example had been delivered at the University of Liverpool by A. Lloyd James, the BBC's linguistic adviser and Reader in Phonetics, in a speech to trainee teachers. Defending the BBC against charges that its 'baneful influence' was 'crushing the life out of historic English dialects' by attempting to 'standardise English', James played his audience a recording of the speech of London schoolchildren (before they had taken a course in speech training). His commentary, which might have been delivered by George Bernard Shaw's Henry Higgins, was typical of attitudes at the time.[42]

> That may be alright in the Cockney's own milieu, but not outside it. That stuff keeps anybody in the gutter. If speech is the social criterion we have made of it, then for Heaven's sake let us teach it. To turn a child into the world with an accent you have heard on that record is a ghastly mistake. You might just as well turn it out dirty, or unconscious of the elements of public conduct. (Anon 1931b: 4)

Farrell's point about linguistic prejudice was reinforced by Raymond Williams' comment in an influential essay published in 1961, that 'the importance of speech as an indicator of social class is not likely to be underestimated by anyone who has lived in England' (a sentiment scarcely less true today than it was then) (Williams 1965: 237). More importantly, in the same seminal work, Williams considered at length the politics surrounding linguistic variation in modern Britain, including the first extended critical treatment of the term and concept 'standard English'.[43] The significance of his work lay in the emphasis on the distinction between 'standard English' as a phrase that referred to a system of writing – a historically specifiable and codified form – and 'standard English' as a term that connoted speech – a cultural form identified by the social status of its speakers rather than any specific linguistic features per se. To put the point simply, although a standard form of written English (in the sense of a relatively stable, though evolving, system of writing that was commonly used across the national space) may have been forged over the centuries, there was no similar form at the level of speech. Even the *OED* account of the term in the 1933 Supplement (the authoritative definition before the changes made in the 1989 revised edition) made that clear. 'Standard English', the dictionary stipulated, was the phrase

> applied to a variety of the speech of a country which, by reason of its cultural status and currency, is held to represent the best form of that speech. *Standard English*: that form of the English language which is spoken (with modifications individual or local), by the generality of the cultured people of Great Britain.

'Standard English', at least in terms of speech, was an evaluative rather than a descriptive term (its classificatory power depended on the value-laden link between 'the best speech' and 'cultured people'). As the quotation used to exemplify the *OED* definition evinced, 'Standard English, like Standard French, is now a class dialect more than a local dialect, it is the language of the educated all over Great Britain' (Sweet 1908: 7). Interestingly, Farrell reiterated this very point in his account of Liverpool English: 'everyone speaks some sort of dialect. The so-called Standard or Received Pronunciation is merely a Class Dialect as opposed to a local form' (Farrell 1950a: 4). Such a statement amounted to a significant declaration of support for local vernacular speech against a model of centralization and class-based distinction that was based on a false parallel between speech and writing.[44]

In an important development, Farrell noted that there was some confusion over the use of the terms 'accent' and 'dialect' (difficulties that, as will become clear later, were not confined to the realm of non-professional commentary on language). His own account proposed a distinction: 'a person speaks with an accent when his standard pronunciation is modified by traces of another speech form', whereas a dialect is 'distinguished from the standard by differences in vowel quality, in vowel formation and distribution, in consonant quality and distribution, in idiom, vocabulary and speech melody'. Such an analysis led him to assert that 'the native speech of Liverpool should be described as a dialect, as the distinguishing features are enough to give it a special character'. Farrell was, however, sensitive to the fact that the usual category used to describe the distinctive language of Liverpool was 'accent' – and that this was 'in such widespread and common use that it is pointless not to accept it'. This was an acute observation and it points to a long-standing and somewhat peculiar attitude towards the status of Liverpool English as will become clear later. But it was not the only pertinent critical comment to appear in Farrell's essay. For as he points out, the common characterization of Liverpool speech as 'adenoidal and nasalised' is, medically speaking, something of an improbability; 'mixed nasality', to use the term used by speech pathologists and paediatricians, is usually caused by organic deficiency (Farrell 1950a: 4).[45]

Farrell's account of the dialect of Liverpool in his first article referred to many lexical items, phrases and specific pronunciations that were (as will become clear in the next chapter) to form the standard material for the workers of the Scouse industry. Thus he was one of the earliest commentators to note the 'interchangeable' pronunciation of 'fair' – 'fur' ('a fur-hurred lady in a fair coat'); 'the prolonged short i... as in thiid, retiin, Hamilton squur'; the displacement of neutral schwa by [e] in final position in words such as China, reader and dock-worker ('dock-wiike'); and the pronouncing of 'neighborhood' as two syllables ('as Queen Victoria did'). And he drew attention to the common features of elision, assimilation, apocopation and consonantal variation (t/d) with examples such as 'wassemarrewichew', 'dese', 'hospiddle', 'Norris Kreen', 'wicket', 'savvy', 'isavvy', 'leccy' (electric tram), 'Scotty Rd', 'Lanny' (Landing Stage) (as in 'he skipped a leccy down Scottie Road to get to the Lanny'). He also instanced words and phrases heard in Liverpool: 'to jump' (to board a bus or tram); 'Aagho wacker' ('How goes it partner?'); 'Hello La' ('Hello lad'); 'Hey you girl'; and the use of 'our' for 'my' 'when speaking of members of the family' ('our Alice', 'our kid's gone to get me a speck' – 'my brother has gone ahead to reserve me a space'). Such features were (and often are) stigmatized, but in Farrell's somewhat advanced essay, prescriptivism was given short shrift:

> lest there be some readers who are tempted to dismiss the speech of their city as 'bad English', it should be pointed out that dialect is not of itself bad speech. Any speech is bad which is inaudible or unintelligible to people who ought to be able to hear and understand it […] The tendency to regard dialect as a free source of laughter is to be deplored. It is undeniable that there are lots of intelligent people who look on any speaker of dialect as ill-bred and misunderstood. They should have more sense. (Farrell 1950a: 4)

Colman, writing in the next day's *Daily Post*, was slightly less permissive and noted that 'on occasion one native will address another in tones which appear to be understood by the recipient, but which are quite unintelligible to the bystander' (Colman 1950: 4). But Farrell's position was largely supported by another correspondent in the same edition, Notan, who declared that 'of course there is a Liverpool accent if by accent one means a characteristic pronunciation of certain vowels or consonants'. Citing the 'unusual pronunciation' of 't-ts; k-kh; short i in manner of short e; and u as oo or er', Notan claimed that

The characteristic pronunciations of Liverpool speech appear to derive in the main from Lancashire and Irish pronunciations. There seems to be no trace of Welsh influence in the way Liverpool people speak vowels and consonants, but there is obviously a large Welsh influence in another peculiarity of Liverpool speech, the lilting intonation that is even more characteristic of the accent proper in that it persists in almost all classes and at almost any remove, however distant and lengthy, from the district. (Notan 1950: 4)

The voiceless alveolar affricate [ts] was said to have 'excited' Kuno Meyer, the noted Professor of Celtic (and Teutonic languages) at Liverpool University. It was no doubt one of the features that led one of his students to declare that the Liverpool dialect is 'not merely a matter of words. There is an intonation difficult to define but quite impossible to miss in whatever part of the world one hears it' (Chalmers Lyon 1955: 6).

If Farrell's first article amounted to a defence of the Liverpool vernacular, his second – 'A Guide to the Slang of Merseyside. This Half-Secret Tongue of Liverpool' (*Daily Post*, 25 August 1950) – was almost an encomium to it. 'Slang', he noted, is 'rough poetry' which is not safe from 'the censure of the careful parent or the literary purist, and what is pedantically called the "substandard urban locution", must bear the shame of not being in polite use'. Be that as it may, Farrell's essay was a celebration of specific features of Liverpool speech. Thus the tendency to hyperbolize was exemplified by sayings such as 'come in outa the rain… or ye'll get wringin', soppin' wet. Charlie's just come home drowned. That's the second time he's been drowned this week.' Likewise, a punishment or beating could be 'murdering or half-murdering' someone (no distinction between the two), while 'murdered' could also mean to be beaten comprehensively in competition – as could 'to be eaten' ('yiz'll ge ret'). Other versions of punishing someone included 'to paralyse', 'to marmalise' and 'to stiffen' ('if ah stayed out that late me dad id stiffen me'). Variations on 'feller' were also creatively nuanced: 'old feller; owld feller; owl feller' all referred to someone's father; 'the queer feller', 'the quare feller' and 'the soft feller' were used disparagingly of someone who was disapproved of or pitied (in contrast with the more positive 'the big feller'); 'feller' was also used to refer to occupations – 'the bread feller', 'the coal feller' and the 'insurance feller' for example (also known as 'the clubman'). Last but not least was 'me feller', as in 'Ah'm goin' out wi' me feller' (boyfriend or husband). There were of course corresponding female forms. For 'mother', 'old lady', 'old woman' and 'old girl' were described as 'respectful' (as opposed to 'the old one', 'owld one' and 'owl one'); while 'his girl', 'his judy' and 'the one he goes out with' all meant girlfriend (or wife in the first two cases). Other aspects of relationships were covered by 'the lads' (a regular set of male friends), 'barney' (fight) and 'chucked' (jilted) (Farrell 1950b: 4).

Interestingly under terms for 'scoff' or 'scran' (food), 'scouse' was defined as 'the local stew [which] gave to native members of the armed forces (NCOs and men) the name "Scousers"' – a term that Farrell described as 'hardly ever used as a mark of affection' ('whacker' and 'whack', he noted, were more common in the 1950s).[46] 'Lunch' was reserved strictly for 'sandwiches made at home for mid morning', whereas the midday meal was 'dinner' or 'carrying out'; 'tea' of course was the evening meal. Meanwhile 'bad' was used for varying degrees of sickness; 'off bad' meant absent from work sick, while 'very bad' usually meant very ill (likewise 'poorly'). And there were a number of senses of 'sweating'. 'To sweat on something' meant to be anxious about a result of some kind (as in 'sweating on' the three-thirty at Doncaster), while in a related sense 'sweating cobs' was at one time a reference to excessive anxiety, although it later just meant heavy sweating (as a result of labour). A 'cob' was 'a lump about the size of a fist' ('a cob of coal', or a 'cob of chuck' – bread), though 'to have a cob on' meant to be annoyed or in a bad mood. Hence 'the queer feller had a right cob on this morning' ('that moody fellow, whom nobody can trust, was very irritated about something or other this morning'). One thing that could be a cause of annoyance was 'money' in the sense of wages or pay. The nuances ranged from the happy appreciation of 'good money', through the begrudgingly satisfied 'not bad money', to the plaintive 'poor money'; in any case, the person involved would have 'to go and pick up me money' (or 'go for me coppers') (Farrell 1950b: 4).

As was often the case with observers of Liverpool language, Farrell noted that even at the time of writing, certain words were 'dying out'. He cited 'meg' for threepence, 'win' for a penny, 'jowler' for 'entry', 'cherrywobs' for cherrystones (used as marbles) and 'to be away for slates' (depart in a hurry) – all of which have indeed become obsolete. But he remarked on other cases of older usage that were still in use – 'parapet' for 'pavement' and 'ta-ra well' for 'goodbye' – though in evident danger of passing away ('parapet' was later replaced by 'kerb' or 'side', and although 'ta-ra well' has been retained, its use is often slightly arch today). Perhaps the best examples of this process of retention and rejection are the adjective 'smashing' and the adjectival phrase 'it's the gear'. 'Smashing' (somewhat fancifully derived by some from the Gaelic *'s maith sin* – pronounced [smɑːʃin] – a contraction of *is maith liom é sin* – 'that's great') was described as 'applied wantonly to all pleasurable situations'.[47] 'It's the gear' (or 'de gear') on the other hand, has dropped from use (though 'gear' is sometimes heard), possibly to the relief of Farrell's imaginary stranger in Liverpool since 'its ubiquity irritates […] and [the stranger] begins to see that whenever the local speaker finds joyful satisfaction – the prompt and hospitable bus, the good cup of tea, the uninterrupted view of the football match, "it's the gear" springs from his lips'. Needless to say, if satisfaction were to be replaced by disappointment, then 'hard lines' would be used by way of consolation (Farrell 1950b: 4).[48]

Farrell's sense that specific distinctive features of Liverpool speech were in peril of passing away was a concern that appears to have been common.[49] Yet though this was certainly a worry that was frequently expressed in Liverpool in the 1950s and early 60s, the complaint that local forms of speech were disappearing as a result of other forms of change was in fact a familiar trope in the history of English dialect study. As Lloyd's defence of the BBC (cited earlier) implicitly revealed, one perceived threat was the alleged standardization of speech. Thus Henry Wyld, in a text published while he was Baines Professor of English Language at Liverpool University, argued that 'the main factor in obliterating Regional Dialects is our system of Primary Education' since teachers were trained in 'a uniform scheme' of pronunciation (other factors included the 'speech missionaries' of the Church of England and 'the wonderful increase in facilities of locomotion') (Wyld 1907: 124). Likewise in *Mankind, Nation and the Individual* (1925), the influential linguist Otto Jespersen specified forces that he thought tended to unify speech:

> Greater mutual intercourse owing to the vast development of the means of communication – railways, tramways, motors, steamships, telephones, wireless, etc., cheap books and newspapers in the interest of literary communism – finally the enormous growth of many great cities which attract a population from outside. (Jespersen 1925: 43–44)[50]

The dangers, however, were not simply external, since the perception was that there were other, more local factors that influenced the process. Shaw noted that 'some who are Scousers are ashamed of the fact and do not want their children to be' (Shaw 1957b: 6). And he elaborated on this idea in 'Dialect of a Seaport', a three-part study in the *Journal of the Lancashire Dialect Society* (1958–60): 'many Liverpool people dislike the whole business and see the speech form as nothing but shamefully debased English with not even its decided comicality to recommend it' (Shaw 1958b: 13). It was a stance confirmed by another member of 'the Scouse industry', Glyn Hughes, in his comment that 'the chief hater of the Scouse lingo is a certain type of Liverpudlian who refers to our native mode of speech as common, and to be common in Liverpool is to be inferior or vulgar' (Hughes 1963: 4). But again the form that the anxiety over the apparent changes in Liverpool speech took was one that was familiar from other debates about the shifting relations between language, place and class in modern Britain. Thus, in his *Glossary of Hampshire Words and Phrases* (1883), W.H. Cope reported on shame as a factor in the disappearance of dialects:

> The children of parents who speak among themselves the dialect of the country, are ignorant of the meaning of words commonly used by their fathers. And even among the older people there is a growing disinclination, when speaking to educated persons, to use, what I may call, their vernacular dialect. So that when asked to repeat a word, they frequently – from a sort of false shame – substitute its English equivalent. (Cope 1883: 1)[51]

In view of the perceived threats posed to Liverpool speech from within and without, it is perhaps not surprising (although still remarkable) that Farrell's second article ended with a vindication of Liverpool speech in high-cultural terms:

> Most listeners declare the slang of a big city to be disreputable. No scholar talks about cherishing it. Yet, to the speaker, this half-secret tongue offers many an exclusive delight, not the least of which is a certain recklessness with figurative language, and that quality, in sensitive and cultured minds, lies near the heart of poetry. (Farrell 1950b: 4)

A later correspondent to the *Liverpool Echo*, however, a doctor at Birkenhead General Hospital, though supportive of Farrell's defence in general terms, evinced a more cautious attitude and raised a set of issues that had dogged the study of Liverpool speech (such as it had been) from the start and that were to remain significant. Thus, he argued, 'if the collection and recording of "Liverpool lingo" is to be of genuine value to posterity all words or phrases should be relegated to their proper category within a sharply-defined system of classification, under two main divisions'. These were: '(1) Those of local origin and those whose use is restricted to the area – that is, true Liverpool words. (2) Words common to the district by adoption and frequent usage, and variants, having acquired a local status by dialectal differentiation.' In other words, lexical items needed to be examined according to the categories of 'dialect, idiom, loan word, or slang' (Harvey 1950: 2). This was an important intervention since while it supported research into Liverpool speech, it also brought to the fore the question of the status of the form. As will become clear later, this was an issue that was to remain significantly unresolved.

Conclusion

The aim of this chapter has been to demonstrate that there is good evidence for a long-standing interest, both among the local population and with exiled natives, in forms of language used in Liverpool. This was evinced principally by consideration of letters, articles and features on the use of words and cultural practices that appeared in Liverpool's newspapers from the early to mid twentieth century. What is also clear from an analysis of this material is that in the aftermath of the Second World War in particular (a war that wreaked considerable damage on the city), there was a renewed focus on language in Liverpool. This included the significant work of John Farrell, an unacknowledged pioneer in this area whose achievement was eclipsed by more media-savvy operators, as will become evident. But both the earlier interest and even the more engaged work of the later period amounted to little more than a precursor to the appearance of 'Scouse' – a category that appears to be linguistic and yet that bears (and has always borne) a great deal of cultural, social and indeed political resonance. The next chapter then will turn to an analysis of the process by which Scouse was constructed and disseminated.

Notes

1 H.R. Shaw, 'Liverpool Accent', *Liverpool Echo*, 4 August 1950, 2.
2 Read one way, Benny's journey from urchin to Liverpool gentleman is a story of moral and linguistic progress from the street language of Liverpool to 'speaking correctly' (Hocking 1966: 181).
3 *Dorrie* is the moralistic tale of two sisters and a blind preacher who lives with them in a poor part of Liverpool; one of the sisters, Dorrie, rejects Christianity and falls into hellish sin (the other marries the virtuous preacher on the last page). There are in fact passages of genuine interest in the novel, including some

accomplished writing and vivid depictions of scenes of Liverpool life. But the melodrama is staggering. For example, Dorrie pricks the preacher's hand with a pin, whereupon the arm becomes infected and has to be amputated at a hospital while Dorrie (dressed as a man) watches; she steals the hand, takes it home to her sister, and, after leaving it under the couch for a while, they bury it in the back yard. Dorrie is later drugged and kidnapped by a sinister Bengalese who trafficks her into a dance-prostitution troupe for sailors in Liverpool (the troupe includes a number of mixed-race children); she runs away, joins a theatre, is seduced and elopes with a ne'er-do-well Liverpool clerk whose family is rich, and is abandoned in Manchester. The implication is that she becomes pregnant, kills the child, and returns to Liverpool as a prostitute where she is discovered by the preacher (whose sight has been restored thanks to a Christian benefactor who takes him to Italy for the operation). Her rescue is ill-fated as she becomes depressed, delusional and eventually expires on the breast of her long-lost mother who happens to be the wife of the benefactor (her mother dies at the same moment as Dorrie). In somewhat bathetic fashion, the benefactor retires to Aigburth.

4 The 'Day to Day in Liverpool' column, authored by the anonymous 'Postman', was a regular feature that included pieces of information, speculation, opinion and gossip held to be of interest to the local audience. Its companion piece in the *Liverpool Echo* was 'Echoes and Gossip of the Day'.

5 The phrase may simply be related to doubles such as 'oh-oh', or 'uh-oh', or perhaps the euphemistic 'by heck'.

6 'Postman' noted that 'jowler' meant specifically 'the very narrow type of entry' between back-to-back houses, a distinction that was supported by Harry O'Henry's claim that the difference between a 'jowler' and a 'jigger' was related to their width: the jigger was 4ft 6in wide, the jowler 2ft 3in (O'Hanri 1964: 6). In a letter to the *Daily Post*, Whittington-Egan claimed that 'jowler' had been replaced by 'jigger' which had in turn been displaced by 'cooey' (Whittington-Egan 1955b: 6).

7 Jack Spear claimed that the terms derived from 'the common practice in Liverpool a great many years ago' of slipping out of the back door to the local for 'a jug or jowl of ale (a jowl is an earthenware jug)' – hence going for a 'jugger' or 'jowler' (Spear 1964: 6).

8 This sense is supported in the *OED*. The older phrase 'cheek by cheek' was replaced by 'cheek by jowl' (and the variant 'cheek to cheek'), in the sense of extremely close – 'jowl' meaning 'jaw' and latterly 'cheek'. *Oxford English Dictionary*, 2nd edn (Oxford, 1989), *s.v. jowl* n[1], 4.

9 T.L. Thomas later argued a converse proposition: that 'jigger' was 'the Liverpool name [...] for ledger markers used in a large concern' – because they marked an 'entry' (Thomas 1963: 4).

10 *Green's Dictionary of Slang* (London, 2010), *s.v. jigger* n[1].

11 This is not to say that some terms were not geographically identifiable. 'Postman' noted the use of 'moss nor sand' by the Lancashire coroner, Samuel Brighouse, 'whose mind is a rich store of homely and racy Lancashire colloquialisms'. Returning to the phrase the next day, a correspondent commented that it 'seems to have been unknown in Liverpool, but in districts only three or four miles outside it it has long been known' ('Postman' 1933a, b: 7).

12 *Oxford English Dictionary*, 2nd edn (Oxford, 1989), *s.v. butty* n[2]; *English Dialect Dictionary* (London, 1898–1905), *s.v. butty* sb[2] 1.

13 The tendency to claim specific words as 'unique' to Liverpool and thus culturally distinctive was not always unchallenged. In a letter to the *Liverpool Echo* in the early 1960s, 'Rancid Ronald' denounced the practice of crediting 'the Scouse language with more originality than it deserves' and rejected, on this basis, many of the

standard examples such as 'jigger', 'jowler', 'cooey', 'keep dowse', 'nix', 'judy' and 'scuffers' ('Rancid Ronald' 1963: 8).

14 In J.C. Hotten's *Dictionary of Modern Slang, Cant and Vulgar Words Used at the Present Day in the Streets of London* (1860), a 'dodger' is defined as 'a dram', hence a 'dram glass'.

15 The *English Dialect Dictionary* has no entry for 'tatting', but gives 'tatter', 'a shred, loose hanging rag', as derived from Icelandic 'tötturr', plural 'töttrar', 'rags or tatters'. But the *OED,* citing a 1926 Glaswegian use for 'tatting', defines it as 'rag- or scrap-collecting' and notes the derivation from the verb 'to tat' – 'to gather rags' (and, oddly, provides an earlier use of 'tatting' from Mayhew's *London Labour and the London Poor* in 1851); the verbal form stems from the noun 'tat', whose origin, the *OED* says, is uncertain – though it draws attention to Old English 'tættec', a rag. *Oxford English Dictionary*, 2nd edn (Oxford, 1989), *s.v. tatting* n[2], *tat* v[3]. In *Indian English* Rao claims that 'tat' is Hindi for 'coarse canvas made from various fibres' and cites a recorded use in 1820 (Rao 1954: 132).

16 Earlier and later definitions of the Nelson cake (the *OED* cites it as chiefly found in Liverpool in references from 1909 and 1966) describe it as made up of crushed biscuits and dried fruit soaked in syrup and sandwiched between two layers of pastry. *Oxford English Dictionary*, 2nd edn (Oxford, 1989), *s.v. Nelson* n[1], 3.

17 The author of this letter was T. Jones, of Shrewsbury. One interesting aspect of the interest in Liverpool language is that it was often taken up by Liverpudlians in exile. H.R. Shaw, for example, a staunch defender of the 'Liverpool accent' in the *Liverpool Echo* (4 August 1950) was a 'native of Liverpool, but London resident'. The tendency to believe that at least specific varieties of Liverpool speech were in danger of extermination was widespread. Whittington-Egan's 'Liverpool Dialect is Dying Out', in the *Liverpool Echo* (14 April 1955), asserted that the dialect was not dead but expiring, and that it was now the object of parody rather than use. Shaw (Whittington-Egan's source for matters dialectal) had an article in the *Manchester Guardian* (20 April 1955) simply entitled 'Death of a Dialect'.

18 Stonehouse's work, which originally appeared in the *Liverpool Journal*, was largely derived from earlier local histories such as those of Enfield, Aiken, Troughton, Syers, Baines and Brooke. Interest in local onomastics – particularly street names – was a well-established concern in Liverpool. Stonehouse's work was reissued by the Liverpool Libraries and Information Services in 2002; other works on the subject include Thomas Lloyd-Jones, *Liverpool Street Names* (1981) and Steven Horton, *Street Names of the City of Liverpool* (2002).

19 The correspondent recorded seeing six men dressed as pace-eggers, one with a 'black face and dingily dressed' who fought with another dressed as St George; the Pace (Pasche)-Egg play was a traditional mummers play depicting the legend of St George. In his *Memorials of Liverpool* (1875) Picton had also argued that it was a Lancastrian custom: 'Pasche eggs, Morris dances, and hot cross buns have lingered here with greater perseverance than in most other parts of the country' (Picton 1875: II, 302). For a discussion of 'Judas burning' in the Dingle area, see Frank Turner, 'A Curious Custom: The Judas Penny' (1954), and Carole Sexton, *Confessions of a Judas-burner: A Social History of Judas Burning in the South End of Liverpool* (1996).

20 Liverpool children's songs and games were later collected by Frank Shaw in *You Know Me Anty Nelly? Liverpool Children's Rhymes. Compiled with Notes on Kids' Games and Liverpool Life* (1969). Shaw included the 'Mystery Carol' but noted that it had disappeared by the late 1960s (Shaw 1969: 13).

21 A number of girls formed a circle, facing inwards, inside which would be one girl ('mother') and outside which was Daddy Bunchy. Daddy Bunchy walked rapidly around the circle while the mother chanted 'who's going round my storey-house

tonight?' – to be met with 'only Daddy Bunchy' from the other girls and a further response of 'don't take none of my fine chickens' from the mother. Daddy Bunchy meanwhile would shout 'only, only, only, only... this little one' – 'this little one' being one of the girls in the circle who would then stand outside the ring (Lovgreen 1955: 6).

22 Shaw noted that this was a serious game in Liverpool – 'the only place [...] where grown-up men play marbles called ollies' (Shaw 1966c: 4).

23 The brass buttons were in all likelihood from blazers made at Fleming's the tailors; see the clarification of the phrase 'Fleming's up the steps' on p. 45.

24 F.G. Holbrow made the point that 'soldiers or other servicemen were responsible for many Hindustani phrases, the most popular of course being "char" for tea' (Holbrow 1964: 6).

25 In Wallace's *General and Descriptive History* (1795), he noted that 'the streets are in general well, but not pleasantly paved; the foot paths, called here parapets, are disagreeable and offensive, they are all laid with small sharp pebbles, that render walking in the town very disagreeable, particularly to ladies' (Wallace 1795: 273).

26 The *OED* gives one sense of 'loggerhead' as 'an iron instrument with a long handle and a ball or bulb at the end used, when heated in the fire, for melting pitch and for heating liquids'; 'loggerheads' were used for heating tar for ship repair. *Oxford English Dictionary*, 2nd edn (Oxford, 1989), *s.v. loggerhead* n3, a.

27 The *OED* has 'nipper' as a nineteenth-century usage: 'a boy who assists a coster-monger, carter, etc. Later (more generally): the most junior member of a group of workmen, *esp.* one employed in menial tasks.' However, another sense of the term, specifically nautical, referred to 'a short piece of rope used to bind one rope to another temporarily, as an anchor cable and its associated messenger cable during the lifting of the anchor'. *Oxford English Dictionary*, 2nd edn (Oxford, 1989), *s.v. nipper* n¹, 4 a; 7 a. A citation supporting the latter sense is given to Falconer's *Universal Dictionary of the Marine* (1769): 'The persons employed to bind the nippers about the cable and voyal, are called nipper-men.' It is possible that 'nipper', as the *Liverpool Echo* etymology suggests, referred to the boys who were used to tie the 'nipper' ropes .

28 *OED* gives one sense of 'brace' as 'a rope attached to the yard of a vessel for the purpose of "trimming" the sail', *Oxford English Dictionary*, 2nd edn (Oxford, 1989), *s.v. brace* n³, a.

29 *OED* categorizes this phrase as nautical and gives Smith's *Sea Grammar* (1627) as its first authority: 'a Bitter is but the turne of a Cable about the Bits, and veare it out by little and little. And the Bitters end is that part of the Cable doth stay within boord.' *Oxford English Dictionary*, 2nd edn (Oxford, 1989), *s.v. bitter* n³, 6b.

30 The *OED* gives no support to this account and dates the nominal 'carry on' in a negative sense as a nineteenth-century Americanism; it also gives 'to carry on', in the positive sense of continue on one's way, as a nautical term – also dated as nine-teenth century. *Oxford English Dictionary*, 2nd edn (Oxford, 1989), *s.v. carry-on* n; *to carry-on*, v 4.

31 *Oxford English Dictionary*, 2nd edn (Oxford, 1989), *s.v. marmalize* v. The diction-ary categorizes the word as slang and defines it as 'to thrash; to crush or destroy. Also *fig.*: to defeat decisively.' The primary reference is to the first of the *Lern Yerself Scouse* books published in 1966, to which Shaw was the principal contributor. The word was popularized by the Liverpool comedian Ken Dodd who was also thought to be responsible for the coinage of 'diddy' to mean small or tiny (as in the 'diddy men' from Knotty Ash). This is not to be confused with another Liverpool use of the term 'diddy', meaning 'breast, nipple', taken from Irish-English, originally Gaelic *dide* (plural, *didí*), 'nipple'.

32 *Foclóir Gaeilge-Béarla* (Ó Dónaill, 2005), *s.v. gámaí, gamal, modar, modarthacht*.
    'Mam' is probably from the Latin 'mamma', cognate with Greek μάμμη, 'mother,
    mother's breast' (hence 'mammary'). 'Dug' is first recorded in English in the six-
    teenth century – in John Palsgrave's *L'Eclaircissement de la Langue Française* (1530),
    a guide to French written in English (despite the title) for English gentlemen: 'Tete,
    pappe, or dugge, a womans brest'. The etymology is unclear, but possibly radically
    derived from Swedish *dægga*, Danish *dægge* to suckle (a child). *Oxford English
    Dictionary*, 2nd edn (Oxford, 1989), *s.v. dug* n[1]a.

33 The examples here range from the possible – 'gob', 'puck' and 'lug' – to the ingenious
    but highly implausible – 'scuffer' and 'kewin' – to the nonsensical – 'cod'. There is
    no 'scuffer' in Irish-English, and 'kewin' meant 'winkle' in Liverpool, but O'Hanri's
    analysis of these two terms suggests that he was more familiar with Gaelic than
    with Irish-English or Liverpool English, though this is slightly undermined by the
    fact that he signed himself 'an scríob', which means 'scrape, scratch'; the Irish word
    for 'scribe' is *scríobhaí* (*scríobhaidhe* in the pre-1957 spelling system). An even more
    ingenious origin for 'scuffer' was offered by 'Mistrolis', who traced it to redundant
    soldiers who, after the Napoleonic Wars, joined local constabularies. These ex-
    officers, having been in France, played on the French 'escoffier' – 'someone able
    and ready to "cook your goose"' – taken from the name of Auguste Escoffier, the
    famous French chef and restaurateur (Mistrolis 1964: 8). Sadly, the chronology is
    awry; Escoffier only rose to fame in the late nineteenth century.

34 *Slapóg*, in the sense of 'slut', may be the origin of the modern English 'slapper',
    though the *OED* cites 'slapper' in the sense of 'a big, strapping or overgrown person'
    in northern dialect dictionaries from the eighteenth century – the first use specific-
    ally to refer to 'over-grown females' is in the mid nineteenth century. The *OED*
    suggests a possible Yiddish origin – 'schlepper', one of whose meanings is 'slovenly
    or immoral woman', but the Gaelic importation seems as likely.

35 One of Shaw's reasons for claiming that Gaelic had little direct influence on 'the
    Liverpool way of speech' was that 'very few of the Irish emigrants to Liverpool could
    speak that language' (Shaw 1951: 2). There is in fact no research to show that Shaw's
    claim was accurate (though it has often been repeated); given the profile of many of
    the emigrants – rural and therefore poor – it seems likely that some of them must
    have spoken Irish, particularly in the 1840s and 50s before the full impact of the
    Famine on the Irish-speaking districts was felt.

36 Oakes Hirst was the co-author, with Henry Wyld, of *The Place Names of Lancashire.
    Their Origin and History* (1911).

37 Large numbers of Irish people settled in Woolton in the late nineteenth century
    (24% of the area's population according to the 1851 census), in order to work in the
    local quarries.

38 'Tearing', in the sense of 'rowdy or reckless', was a seventeenth-century coinage;
    'gab' is of obscure etymological origins, though the 'Old Norse, common Northern
    English and Lowland Scots use' suggested in the article seems plausible. 'Scuffer'
    might be derived from Scots/Northern English 'scuff' – 'nape or "scruff" of the
    neck', or 'to strike with an open hand', or even Scots 'mean, sordid fellow; the
    "scum" of the people' – all from the nineteenth century. *English Dialect Dictionary*
    (1898–1905) *s.v. scuff* sb[1] and v[1]; v[2] 3; sb[4].

39 *The Scab* (1952) dealt with the impact of the General Strike on the family of a
    Liverpool docker (a topic treated in the Liverpool novelist James Hanley's *The
    Furys* in 1935). Shaw's own description of his work was that it was 'a one-act play of
    Liverpool working-class life written, largely in Liverpoolese'. The drama was per-
    formed at the Unity Theatre, Liverpool, and the Free Trade Hall, Manchester, as well
    as at the National Drama Festival at the David Lewis Theatre in March 1953. For the

Festival, the text was censored by the Lord Chamberlain's Office; it insisted on the deletion of the word 'sod' (Shaw 1952).

40   Frank Shaw described Farrell as a 'Liverpool speech teacher' but supplied no further details (Shaw 1963b: 6).

41   A feature in the *Liverpool Daily Post* (5 May 1954), 'Play Posed Accent Problems But… BBC Found Liverpool as It Is Spoken', noted the BBC's difficulties with James Hanley's radio adaptation of one of his novels, *Sailor's Song* (1943), which featured Liverpool seamen. The report commented: 'because Liverpool is one of Britain's principal gateways, the accent of its sons is known throughout the world, but to the uninitiated, it is an inflexion – like that heard in Northumberland – which is extremely difficult for the non-natives to reproduce adequately' (Anon 1954a: 1). The answer was to recruit Liverpool actors; the play was broadcast on the Home Service on 16 May 1955.

42   Henry Higgins was the protagonist in George Bernard Shaw's satire on the relations between language, class and gender in early twentieth-century Britain, *Pygmalion* (1912).

43   For a discussion of the complex and often misleading uses of the phrase 'standard English', see Tony Crowley, *Standard English and the Politics of Language* (2003).

44   In a letter to the *Liverpool Echo*, Isenberg asserted that while 'there is no reason why "Scouse" should be eliminated completely […] everyone ought to have the opportunity of having a second language – Standard English', something which 'can never be done until more provision is given to the training of speech to children by trained speech trainers' (the writer was a Southport-based speech-trainer). He observed such 'noticeable faults' as the 'gutteral "ch"' which is not found at all in English proper' and commented that 'if a foreigner landed at Liverpool airport with a Diploma in English, he would tear it up before he reached the city centre'. He concluded that 'Liverpool speech is unlovely, but how could it be anything else when it is such a hybrid dialect' (Isenberg 1962: 6). The prioritization of standard English had respectable support. Henry Wyld, the erstwhile Baines Professor of English Language and Philology at Liverpool University, later Merton Professor of English Language and Literature at Oxford, advised in his *Elementary Lessons in English Grammar* (1909): 'The best thing to do, if you have a Provincial Dialect, is to stick to it, and speak it in its proper place, but to learn also Standard English' (Wyld 1909: 208).

45   'Adenoidal speech', a condition produced if the adenoids are excessively large, is more accurately known as hyponasal speech; the effect is to decrease nasal resonance and thus to muffle the nasals [m], [n], [ng]. 'Mixed nasality' is usually the effect of a combination of factors such as paresis of the palate and enlarged adenoids; it isn't common.

46   John Kerr made much the same point: 'When I was a boy Scouser was an insult used by non-Liverpudlians to describe a [*sic*] people whose standard of living was so low that they were reputed to exist on a diet of blind scouse – "taters and water"' (Kerr 1966: 6).

47   'Smashing' has endured and is still used. The *OED* etymological explanation is scarcely less fanciful than the Gaelic version: from the verb 'smash', 'probably imitative: compare Norwegian dialect *smaska* to crush, *slaa i smask* to knock to smash'. *Oxford English Dictionary*, 2nd edn (Oxford, 1989), *s.v. smash*, v1. The Gaelic derivation of 'smashing' is given in *How the Irish Invented Slang* (Cassidy 2007: 268)

48   The *OED* gives 'that's (or it's) the gear' as 'an expression of approval. Hence as adj., good, excellent, "great"', and cites E. Fraser and J. Gibbons, *Soldier & Sailor Words and Phrases* (1925): '*Gear*, apparatus generally […] Also used as a colloquial term for anything giving satisfaction—*e.g.*, "That's it, that's the gear!"' The sense of 'gear'

as apparatus dates to the early fourteenth century, as does the use of the term to refer to items of clothing. 'Hard lines', with the meaning of 'ill luck, bad fortune', is also described as probably nautical in origin; 'hard line money' was nautical usage for money received in compensation for difficult duties. 'Line' may, however, refer to the biblical sense of 'lot in life', as in Psalms 16:6: 'The lines are fallen vnto mee in pleasant places; yea, I haue a goodly heritage' (Authorized Version). *Oxford English Dictionary*, 2nd edn (Oxford, 1989), *s.v. gear* n 1a, 5e; *line* n² 4c, 6.

49 In a letter to the *Liverpool Echo*, Jack Welsh asserted that 'many "Scouse" expressions have disappeared forever and many more are just fading fast away'. His examples included 'cosher', a street paper-seller; 'sticking out', the use of specific streets in which to sell the paper; 'Echo Belt', a belt worn by licensed paper-sellers (Welsh 1964: 8).

50 Jespersen's argument here illustrates the tendency to think that dialects existed in rural areas only. His point that population movements into urban areas resulted in the eradication of local difference is predicated on the widely held assumption that such locations would not produce dialects of their own; see chapter four below.

51 Shame was also cited as a central factor in the eradication of the native language in the predominantly Irish-speaking districts of rural Ireland in the late nineteenth century. For a discussion of this and other – material and affective – factors involved in the disappearance of Gaelic, see Crowley 2005: chs 4–5.

4

Frank Shaw and the founding of the 'Scouse industry'

It seems fairly certain that Liverpoolese is of comparatively recent origin. (Richard Whittington-Egan, 'Is Liverpool Dialect Dying Out?', 1955)[1]

The previous chapter illustrated the local interest in language in Liverpool in the early to mid twentieth century together with a number of the problems associated with its categorization. The account also presented evidence from the early 1950s onwards of an emerging link between a representation of the language of the city and the 'Scouser' (a cultural category that had existed for a considerable period but that was not in common use at the time). The connection was exemplified in *Liverpool*, the book marking Liverpool's 750th anniversary, which was written by the city's official historian (and librarian) George Chandler. Noting the importance of popular culture as a medium in which representations of the language and inhabitants of Liverpool were propagated, Chandler commented that 'the speaker of the Liverpool dialect is through Music Hall fame widely known as a scouser' (Chandler 1957: 423). And yet, as demonstrated earlier, one of the most striking things about the use of the term 'Scouse' to refer to the language of Liverpool is how recently it was coined. According to the lexicographical record at least, 'Scouse' in the sense of 'the dialect of English spoken in Liverpool', is a coinage of the 1960s.[2] In fact, as the analysis in the last chapter began to show, 'Scouse' as a term used to denote the language of Liverpool started to appear in the 1950s in the correspondence, articles and features that focused on language in local newspapers and journals. But given that this was the case, how did a term that was apparently invented only in the 1950s become so lodged in popular cultural imagination as to be almost metonymic in relation to the city and its inhabitants? In other words, what were the means by which Liverpool and its people became so firmly associated with Scouse? Though it will not be possible to explore all of the significant factors in great detail, it is clear that the process depended on a variety of circumstances, ranging from global economic shifts that had a direct impact on Liverpool (the decline of the port), to the emergence of the international phenomenon of pop culture (which facilitated a particular type of cultural representation), to the contradictory experience of the inhabitants of a city that boomed culturally and yet stagnated economically and politically (from Mersey Beat to Liverpool battered). But among these macro-level developments, there was one that took place on a different plane altogether and that will form the focus of this chapter: the activities of a small group of culturally motivated men whose efforts largely established the Scouse industry.

The work of Frank Shaw: history and preservation

In 'Save Our Scouse – The Dying Language of Liverpool' (*Daily Post*, 2 December 1960), Kenneth Hodgkinson asserted the need for a contemporary Cecil Sharp to record the 'subtle features' of language in the city, 'with examples taken from the wacker's mouth', before they passed away (1960: 11). Given his primarily rural focus (as the founding figure of the folklore revival in early twentieth-century England), Sharp was a slightly unlikely figure to invoke in this context. A more appropriate model offered itself in the guise of the journalist and writer Damon Runyon, the sharp observer of Prohibition-era New York whose work captured the language of the street in its depiction of the rough urban world of the great metropolis. It was fitting, then, that a similarity was drawn between Runyon and the central character in the story of the establishment of the Scouse industry: Frank Shaw.[3] Liverpool-born, though raised in Ireland during his early years, Shaw was a customs officer in the port of Liverpool for most of his working career (a role that brought him into daily contact with the dockers who were to be one of the main sources of his material).[4] And while Shaw was no Runyon in terms of the quality of his literary output, he was nonetheless, more than any other individual, responsible for an unrelenting campaign to present Scouse as the language of Liverpool.

As noted in the previous chapter, the publication of Farrell's two long articles – 'About that Liverpool Accent (or Dialect)' and 'A Guide to the Slang of Merseyside. This Half-Secret Tongue of Liverpool' – was an important development in the historiography of language in Liverpool. Significantly, Farrell's call to arms was recognized by Frank Shaw in 'Liverpool Dialect', a letter to the *Daily Post* in which he appealed to readers of Farrell's essays 'to help with the compilation of words and phrases' (of which he already had 'ten pages worth') for a glossary that visitors to Liverpool in the Royal Festival Year might find useful (Shaw 1950a: 4). This in turn led to an article on Shaw's own work, 'Liverpool's Dialect is his Hobby', in which he announced the inaugural meeting of the Liverpool Dialect Society. Its goal was:

> to foster the study of the Liverpool dialect among Liverpolitans and visitors, by discussion, the reading of papers on the origins of words and phrases, and by comparisons with other dialects. One of our aims will be to protect our dialect against misuse. It is a serious error to represent Liverpool people speaking with a Lancashire accent, as has been done in recent films and plays. (Shaw 1950b: 5)[5]

Yet notwithstanding the issuing of more than two hundred invitations, a telegram of support from Deryck Guyler (who played Liverpool character Frisby

Dyke in Tommy Handley's *ITMA* radio show), and expressions of interest from the Liverpool Civic Society, Liverpool University Undergraduates' Guild and Eric Partridge (the great lexicographer of slang), the planned meeting was a flop.[6] As noted in 'Propurorful: Liverpool Is Dialect Shy', the report of the non-event held at the Bluecoat in March 1951, it couldn't be said that 'dur wus millions er peopil, y cud walk on der 'eads'. In fact only three people (apart from Shaw and the press) turned up to listen to Shaw announcing over 'a recording machine', 'I don wan any ciggies, I've got thousins uv thim', along with other phrases from a book he hoped to publish on the 'lingo of Scouseland' (Shaw 1950b: 5).

Despite this inauspicious start, Shaw nonetheless embarked upon a prodigious campaign over the next twenty years or so to popularize, celebrate and preserve aspects of the language and culture of Liverpool. Indeed the sheer volume of his writing was implicitly acknowledged by Shaw himself in his comment that he had worked for HM Customs 'full-time [...] for forty years while being a part-time writer. Unkind superiors put it the other way about' (Shaw 1971: 237). The net effect of Shaw's productivity was that he became the central figure in the shaping of the debates around language in Liverpool in the 1950s and 60s, most importantly in the establishment of a putative history for Scouse (a discursive achievement that had influential consequences, as noted in chapter two). Thus in 'Scouse Lingo – How It All Began', Shaw asserted that 'many of the words and phrases you hear daily in Liverpool [...] give, in a way, the history of the city'. It followed, he argued, that 'the basis of the "lingo" is the Lancashire dialect of which very little is now left. Yet there is much more of Lancashire than some people realise.' He then made the crucial claim (supporting it with reference to the text upon which so much of the subsequent historiography hung) that, as we saw earlier, was taken up without acknowledgement by Whittington-Egan and then Knowles: 'probably until about one hundred years ago Liverpolitans spoke as they do in Bolton, or even in nearby Prescot. Certainly in 1830, according to Syers' *History of Everton* (which was where the Liverpool "nobles" lived) a broad Lancashire dialect was spoken by all' (Shaw 1950c: 4). But how, according to Shaw, did the shift from Lancashire dialect to Scouse take place? The principal causes of the change to the use of 'the nasal manner' of 'the peculiar and universally recognized Frisby Dyke style' were cited as 'the Industrial Revolution' together with 'the famine in Ireland [...] and the consequential inflow of poor Irish immigrants'. Other elements were, at least from this perspective, secondary: 'there are many Welsh and Scottish in the city but their influence has not equalled that of the Irish'. The 'sing-song tone' of the Welsh gave Liverpool English its 'lilt' and often made 'Dicky Sam [...] the chanty man' (the ship-board singer), and the principality may have donated the word 'kecks' (trousers), but as far as the impact of Scottish immigrants was concerned, 'characteristically the Scots gave nothing'.[7] The only other factor mentioned by Shaw was the effect of 'trade with America and the world', which gave 'fresh largesse to the Lancashire-cum-Irish mint'; even then, he noted, especially in relation to words borrowed from New York, it was often the case that their origin lay with Irish immigrants (Shaw 1950c: 4).

What is particularly striking about Shaw's account was the tenacity with which he repeated it until it simply became the established narrative. Another example appeared in 'Death of a Dialect' in the *Manchester Guardian*, a national daily, in which he reiterated that the 'debased English of most of our big cities has, as a basis, the original regional dialect'. And while this was 'clearly evident in Manchester', 'the keen-eared listener in Liverpool will detect the Lancashire on which has been piled the Anglo-Irish of generations of Irish immigrants'. Liverpool English, Shaw argued, was in effect the product of Lancashire + Anglo-Irish + cosmopolitan influences. It was 'a palimpsest, for on top again are all the speech habits and slang from all over the world, imported by the much-travelled natives of Merseyside, and especially from the U.S., with which the port had close contact before any other port in the country' (Shaw 1955b: 18).[8] For Shaw the most important factor in the displacement of the Lancashire dialect as the spoken vernacular of Liverpool was Irish immigration from the 1840s on. But apart from the Irish examples that he identified in 'Scouse Lingo', what is interesting in this early article was the specification of a whole set of terms and phrases that, it was claimed, illustrated the uniqueness of 'Scouse' ('the weird and wonderful dialect which only Merseyside can produce' as Don Smith described it in the *Daily Herald*) (Smith 1955: 5). Significantly, many of the examples cited in Shaw's essay were borrowed from Farrell and other sources, and a large number were to be recycled over the years by Shaw and others in various formats (great use was made of a relatively limited stock of material). Items included 'to snitch' ('to inform' – though 'snitch' was cited in Vaux's *New and Comprehensive Vocabulary of the Flash Slang*, 1819); 'judy' ('girl, woman' – also found in Vaux's *Vocabulary*, possibly from 'Punch and Judy'); 'chatty' ('lousy' – Vaux); 'whack' ('share' – Vaux, and see chapter three above); 'have a cob on' (cited by Farrell, etymology unknown); 'the gear' and 'smashing' (both also given by Farrell); blocker' ('bowler hat' – worn by dock foremen); 'climp' ('an old Liverpool word of approval' – not found in the *OED*, *EDD* or any of the major dictionaries of slang); 'down the banks' ('remonstrate, argue, fight' – also not in the standard reference texts); 'scuffer' ('policeman', which Shaw derived from Partridge's suggestion of 'scufter', from the German 'scuffe', 'to throw up dust while walking'); 'scoff' ('food' – mentioned by Farrell, though Shaw correctly indicated its South African origin, by way of Dutch 'schoft', 'quarter of a day', hence one of four meals); 'clat', 'douse', 'eck, eck', 'jowler', 'nix', 'sag' and 'tatting' (all of which had been noted in the correspondence in local papers, see chapter three above); 'cod' ('pretence, joke', a word that Shaw claimed was Norwegian for 'empty husk', though it was used in Irish-English, as in Joyce's *Portrait of the Artist as a Young Man* – 'some fellows had drawn it there for a cod'); 'bevvy' ('alcoholic drink, beer', a nineteenth-century term from 'beverage', ultimately from *bibere*, Latin, 'to drink'); 'old shawlie' and 'Mary Ellen' (both terms used in a primary sense to mean an older working-class woman), 'Mary Ann' ('man who does housework', and thus, in a sense described as 'most offensive' by Shaw, an effeminate or homosexual man); 'dig' (as in 'a dig in the chin', 'blow, punch, hit', probably from nineteenth-century Irish-English); 'growler' ('a tin for food for dockers', a word that may be derived from a nineteenth-century Americanism meaning 'a vessel in which beer is brought from a bar'); 'tart' ('girl, woman, girlfriend, wife' – Shaw gives it as an abbreviation of 'sweetheart' and notes that 'it has remained pleasant in Liverpool', though 'tart' was used widely from the mid nineteenth century both in its general sense and with the meaning of 'prostitute'); 'gammy' ('bad', possibly from 'cam' in Welsh, 'crooked or 'wrong''); 'jangle' ('gossip' – a very old word in the sense of 'idle talk or chatter', though still used in Liverpool, as in the poet Matt Simpson's 'Prufrock Scoused' from the collection *Catching up with History* (1995) – 'Ders diss posh do wid lah-di-dah judies/janglin about ow thee once-t knew John Lenin').[9] Other terms stumped even Shaw's lively etymological imagination: 'kewin' ('winkle'), 'bannymug' ('thick brown pottery'), 'whicker' ('suit'), 'welt' (an unauthorized break at work) and 'Joe Gerks' (jail, usually Walton prison) (Shaw 1950c: 4).

Having postulated the history and uniqueness of Scouse, another of Shaw's imperatives was preservation. As he made clear in 'Scouse Lingo is Preserved for Posterity' (penned by 'An Unashamed Scouser'), from his perspective at least 'there are fewer Scousers every year'. In part, he argued, this was caused by general cultural developments since 'those factors which are driving our regional speech elsewhere are operating here' (Shaw 1957b: 6). Given the danger of eradication by such forces, Shaw evidently felt that there was a clear imperative to record if not preserve Scouse for posterity. To that end Shaw was involved in several projects, apart from his journalistic contributions, that aimed to register Scouse as a linguistic and cultural form. These included the first dramatic text written entirely in Scouse (or 'Liverpoolese'), *The Scab* (1952), and a series of *Scouse Talks* (1957), a collaborative effort with the actor Jack Gordon of Unity Theatre which consisted of tape recordings made in Liverpool City Library with accompanying texts and 'translations'.[10] These fictionalized talks on various aspects of Liverpool life aimed to represent Scouse and addressed topics such as children's games, street and other rhymes, 'are [our] family', the ballad of Maggie May, 'at the back of the market', 'the cruise of the Calibar', 'round the town with Dicky Sam' and 'the rabbit pie'. The first talk, 'Children's Games of an Older Day', delivered by a middle-aged man, began:

> The're 'avin' a do at are kid's for he's lad's twenny-first so natch he's judy comes round wid him to are place to borry a few t'ings to make the blomonge an' all like dat like and when he's tart and mine get janglin' we 'ave the right old chin wang about when us two was lads and dat's goin' back a bit. The was gear dos in them days, jars out, beer for dogs, lashin's a chuck an' ninety-nine times outa ten finishin' up wid a barny, skin and 'air flyin'.

The accompanying rather stilted 'translation' read:

> There [*sic*] are to have a party at my brother's for his son's twenty-first birthday and, naturally, his wife came round with him to borrow a few things to make the blanc-mange etc. and when his wife and mine began to gossip we had a grand talk about when we were young which is a long time ago. There were great parties in those days, drink for consumption off the premises, plenty of beer, more than enough food and, very often, it finished with a row, all in. (Shaw 1957a: 1, 3)

In addition to these projects, Shaw's other main archival work on language was the study for the *Journal of the Lancashire Dialect Society* (1958–60) mentioned earlier. 'Dialect of a Seaport' was the most sustained analysis of Scouse that Shaw undertook and it consisted of three related essays: (i) 'Dicky Sam, Frisby Dyke, and Scouse'; (ii) an untitled piece on names for clothes, 'a bevy and a rowdy do' and 'fighting and other pastimes'; and (iii) 'Rhymes, Games, Pub Names'. In fact, as Shaw himself noted, the focus in the essays tended to stray away from language per se and on to other forms of cultural practice. This interest was pursued a decade or so later in *You Know Me Anty Nelly? Liverpool Children's Rhymes. Compiled with Notes on Kids' Games and Liverpool Life* (1969). As with the earlier work, the justification for this collection (of more than two hundred rhymes) was again the danger of cultural eradication: 'so much of old Liverpool is passing, all the forces making a great and idiosyncratic city and people like ours the same as any other (*almost, we shall not be moved – completely*), something of its spirit must be recorded before it is too late' (Shaw 1969: 71).[11] The desire to record a culture that was perceived as dying was combined with a clear sense of the historical significance of the folklore that was being preserved (Shaw cited the German Romantic philosopher J.G. Herder's comment that 'it is no reproach to the noblest of poetry to say that it is heard on the lips of the common people') (1969: 72). It was a belief supported by the major British folklorist Peter Opie (co-author with Iona Opie of the groundbreaking *Lore and Language of Schoolchildren* in 1959) in a preface to the second edition of *You Know Me Anty Nelly*. Opie paid Shaw the huge compliment of distinguishing his contribution from the dominant work in the field by noting that 'almost all writers who have set out to record some part of our oral lore have been outsiders' ('scholar-maggots who can feed on a body only when it is cool'), whereas Shaw was an insider who conveyed the vitality of the tradition in a text in which 'rhyme and commentary are almost indistinguishable, spoken in the same voice' (Shaw 1970: viii).

Other projects were not explicitly concerned with the recording of Scouse per se, but did nonetheless feature it in various ways. For example, Shaw was involved as a researcher for a BBC North radio feature, *The Talking Streets*, produced by the innovative documentary-maker Dennis Mitchell (broadcast 27 October 1958).[12] The work, based on two weeks of interviews in Liverpool, was one of the first to portray the realities of poverty in post-war Britain and to present the city as still suffering from the ravages of poor housing in particular. It was, as Shaw noted in an article on the work, 'The Talking Streets of Liverpool', a chastening experience: 'we penetrated into places which were not so nice and I who thought I knew my city found houses lived in by human beings I would never have guessed at and which are a disgrace to any civilized community in the year 1958' (Shaw 1958d: 6). Nonetheless, the success of the programme led to a further collaboration between Shaw and Mitchell the following year on the award-winning BBC TV documentary *Morning in the Streets* (broadcast 25 March 1959), a pioneering work that offered an 'impression of life and opinions in the back streets of a Northern City in the morning' (in fact the scenes were shot in Liverpool, Salford, Manchester and Stockport) (Shaw 1971: 219).[13]

Consisting of a montage of social observation and staging in the four locations, the film creates a strikingly moving, surprising and often funny depiction of the texture of northern working-class life.

'Proper Scouse': its use and abuse

Despite Shaw's efforts to preserve and gain cultural recognition for Scouse, there is a curious strain of ambivalence towards various forms of language used in Liverpool that appears consistently throughout his work. In 'Death of a Dialect', for example, while noting that the change from Lancashire dialect to Scouse was 'not one for the better, for there are some very ugly locutions', he also commented that 'the Anglo-Irish influence has certainly contributed a lively vocabulary and numerous very funny phrases' (Shaw 1955b: 18). Likewise Shaw described 'the shudder the sensitive visitor must feel when he hears a bus conductor say "Furs, please"', or 'youse' (you plural), or the 'bad tendency to apocope', or examples such as 'Toosdy' (Tuesday), 'Sintantnee' (Saint Anthony), 'Pivvy' (Pavillion), 'neighbrood' (neighborhood), 'Lanny' (landing stage), 'Leckie' (electric tram), 'you was' and 'you should hav went'. Nonetheless he asserted 'the importance of being parochial' and informed his readers that

> you will be pleased to find that the city has resisted the tendency to dead level which is one of the bad things the BBC has brought about – by keeping its own name for a number of everyday things such as 'casey' for football, 'olly' for marble, 'kewin' for winkle, 'scouse' for stew, 'cokes' for restaurant, 'bevvy' for drink, 'jigger' for back entry of a house, 'judy' for a female, 'blocker' for bowler hat, 'whicker' for a suit. (Shaw 1955b: 18)[14]

The culture of the parish extended not just to individual words but to idiomatic phrases such as 'she's the talk of the wash-house', 'that wan's dirty when she's dollied', 'put the top hat on it' and 'I had a cob on so I gave him high ding dong; we had down the banks and the queer fella didden like it I telly.'

As the comments above indicate, Shaw's approach to Scouse was an odd mix of folkloristic pride and humorous mockery that sometimes veered towards cultural condescension. Indeed on occasion Shaw's stance became markedly negative, though in this regard he was following in a well-established tradition in terms of attitudes towards language use in Liverpool. As noted in chapter two, Maria Edgeworth commented in 1813 that William Roscoe, an important figure in the history of the city, 'speaks excellent language but with a strong provincial accent which at once destroys all idea of elegance' (Colvin 1971: 10–11). And in Tirebuck's *Dorrie* (1891), a stage impresario interviews the eponymous heroine and decides that 'he didn't like the common Liverpool twang about her pronunciation' (1891: 189). J.B. Priestley's *English Journey* gave him the opportunity to observe that 'Liverpool is simply Liverpool. Its people – or at least the uneducated among them – have an accent of their own; a thick, adenoidy, cold-in-the-head accent, very unpleasant to hear' (1934: 200). An even more explicit attack (with which Shaw was familiar) on Liverpool speech was made by the Liverpool novelist John Brophy in *City of Departures* (1946). Responding to an exchange with a paper-seller in Lime Street, one of the characters reflects:

> The words, emerging as a sustained shrill note between scarcely moving lips, at first were unintelligible to him, meaningless, hardly recognizable as human speech. He had forgotten the ugliness of the Liverpool accent: his ears were not attuned to its adenoidal whine, its flat vowel sounds and slurred consonants, its monotonous rhythms compounded of distant memories of Dublin slums and Welsh villages, but all debased, forced through nasal and oral passages chronically afflicted with catarrh. Liverpool had the ugliest English accent in the world, unless the Bowery in New York or the Cicero district of Chicago could produce something more repulsive. Thorneycroft wondered if his own speech had ever marked him as Liverpool-born. He hoped not. (Brophy 1946: 21)[15]

Brophy's word 'debased' was used repeatedly by Shaw in references to language in Liverpool and the sentiment was reinforced by a number of other declarations that appear at first sight to be puzzling.[16] Thus he described 'the nasty way we say' things and asserted that 'it is laziness which debases all standard language'; he also admitted that 'as a lover of words and wit [...] I hate the ugliness of Liverpool speech, especially the slurring and the mangling of vowels such as the "ai" sound in lovely words like "Mary, fairy"' (Shaw 1962a: 9; 1959b: 4).[17] This stance was articulated most clearly in 'Liverpoolese, Yes, But I Don't Like Scouse', an article written in response to a debate with 'Mrs. Richard Clarke' [*sic*], principal of an Ormskirk school of speech and drama tasked with teaching 'correct vowel pronunciation to Schoolgirls at Kirkby' (Shaw 1962b: 8). Given his previous (and later) work, Shaw's central claim was striking: 'I was for Liverpoolese. I still am. But I don't see how anyone with two ears and a moderate education can like what has come to be known as Scouse.' His gloss on this comment was that 'it may seem like the statement of a renegade', but his explanation was revealing. Declaring that 'I love the Liverpool wit', he noted ruefully the consequences attached to his status as 'an authority on Liverpool speech': 'people come up to me in the street, on a bus, or in a pub with the latest piece of mangled vowel enshrined in bad grammar and I dutifully grin'. But, he asserted, 'I am in no way proud of our mispronunciations' and, returning to Liverpool after a period away and hearing 'that catarrhal, adenoidal singsong, containing the worst of Welsh, English and Irish English, I wince' (a reaction that was also prompted by hearing his own voice) (1962b: 8). This was not to say that he valued the 'standard' form per se, since 'standard or B.B.C. English is only a dialect – the one that won out and that can hit the ear harshly, too, with "huntin'" and lawra norder and the Empah'. But, he argued, 'we have some very ugly sounds in this city I would like to see eliminated' (examples included 'Mary' pronounced as 'Murry', bus conductors asking for 'Furs please', and an advert on local transport which rhymed 'Treat us fairly, travel early').[18] And so, he concluded, 'let us avoid the clipping and elision, the foul dipthong vowels, the too-longdrawn final consonants, the excessive use of "y'know" and "well", mispronunciations like chimbley and somethink and the sheer false syntax of "You was" and "I never done ut"' (1962b: 8). Such strictures fell on one group in particular: the young women of Liverpool. In a commonly expressed sentiment that highlights a significant gender demarcation, their language was particularly disturbing. Thus in 'Liverpoolese, Yes...' (which cited a headline from a previous piece – 'Model Girls... Until You Hear Them Speak!'), Shaw recalled Chesterton's comment that Broadway's neon signs would be beautiful even to an illiterate. Likewise, he remarked, 'I feel at times Liverpool girls would be lovely if one could not hear' ('gorgeous until they open their mouths' was the more common expression of this attitude) (1962b: 8).[19]

A follow-up article by Clarke – 'Let's Have Good Sensible Speech' – developed the debate. Asserting the need for 'vigorous, pleasant, clear and concise speech', Clarke declared: 'what I dislike first and foremost is unintelligibility – this brings me to the Scouser accent, which is unpleasant and distorted. I agree with Frank Shaw to the extent that in the first instant it is a doctor and NOT the elocutionist that is required' (a doctor could address adenoidal problems presumably, though given medics' propensity to be busy, elocutionists were proposed as the more likely source of a remedy). Interestingly, Clarke followed Shaw's anti-standardization tendency when she proposed that 'there is little fear of losing local colour as long as turns of phrase, local abbreviations and use of words persist'. 'Liverpool's native wit and lively sense of the ridiculous,' she added, would 'take care of the character of its speech with or without the Scouser accent'. She also contended that

> The Scouser accent seems to me to be by no means the most unpleasant in the United Kingdom. It may be the result of a lifetime of hearing it, but to me it is less unlovely – which is more truthful than saying lovelier – in my ears than the Birmingham accent, or the unique Tyneside accent, which rivals Liverpool in its utter incomprehensibility. As for Cockney, traditional though it is to praise its liveliness and wit, I am reminded more of nocturnal cats than human speech. (Clarke 1962: 6)

Not the worst then, but objectionable all the same since in Liverpool 'the AIR sound' is 'flat and ugly': 'thus "Go and sit on the chair over there" would sound something like: "Go 'n sit on the cher ovur ther". This is just laziness.' And laziness could be cured by good teaching – a fact, apparently, much appreciated by the young women of Kirkby.[20] Despite their apparent differences, then, the arguments of Shaw and Clarke were close on a number of points, a conclusion further demonstrated in Shaw's 'Merseyside should nurse its Scouse, but reject bad English' (Shaw 1963a: 6). There was one respect in which they differed, however, which related to Shaw's desire to distinguish between what he considered to be real, genuine or 'proper Scouse' (which needed to be recorded for posterity), as opposed to the 'bad English' of contemporary usage in Liverpool. Unlike Clarke, whose focus was primarily elocution, Shaw's aim was to have 'the worst locutions scrubbed' and to return instead to a less 'debased' form, on the grounds that 'the North Country form of speech, for Liverpoolese has never lost its Lancashire association, is no worse than South Country'. If this could be done, he argued, then there could be new uses for the language of

Liverpool: 'Good Irish, good Scottish, and even during the war good Yorkshire, were acceptable to the B.B.C. Why not good Scouse?' (Shaw 1963a: 6).

Shaw's concern with 'good Scouse' led him to demarcate two types of inhabitant of the city of Liverpool: the Liverpolitan and the Liverpudlian (or 'Pol' and 'Pud') (Shaw 1958b: 13). The 'Pols' were identified with 'posh or snotty types living in the better suburbs (say, Mossley Hill...) more pretentious in their social habits, professing higher cultural aspirations than their own humble origins usually justified' (Shaw 1971: 20).[21] Moreover, along with their pretentiousness, they were somewhat fraudulent (or self-deluding): 'the Liverpolitan is he who, though he might eat it, will not talk about Scouse or admit to liking it and assert vehemently, in pure Scouse, that he does not talk like a Scouser either'; they were members of 'the "bay-window" classes... ("Plus fours an' no Breckfist")' (Shaw 1958b: 13). The 'Puds' on the other hand were the real thing: 'Liverpudlian as a word, with the North country vowelled Pud like an exploding black-pudden, suggests the real Scouser' (Shaw 1971: 20). The differentiation was apparently intended to be humorous, and Shaw had a piece in *Punch*, 'The Liverpool Indicator', that continued the joke. Based on the linguistic and cultural distinction between 'U' and 'non-U' first articulated by a linguist (A.S.C. Ross) and then taken up by Nancy Mitford in her collection *Noblesse Oblige* (1956), Shaw drew up a corresponding list of Scouse and non-Scouse – 's' and 'non-s' – words and cultural practices.[22]

> It is s either to apologise when giving a large coin for a small fare to a bus conductor or to say, if given by him a large number of coppers: "They'll do for church".
>   It is s to eat your chips from their paper on the main road. Non-s folk use side streets...
>   Definitely (pronounced by s fellows 'defanely') non-s locutions are "Long time no see", "Pleased to meet you" (s is "How do, whack'), "Who do you think you're pushing?" (usually said to s individuals), "Here's looking at you" (s "I paid for the last, whack") [...]
>   Best clothes on Sunday is, above all, the clearest s indicator. (Shaw 1971: 14–15)

One characteristic of both the Pols and Puds was the propensity to produce 'Malapudlianisms', a coinage explained by Shaw by analogy with Irish Bulls ('it must be the Irish in us') and Malapropisms (Shaw 1958e: 6). Malapudlianisms were a creative use of language (otherwise known as a solecism) that had 'a sort of wild sense of its own', produced by 'the exuberant Liverpudlian who loves words, but [who], as often happens [...] is not as familiar with what he loves as he might be' (Shaw 1960b: 5). They were 'caused by a rush of Scouse to the head' (Shaw 1966b: 8). Bullish examples in the initial article included 'alive with dead rats', '99 times out of 10', 'if the Lord spares me I'll be buried at Ford Cemetery' and 'I hate the sight of his voice'. They were accompanied by various Malapropisms: 'undulated with letters' (inundated), 'the horns of a diploma' (dilemma), 'run Bismarck' (amok), 'I can't transcribe it' (describe), 'throw an accordion round' (cordon), 'too small to perform me absolutions' (ablutions), 'no confluence' (confidence), 'an impassive speech' (impressive) and 'state of kiosk' (chaos) (Shaw 1958e: 6).[23] The essay evidently touched a nerve and was followed by a series of letters to the *Liverpool Echo* citing other examples (correspondents may have been encouraged by the promise of a guinea for each 'Malapudlian letter').[24] And yet though Shaw claimed that Malapudlianisms were the prerogative of both Pols and Puds, his tendency was to specify that only a particular class (and indeed a job-related group within a class) produced the genuine article. As the subtitle of an article entitled 'Ink, Lino and the Lenient Judge' asserted, 'They're all there at the docks, the richest breeding ground for Malapudlianisms' (Shaw 1960b: 5). And if the docks were the place to find Malapudlianisms, they were also the source of another mode of linguistic creativity: the nickname. This was a theme to which Shaw returned many times in his works (often with the same examples). Thus in 'Beware of a "Destroyer" when at the Docks... He may be after a Sub', Shaw gave several instances: 'the destroyer' ('a man without money looking for a sub' – short for 'subvention'), 'the plumber's mate' ('no intention of doing a tap'), 'the ringer' ('always on the phone'), 'Max Factor' ('man assigned to "make up" the gang'), 'the lenient judge' ('a docker who says "let that go" on the job'), 'sell the bed' ('nightworker'), 'wailing wall' ('moaner') and 'Oliver Twist' (man with 'sprained wrist after picking up good week's wages') (Shaw 1958a: 3). Other examples included 'Stanley Matthews' (manning a hatch, he says 'I'll take dis corner'), 'the Sheriff' (foreman who says 'what's the hold up, lads'), 'the Baker' (talks about 'me and me tart'), 'the Surgeon' (says 'cut that out' repeatedly), 'the Parish Priest' ('works every Sunday'), 'the Spaceman' ('going to Ma's [Mars] for dinner'), 'the Balloon' ('foreman who says "don't let me down lads"') and 'Cinderella' (always has to be home by twelve) (Shaw 1971: 32).

If an inquisitive researcher had asked the question, 'where can real Scousers, with all their linguistic creativity be found?', the answer might have been: everywhere, but one location in particular. For as Shaw made clear in 'A Skinful of Words', 'Scousers can be found drunk in charge of words in cafes or milk-bars, on dock quays, on buses, even outside church; young and old, men and women, of all classes.' With regard to Scouse however, 'it is from dockers and folk of what used to be called the poorer classes that one gets it in greatest abundance' (1962c: 6). This was a key delimitation and one that had a significant influence on thinking about language in Liverpool; it was a point that Shaw made repeatedly. In 'A Proper Jangle in Scouser Lingo' – a report on a talk by Shaw to the Ramblers' Association ('a linguistic hike round the docks'), he was quoted as asserting that 'Liverpoolese' was 'maintained and nourished' in the Liverpool docks (Shaw's other term for the form was 'doxology'). 'Like other dialects it was dying', he claimed, 'but it was nurtured in lusty health still by the dockers, who often keep themselves cut off from the world of the Oxford accent' (Anon 1955: 6). Despite the oddity of the expression here (did dockers have to go out of their way to avoid 'the world of the Oxford accent'?), much the same sentiments were expressed in '[The] Strange Charm of the Lingo of Liverpool's Dockland'. Proposing that 'the lingo came from dockland in the first place', Shaw argued that its reproduction was caused by a number of factors that made it largely the preserve of the male working-class employees of the

Port of Liverpool. Dock work was 'one of the few father and son occupations left'; dockers 'lived near each other till recently'; and 'even under the Port Labour Scheme, dockers tend to work in the same gangs, under the same stevedores and "cod bosses", [which] makes them a homogeneous body with uniform customs and speech habits' (Shaw 1959b: 6).[25] This was an interesting suggestion, pointing to what was later to become known as a linguistic network, although it is implausible to think that this alone can explain the origin, maintenance and propagation of Scouse per se.[26] Nonetheless, although Scouse was considered by Shaw to be passing 'in most parts of the city' by dint of 'the forces of radio, films and such which are killing regional speech' (as well as the effects of the slum clearance schemes that were to have such an effect on the character of Liverpool's urban space), it still lived 'among Liverpool's thirty eight miles of quay space. And all who hate uniformity will say let it live.' The docks were the location of 'Scouse at its ripest' and even in the late 1950s that must have appeared to be some sort of guarantee of its survival.[27] The sentiment was explicit in Shaw's horribly inaccurate estimation of the impact of technology on dock employment: 'Liverpoolese will never die as long as the port has dockers, and it will be a long time before their work can be wholly done by automation' (Shaw 1959b: 6).

Staging and inscribing Scouse

Thus far in this chapter it has been argued that Frank Shaw was the most important figure in the development of a discourse around Scouse. But though his contribution was fundamental, it would be a mistake to think that the Scouse industry was either a one-man operation, or that it worked simply through the dissemination of articles and essays in newspapers and journals. In fact if it had been limited in either of these ways, it is doubtful that the industry would have developed into the influential force it later became. For while Shaw's work was indispensable, it was only one element in the articulation of a discourse that took various forms, some of which tapped into established aspects of the Liverpool cultural scene (such as the local folk music tradition), and some of which were enabled by the new possibilities offered by modern popular culture (such as Shaw's collaboration on radio and TV documentaries).[28] Moreover, although Shaw was the leading light, there were others who played crucial roles, including musicians and writers such as Glyn Hughes and Stan Kelly (known later as Stan Kelly Bootle), broadcaster and writer Peter Moloney – described by Shaw as 'my rival in the Scouse industry' – and last but not least, musician, writer, publisher and impresario Fritz Spiegl.[29] All were participants in an enterprise that, while it was culturally motivated, was also economically profitable (Shaw declared once that 'scouse itself has brought me quite a few guineas') (Shaw 1955c: 6).[30] Needless to say, as with Shaw's contribution, the work of these figures was not in itself sufficient to gain cultural and social recognition for Scouse, for if their activities had not been taken up by larger forces operating at the national level, they might have remained nothing more

than a symptom of the 'second revival' of interest in British folklore, music
and song that occurred from around the end of the Second World War to the
end of the 1960s. Despite this, however, the contribution of what amounts
to a relatively small group of men (very few women were involved at the
public level, a fact that undoubtedly influenced the tendency to focus on the
working-class man as the archetypal Scouser) became the foundation for a
great deal of the representation of Liverpool in popular culture in the 1960s
and 70s. In that respect, although the Beatles phenomenon gained enormous,
worldwide attention for Liverpool, the perception of the city at a national
level was equally derived from the depiction of the Scousers who appeared in
Z-Cars and *The Liver Birds* (to cite but two examples, though they were among
the most popular series of the 1960s and 70s on British television). And those
Scousers often conformed to the cultural, linguistic and social representations
that had been set out by the founders of the Scouse industry.

Scouse was literally staged in the early 1960s with a series of performances
involving a host of familiar names. One of the earliest of these concerts – a
combination of music, song, anecdote and story – was reported in an article
in the *Daily Post* (6 January 1961) under the heading 'Dese Scousers, Like,
Said De Scouse Was Gear'. The article began: 'So der's dese wackers, like, in
dis cooey in Canning Dock last night – an' well like dey 'ad dis Paddy wack
an' a pan of Scouse an' a wet nella' an' kewins an' a cob of chuck. Den dis fella
Stan Kelly wi' de singin' an' dey all ad a good jangle an' a few bevies an' dey
all said it was de gear' (Anon 1961: 3).[31] The performers, in a nightclub on the
old Royal Naval landing craft *Landfall* which was moored in Canning Dock,
were Kelly and Shaw. Kelly, an important figure in Scouse circles and author of
'Liverpool Lullaby' (1959) and 'I Wish I Was Back in Liverpool' (1960), provided
the music.[32] Shaw's party-piece was a 'rhyming fable on the origin of Scouse',
a *Macbeth* parody featuring 'three shawlies round a cauldron on the Cast Iron
Shore'. A later version appeared in Shaw's memoir *My Liverpool*:

> *First* [shawlie]: Eye of newt and toe of frog.
> *Second*: Six spare-ribs and some Mersey fog.
> *Third*: Ringo's ringlets, Lennon's larynx, glottal stop from Cilla's pharynx…
> *First*: Rhody bacon, foot of pig,
>   Bessie's bustle, Laski's wig.
> *Second*: Cob a chuck, a gill of ale,
>   Warder's key from Walton gaol.
> *Third*: Sargent's baton, docker's hook,
>   Pages from a ha'penny book…
> *First*: Stink bomb from the Wizzid's Den,
>   Splinter from the docker's pen.
> *Second*: Here's a scuffer, scarper douse!
> *They taste brew.* Good gees, Maggie, we've invented Scouse! (Shaw 1971: 101–05)[33]

Shaw made explicit reference to the importance of the music hall tradition
in Liverpool and its influence was clear in this and later concerts devised and
hosted by Fritz Spiegl in the more formal surroundings of the Bluecoat (25
November 1961) and the Philharmonic Hall (3 March 1962).[34] At the Bluecoat

the performers were Kelly, A.L. (Bert) Lloyd (a key figure in the folk revival of the 1950s and 60s and a political activist), Stan Hugill (Hoylake-born singer and historian of the sea-shanty – known as 'the last shantyman'), Glyn Hughes (singer and author of 'Whiskey on a Sunday') and 'the Ivor Novello of Scottie Road' (Spiegl's title for Frank Shaw).[35] At the Philharmonic the artists included Kelly, Hughes, Shaw, the Spinners and of course Spiegl himself as conductor.[36] The performances were officially titled 'Scouser Songs: An Entertaining Evening of Old Liverpool Street Ballads, Sea Shanties and Folk Songs' (though in homage to Spiegl's Austrian origins, Shaw nicknamed them the 'Scouse-and-Strauss concerts'). In both cases the programme was much the same: a medley of new and old favourites such as 'Maggie May', 'A Liverpool ABC', 'The Liverpool Dustman', 'The Liverpool Labour Exchange', 'The Liverpool Do', 'The Liverpool Girls', 'The Ballad of Johnny Todd' and 'Seth Davy of Bevington Bush (Whiskey on a Sunday)' (Spiegl 1962).

As Shaw's 'Macbeth' parody indicates, Scouse was represented in such performances by the repeated use of key words and phrases, all of which were presented as being endangered by the forces of modernization. The songs also often embodied idealized images of historical moments or conditions that had passed (or were passing) and that had to be recalled in order to preserve Scouse culture. Kelly's 'I Wish I Was Back in Liverpool', for example, described by the author as a 'soggy mess of neuralgia for the cultural mecca of the world', included two final verses that demonstrated the point:

> There's every race and colour of face and every kind of name,
> But the pigeons on the pierhead, they treat you all the same.
> And if you walk up Upper Parliament Street, there's people black and brown,
> And I've also seen them orange and green in dear old Liverpool town.
>
> I wish I was back in Liverpool, Liverpool town where I was born.
> There isn't no trees, no scented breeze, no fields of waving corn.
> But there's lots of girls with peroxide curls and the black-and-tan flows free,
> With six in a bed by the old pierhead, and it's Liverpool town for me.
> (Kelly 1964: 12)

The tone of this encomium-all-ye was more tempered in Kelly's 'Liverpool Lullaby' (recorded by Cilla Black in 1969), which took the form of a mother's lament:

> It's quite a struggle every day
> Living on your father's pay,
> The bugger drinks it all away
> And leaves me without any.
>
> [*refrain*]:
> Oh you are a mucky kid,
> Dirty as a dustbin lid,
> When he hears the things you did
> You'll get a belt from your dad.

Perhaps one day we'll have a splash,
When Littlewoods provides the cash,
We'll get a house in Knotty Ash
And buy your dad a brewery.
(Kelly 1964: 5)

But the curious mix of nostalgia, pride and, when the sentiments are decoded, brutal reality (poverty, crime, war, ignorance, urban redevelopment, violence and sectarianism) was probably best illustrated in Pete McGovern's 'In My Liverpool Home' (1961), made famous initially by the Spinners.[37]

I was born in Liverpool, down by the docks,
Me religion was Catholic, occupation hard knocks,
At stealing from lorries I was adept,
And under old overcoats each night I slept.

Way back in the forties the world it went mad,
Mister Hitler threw at us everything that he had,
When the smoke and the dust had all cleared from the air,
'Thank God' said the auld fella, 'The Pier Head's still there.'

When I grew up I met Bridget McGann,
She said 'You're not much but I'm needin a man.
Well a want sixteen kids and an 'ouse out in Speke.'
Well the spirit was willing but the flesh it was weak.

There's a place in dis city were the nits de wear clogs,
They've six million kids and ten million dogs,
De play tick with hatchets and I'll tell you no lie,
A man is a coward if he's more than one eye.

The Green and the Orange have battled for years,
They've given us some laughs and they've given us some tears,
But Scousers don't want a heavenly reward,
They just want the green card to get into Fords.

It was, however, the chorus that became perhaps the mostly widely recognized stanza of verse on Liverpool:

In my Liverpool home,
In my Liverpool home,
We speak with an accent exceedingly rare,
Meet under a statue exceedingly bare,
And if you want a cathedral, we've got one to spare
In my Liverpool home...[38]

Scouse culture, then, was staged, sung, celebrated and, literally, turned into an object of knowledge (Shaw set 'Twenty Scouser Questions – How Well Do You Know Your Liverpoolese?' in the *Liverpool Echo*) (1962e: 6).[39] Most importantly, however, its language was represented and indeed codified in specific ways. As noted previously, there were a number of minor attempts to transcribe

Scouse in the 1950s. In his early defences of Liverpool English, for example, Farrell gave examples such as 'wassemarrewichew', 'dese', 'hospiddle', 'Norris Kreen', 'wicket', 'savvy', 'Aagho whacker' and 'Hello La' (1950a: 4). A number of these were repeated in Whittington-Egan's 'Is Liverpool Dialect Dying Out?': '"Ello, la" and "Aago, whack?"' are greetings 'familiar to all' Liverpudlians (1955c: 216, 220). And Whittington-Egan also produced a short passage in Scouse in the same essay: 'De quare-fellow in de green gansey got lushed-up an wen in de cokes fer a wet neller, but e' wooden cod on wen I wanned mugging, aldo I wus skint' (1955c: 216). Likewise, a little later, Hodgkinson's 'Save Our Scouse – The Dying Language of Liverpool' offered a version of Scouse: 'Eh yew ahr Nellie, werd ye purrahr kid's cozzy' and 'a jewdy along Brreckh Roadz withouts a muffler' (1960: 11). But again, the main protagonist in the project to codify and register Scouse was Frank Shaw; *The Scab* (1952) and *Scouse Talks* (1957) were early examples of his contribution in this regard. Yet it was the piece 'Do You Want to Speak Scouse?' that manifested an idea that was to be realized with such great success later. In the article Shaw gave 'guidance on how to speak Scouse' for those who 'don't speak it and want it as a parlour accomplishment': 'we slur our words, merge syllables, drop them altogether, clip vowels and drop final consonants'. Mostly by way of examples, the essay advised the learner to 'note from among many other abuses': 'ow for o', 'd for t', 'me for my', 't'morra', 'minnit', 'book instead of buk (though it can be the horrible bewk)', 'i for o in words like work, u for ai in words like fairy, is for es in words like bosses, are for our (are kid wears a green gansey), ter for to (I 'ave ter ask me mam), the for they, pleece, alwis' (Shaw 1955a: 6). The weakness of the analysis for practical purposes lay in the absence of phonetic transcription, since Shaw presumed, no doubt correctly, that his readership would be unfamiliar with the International Phonetic Alphabet (although in the same essay he was prepared to use technical linguistic terms such as synaeresis, catachresis, hypallage, anastrophe and brachylogy). It was an issue that Shaw addressed in a later article, 'Parlez Vous Scouse, La?', in which he noted the problem of teaching pronunciation 'without recourse to symbols which look like the alphabet has been on the booze' (Shaw 1962d: 12).[40] But despite this methodological difficulty, the real significance of 'Do You Want to Speak Scouse?' lay in the idea that Scouse could be set out for those who didn't speak it but who wanted to acquire it.

Shaw's efforts in this respect were somewhat opportunistic in the sense that at three significant historical moments he called for work on Scouse to be made available to visitors to the city. The first, as noted earlier in this chapter, was his appeal for a glossary for visitors to the city in 1951 for the Liverpool Festival (part of the Festival of Britain). The second was prompted by the possibility of Britain's entry into the European Common Market (later the EU) in the early 1960s, though his intervention in this case was stimulated by Sonia Goldrein's call in the *Liverpool Echo* for booklets for 'foreigners' aimed at teaching regional dialects – 'Teach Yourself Geordie' or 'Teach Yourself Wacker' (Goldrein 1962: 10). Shaw's response in 'Parlez Vous Scouse, La?' was to support this call (in fact he asserted that a 'Wacker' work already existed) and to argue that various Europeans would find Scouse easily attainable. For example, he noted the use of the glottal stop and the voiceless alveolar affricate [ts] in Liverpool as helpful to Germans, while the French vocalic sound in 'mère' was claimed to be 'identical with our e in Mersey or the i in girl' and 'their oo sound in *vous* is ours in "schewl bewk"'. At the macro-level, moreover, the Belgians would be familiar with the diglossic situation in Liverpool since just as 'the Walloons and the Flemings have two separate languages, one resembling German, the other French, so we have one resembling Lancashire-Irish, the other resembling English'. Scouse vocabulary, however, 'often so independent of that found elsewhere in the United Kingdom, is sure to be the biggest stumbling block' for our European partners. Hence the need to devise 'a set of handy phrases for use in the rues (jowlers) and strasses (cooeys) of Scouseland'. The article ended with a flourish: 'it is time, mesdames et messieurs (judies and fellas) to say au revoir (tarrah well). Wackers of the world, unite!' (Shaw 1962d: 12).

Yet if the Festival of Britain and Britain's possible entry into Europe were responsible for Shaw's interest in encoding Scouse in a particular way, it was the staging of a number of matches of the 1966 World Cup in Liverpool that prompted the most successful realization of his project: the first volume of the *Lern Yerself Scouse* series, *Lern Yerself Scouse. How to Talk Proper in Liverpool* (a text that Shaw had implicitly promised in the 'Parlez Vous Scouse, La?' article).[41] Though this was a collaborative project with Fritz Spiegl (who edited it and wrote the foreword) and Stan Kelly (who contributed 'a Scouse pome'), the work was essentially authored by Shaw and was in effect the summation of the work of the previous twenty years or so.[42] Other volumes followed. Volume two, *The ABZ of Scouse*, written by Linacre Lane (later 'revealed' to be E.F. Hughes – both names being jokes, the latter a rude one) also appeared in 1966 and dealt primarily with 'North End and Bootle Scouse' (in contrast to Shaw's first volume, which had mainly considered 'Dingle Scouse, from the south end'). Volume three, *Wersia Sensa Yuma?* (1972), by Brian Minard, focused on 'anarchic Maritime Scouse'. Volume four, *The Language of Laura Norder* (1989) (originally titled 'Scally Scouse'), composed by Spiegl, concerned itself with 'the speech of thieves and rogues but also of police and lawyers'. And finally, volume five, *Scouse International* (2000), a collaborative effort between Spiegl and various translators, concentrated on 'the language the Beatles spoke in their heyday [...] translated into five languages: Scouse, Posh English, French, German and Japanese'. But it was Shaw's volume, read by exiles, visitors and Scousers themselves, which became the touchstone for the Scouse industry. As Spiegl noted in the millennial reprint (the sixteenth): 'it is no exaggeration to say that the first edition of this booklet in 1966 took the country by storm. Although its commercial distribution was (and still is) chiefly local, word soon spread among the many exiled Liverpudlians, both nationally and internationally, and orders began to come from all over the world' (Shaw et al. 2000). Perhaps the claim that *Lern Yerself Scouse* took the country by storm is an exaggeration, but it is worth noting the welcome given to it by no less an organ of influence than the lead article in *The Times Literary Supplement* on 25 August 1966. Noting that the work was 'produced ostensibly for the benefit of visitors to Goodison Park' during the World Cup, the leader-writer (John Willett, later the author of the acclaimed account of artistic creativity in Liverpool, *Art in a City*, 1967) opined that 'at a time when there are so many reasons for language to become tediously standardized, it is heartening to feel that there are parts of England where words are still alive'. Southern readers, he noted, would be 'staggered by the splendor, sometimes of the sounds themselves [...] sometimes by the poetic vision' of Scouse (Willett 1966: 763).

Conclusion

This chapter has attempted to analyse the process by which a discourse around Scouse was articulated and disseminated in the 1950s and 1960s. The work of Frank Shaw was evidently central to this phenomenon, though as has been argued, he was but the most influential member of a number of people working across disparate though related media. These included newspaper letters and articles, books, musical concerts, collections of song, poetry, radio and television broadcasts, and of course comedy performances (everything from the staging of Shaw's 'Malapudlianisms' to Ken Dodd's Knotty Ash Diddymen). There is, of course, an irony in all this, since Shaw and his associates often proclaimed the death of Scouse culture – the traditional language and practices of Liverpool – in part as a consequence of modern popular culture. Yet in fact the modes of popular culture were precisely those through which Scouse was propagated and through which it was given cultural status and recognition. There was no more skilful user of newspapers, radio, television and the rest than Frank Shaw. The Scouse industry, then, was founded in the period under consideration in this chapter, but this fact in itself raises a number of further questions. What lay behind the postulation of Scouse and why did it appear in the form it did, when it did? What was at stake in the transformation of what William Tirebuck in 1891 called 'Liverpudlian English' into 'Scouse'? Most important of all, perhaps, what is 'Scouse'?

Notes

1   Richard Whittington-Egan, 'Is Liverpool Dialect Dying Out?', in *Liverpool Colonnade* (1955), 216.
2   *Oxford English Dictionary*, 2nd edn (Oxford, 1989), *s.v. scouse n 2b*.
3   In Whittington-Egan's essay 'Liverpool Dialect is Dying Out' he referred to Shaw as 'the Damon Runyon of Liverpoolese', though this was not the only sobriquet that Shaw attracted. In the advertising for a concert of 'Scouser Songs' at the Bluecoat Hall Fritz Spiegl called him 'The Ivor Novello of Scottie Road' (Whittington-Egan 1955a: 6; Spiegl 1962).
4   Shaw was born in Liverpool but raised in Tralee before returning to his home city. An employee of HM Customs for forty years, he was also a councillor for Huyton, broadcaster, researcher, writer, dramatist, trades union official, lexicographer and prime mover behind the *Lern Yerself Scouse* books (a phrase he described as the 'best title I ever created'). For details of Shaw's life, see his memoir, *My Liverpool* (1971).

5   Interestingly, the article noted that 'Mr. Shaw has no trace of a Liverpool accent himself.'

6   Partridge's interest did have a consequence of note: Shaw became the advisor on Liverpool usage for the fifth edition of Partridge's *Dictionary of Slang and Unconventional English* (1961).

7   'Kecks' is probably a variant of 'kicks', an old (1699) canting term for 'trousers'. As evidence of the institutional impact of Shaw's work, two of the OED references for 'kecks' are from the *Lern Yerself Scouse* books.

8   This claim for the cosmopolitan nature of Liverpool and its openness to US influences in particular was to become a commonplace of observations on Liverpudlian culture. It often features in commentaries on the Liverpool music scene from the late 1950s on and is sometimes used as an explanatory factor in the rise of Mersey Beat (including of course the Beatles).

9   James Hardy Vaux, *New and Comprehensive Vocabulary of the Flash Slang* (London, 1819), *s.v. snitch, judy, chatty, wack. Oxford English Dictionary*, 2nd edn (Oxford, 1989), *s.v. blocker n5, scoff n², cod n⁵2, bevy, shawlie, Mary Ann n1, dig n¹4a, growler n4, tart, gammy adj3, jangle*. Eric Partridge, *Dictionary of Slang and Unconventional English* (New York, 1961), *s.v. scufter*. For an alternative account of 'scuffer', see chapter three n. 33. Shaw's definition of 'cod' as Norwegian 'empty husk' may itself have been a 'cod' in the sense of hoax or joke; Joyce uses 'cod' in *Portrait of the Artist as a Young Man* (Joyce 1992b: 43). 'Blocker' is one of the few Liverpool words used in Brophy's *Waterfront* (1934: 204); Shaw later explained it as 'so called because that sort of a hat (a bowler) is made on a block: it is an old draper's slang' (Shaw 1964: 12). The OED accounts of 'have a cob on', 'blocker', 'judy' and 'tart' include citations to the first of the *Lern Yerself Scouse* books (see n. 7 above). For 'Prufrock Scoused', see Simpson 1995: 21.

10   The recordings were made at the behest of George Chandler who was, as noted earlier, the Liverpool City Librarian and official historian; Chandler was also responsible for the invaluable (though incomplete) collection of local newspaper cuttings relating to dialect and slang (1931–1972) that are held in the Liverpool Record Office. In addition, Chandler solicited Shaw's typescript of *The Scab* (which the author, in a letter accompanying the text in 1955 that demonstrates how little he understood of the ways of archivists, asked to be returned 'some time'). Shaw described the recording project in 'Scouse Lingo is Preserved for Posterity' (Shaw 1957b). The first novel that attempts a consistent representation of Liverpool speech is H.J. Cross's *No Language But a Cry* (1951), the title of which is taken from one of the most frequently quoted cantos of Tennyson's 'In Memoriam': 'So runs my dream, but what am I?/An infant crying in the night/An infant crying for the light/ And with no language but a cry.'

11   Shaw's sense that a culture was passing was conveyed in the plaintive 'What Songs will be Sung about Speke and Kirkby?', *Liverpool Echo*, 20 August 1957.

12   Shaw's broadcasting career began with an appearance with the Liverpool comedian Arthur Askey and the local MP Bessie Braddock on a radio programme for Liverpool Civic Week in 1951. He later worked for the BBC, ITV and the Canadian Broadcasting Corporation; he became a regular on BBC Radio Merseyside. Shaw has a good claim to being the first 'professional Scouser'.

13   For a discussion of *Morning in the Streets*, including several passages of the dialogue, see Shaw 1971: 219–24; the Liverpool scenes were shot mostly in the Dingle, Everton and Scotland Road. The film won the prestigious Prix Italia and further enhanced the reputation of the director Dennis Mitchell and the cameraman Roy Harris. Shaw, Mitchell and Harris were all Merseysiders.

14   A 'casey' was a leather-cased football; 'olly' does not appear in any of the standard,

slang or dialect dictionaries; 'ollies' later became used for testicles, as in the Liverpool writer Neville Smith's *Gumshoe*: 'What about that shot Pele hit from way behind the half-way line, eh? Made that goalie drop his ollies' (Smith 1971: 61). 'Coke' was a name for cafés in Liverpool; it derived from institutions originally set up for temperance purposes to sell cocoa to the working class.

15 Linguistic prejudice remains as one of the few socially acceptable prejudices. See, for example, Alan Bennett's comment on Scouse: 'there is a rising inflection in it, particularly at the end of a sentence, that gives even the most formal exchanges a built-in air of grievance...' (cited in Belchem 2000b: 33). What might Bennett's response be to a Scouser who commented on 'the unpleasantly brusque tone of the Leeds accent which makes even acts of politeness sound like expressions of arrogance'? As that silly comment illustrates, the rudeness of Bennett's remark is woefully easy to replicate.

16 Like other cities, Shaw asserted, Liverpool used 'a debased form of dialect' (Anon 1955: 6). In fact, he claimed, its language was a 'debased Lancashire form' (Shaw 1955b: 5) that was viewed by some as 'nothing but shamefully debased English' (Shaw 1958a: 13).

17 As Shaw noted, there were many Liverpool people who detested Scouse; there still are. In 'Lazy Talk', a correspondent to the *Daily Post* described a sixty-year fight against 'the mis-called Liverpool dialect'. A particular source of annoyance apparently was the 'constant failing of even well-educated Liverpolitans [...] to pronounce the terminal "ton" in Walton, Garston &c, making them into Walt'n and Garst'n, an abbreviation which is surely due to the people's plain inability to hear themselves speak' ('Postman' 1955: 4).

18 Shaw may have borrowed this reference from J.C. Colman, whose letter, entitled 'Furly Airly', on 'the existence of a Liverpool accent' was published in the *Daily Post*, 9 August 1950 (Colman 1950: 4).

19 Shaw made several references to women's speech. He noted, for example, in 'Do You Want to Speak Scouse', that 'the females among us – [can] switch in a moment from Rose Hill to Mossley Hill' (Rose Hill is in the impoverished Scotland Road area, Mossley Hill is a middle-class suburb) (Shaw 1955a: 6). Hodgkinson asserted that 'the call of the female of the species is a fertile source of characteristic expression [...] "Me an' me 'usband's goin' t' move out t' Kerby next year. It's gettin' orful common round 'ere"' (Hodgkinson 1960: 11).

20 Clarke claimed that 'the girls who have embarked upon the speech training course are most interested and enthusiastic; they attend classes regularly and, in fact, their numbers have risen since the beginning of the term' (Clarke 1962: 6).

21 The comment is revealing: the idea that people from 'humble origins' could not have 'cultural aspirations' without being described as 'pretentious' is an example of the type of inverted snobbery (and cultural condescension) that marks Shaw's work.

22 Ross's original article, 'Linguistic Class-Indicators in Present-Day English', appeared in the respected language journal *Neuphilologische Mitteilungen* (1954). Both in this essay, and Nancy Mitford's appropriation of it, the concern is with the distinction between upper-class and middle-class language (working-class language does not feature). The debate is best read as an indication of shifting economic and cultural relations in the aftermath of the Second World War. Mitford's collection included a poem by John Betjeman ('How to Get on in Society'), which indicates the tone of the discussion:

> Phone for the fish knives, Norman
> As cook is a little unnerved;
> You kiddies have crumpled the serviettes
> And I must have things daintily served.

Are the requisites all in the toilet?
The frills round the cutlets can wait
Till the girl has replenished the cruets
And switched on the logs in the grate... (Mitford 2002: 105)

23 Both 'Irish Bulls' (the subject of an interesting essay by Maria Edgeworth) and 'Malapropisms' (from Mrs Malaprop, a character in R.B. Sheridan's *The Rivals*, 1775) are more than entertaining 'mis'-uses of language. In both cases there are issues of linguistic colonialism (Edgeworth and Sheridan were Irish) and class involved, while the politics of language in *The Rivals* revolves around gender and class. For an examination of Edgeworth on 'Irish Bulls', see Crowley 2005 ch. 4; for a consideration of language politics in the eighteenth century, see Barrell 1983: ch. 2; Crowley 1996: ch. 3; Sorensen 2000; Mitchell 2001.

24 Examples abounded: 'congratulate' for 'congregate', 'Ulster' for 'ulcer', 'curvaceous' for 'herbaceous', 'content' for 'contempt', 'distinguish' for 'extinguish', 'macarooned' for 'marooned', 'amalgamating' for 'accumulating', 'pelvis' for 'pelmet', 'antique' for 'unique', 'symphony' for 'sympathy', 'ejection' for 'injection', 'antidote' for 'anecdote', 'violation' for 'volition', 'inimical' for 'inimitable' and so on. A couple of the more interesting phrases were 'it would fit Phil Macoo' (Finn Mac Cumhaill, aka Finn Macool, the legendary Irish warrior) and 'Skinn Finnegan' (a Sinn Féin man).

25 On the BBC *Northcountryman* radio programme, broadcast in January 1958, Shaw introduced what he called 'the secret speech of Liverpool dockers' (Harrison 1958: 5).

26 The pioneering work in linguistic network theory (the application of social network analysis to language) was Lesley Milroy's *Language and Social Networks* (1980).

27 Whittington-Egan concurred: 'In the course of my investigations, I have found that it is the poorer districts of Liverpool, and particularly the dock areas, where, incidentally, the docker has a rich additional dialect of his own, that constitutes the last strongholds of our vanishing dialect. In those places it will, I think, survive' (Whittington-Egan 1955a: 6).

28 For a discussion of the cultural significance of the mid-twentieth-century folk revival in Britain, see Michael Brocken, *The British Folk Revival 1944–2002* (2005); Brocken's analysis is based on doctoral work at the Institute of Popular Music at the University of Liverpool (Brocken grew up in the city). For a detailed historical account of music in Liverpool that challenges 'the Beatles-Liverpool narrative', see Brocken's *Other Voices: Hidden Histories of Liverpool's Popular Music Scenes, 1930s–1970s* (2010). For a detailed historical account of music in Liverpool that is based on 'the Beatles-Liverpool narrative', see Paul Du Noyer, *Liverpool: Wondrous Place. Music from the Cavern to the Capital of Culture* (2007).

29 Shaw's comment on Moloney appears in *My Liverpool* (1971: 237). Moloney taught at St Malachy's, Beaufort Street, in the Dingle in the 1950s; his more successful career was as an early 'professional Scouser' in the guise of raconteur, after-dinner speaker, television broadcaster (including his own series, 'Moloney on...') and writer. His *A Plea for Mersey. Or, the Gentle Art of Insinuendo* appeared in 1966 and was followed by an LP, *A Load of Moloney – How to Speak Scouse Proper*, a year later.

30 Shaw also achieved other forms of recognition: at an inaugural meeting of the Warwick Wackers Club at the University of Warwick in 1968, he received an honorary degree in Scouseology (BSc) ('Postman' 1968: 4).

31 Shaw noted that 'the only thing missing from a Liverpool menu are spare ribs and salt fish' (Anon 1961: 3). Salt fish (cod) was a traditional seafarer's dish and a Portuguese speciality – hence the other name 'bacalhoa' (Portuguese 'bacalhau'), which was used in the Dingle; salt fish was popular on Fridays in Catholic areas. The Portuguese influence in the Dingle, or at least in specific streets, may also explain the practice of Judas-burning on Good Friday morning (see chapter three n. 19).

32   Stan Kelly (Stan Kelly-Bootle as he later called himself) had an unusual and varied
     career. A pioneer in computing (he was awarded the first postgraduate diploma in
     computing from Cambridge in 1955) he was a founder-member of the St Lawrence
     Society (the Cambridge folk club) in 1950 and was later involved in a skiffle band
     (skiffle was influential in the development of both the folk scene and beat music –
     John Lennon's Quarrymen was a skiffle band that evolved into a more famous pop
     group). Kelly supplied the music for *The Talking Streets* and *Morning in the Streets*
     and recorded a collection of songs about Liverpool – *Liverpool Packet* (1958); he
     published *Liverpool Lullabies – The Stan Kelly Song Book* (1964) and contributed
     a Scouse 'translation' of *The Rubáiyát of Omar Khayyá*m to the first of the *Lern*
     Yerself Scouse books (1966). Kelly's version of *The Rubaiyat* (based on Edward
     Fitzgerald's mid-nineteenth-century edition of the poetry of the eleventh–twelfth-
     century Persian poet and intellectual Omar Khayyám) began: 'Gerrup dere La! De
     knocker-up sleeps light;/Dawn taps yer winder, ends anudder night;/And Lo! De
     dog-eared moggies from next door/Tear up de jigger fer an early fight' (against
     Fitzgerald's 'Awake! for Morning in the Bowl of Night/Has flung the Stone that puts
     the Stars to Flight:/And Lo! the Hunter of the East has caught/The Sultán's Turret
     in a Noose of Light' ('Postman' 1965a: 4; Fitzgerald 1921: 39). Kelly also worked with
     Shaw ('scholars from Dingle University and Huyton Elysée') on Gray's 'Elegy': 'A
     "curse you" 's on me lips now evr'y day/When evr'yone gets on his bus but me,/So
     all me butties now are well away,/While I'm still waitin' for de ould 10D' ('Postman'
     1965b: 4). In a letter to *The Times Literary Supplement*, Shaw claimed that he and
     Kelly were preparing the *Scousiad*, *King Gear* and *Paradise Street Lost* (Paradise
     Street is one of the oldest in Liverpool city centre) (Shaw 1966e: 781). Kelly later
     compiled *O Liverpool We Love You* (1976), a tribute album to Liverpool Football
     Club (the title song of which is still sung by its fans).
33   'Rhody' meant 'streaky'; pigs' trotters were used in soups – though if someone
     received a blow that was likely to bruise, the observation was often made that 'it
     will look like a pig's foot in the morning'; 'Bessie' is a reference to the redoubtable
     Liverpool MP, Bessie Braddock, while Laski was the name of a Liverpool judge; 'cob'
     is a piece of something, though 'a cob' means a roll; 'chuck' was bread; 'gill' meant
     a half pint in Liverpool, though a quarter pint elsewhere; Sir Malcolm Sargent was
     the conductor of the Royal Liverpool Philharmonic Orchestra; speaking nonsense
     was referred to as 'talking like a halfpenny book'; the Wizard's Den was a famous
     Liverpool joke shop; 'scuffer' was policeman and 'douse' meant 'look out!'
34   As cited in the introduction to this chapter, Chandler noted the significance of
     music hall in the representation of the 'scouser' (Chandler 1957: 423). In 'There's
     Poetry in Liverpool', Shaw commented on the music hall singing tradition in
     Liverpool and its association with 'native ballads' (as well as the custom of Liverpool
     seamen becoming the 'shanty-man' on ships); he also opined that 'it is not therefore
     surprising to learn that many singers in modern dance bands are Scousers' (Shaw
     1958c: 6). Shaw later hosted the 'Pot of Scouse Revue' at the Everyman Theatre in
     1967.
35   Shaw was not the first to bear this title – as noted in chapter three, Seth Davy was
     described as 'the "King" of Scotland Road's entertainers, the "Noel Coward and Ivor
     Novello" (all in one)' (Bailey 1957: 6).
36   Spiegl was a 'kindertransport' refugee from the Nazis who arrived in England
     from Vienna in 1939. He became principal flautist in the Liverpool Philharmonic
     Orchestra and was heavily involved in various Scouse adventures as impresario
     and publisher (he was the founder of the Scouse Press and thus largely respon-
     sible for the *Lern Yerself Scouse* series). Apart from his contributions to the Scouse
     industry, Spiegl was famous for two things in particular: first, his judgement that

'The Liverpool Sound' (by which he meant the Beatles) was 'probably the most successful mass bamboozle since the virgin birth' (Shaw et al. 1966: foreword, n.p.); second, his setting of 'Johnny Todd', a traditional Liverpool sea-shanty, which became the theme tune of *Z-Cars* and Everton Football Club.

37 The Spinners (only one of whose permanent members was born in Liverpool) were formed in 1958, pre-empted the Beatles at the Cavern and became the national face of the Liverpool folk scene through TV appearances, including their own BBC TV series; their first album was *Songs Spun in Liverpool* (1961). The Spinners were unusual in two respects; first, they were multiracial (Cliff Hall was a Cuban-Jamaican); second, one of the women who sang with them, Jacqui Macdonald, became a successful artist in her own right and a mainstay of the Liverpool folk scene (with her singing partner Bridie O'Donnell). The Spinners used Kelly's 'I Wish I Was Back in Liverpool' (1960) as their signature tune.

38 The second verse refers to the Liverpool Blitz (1940–41), in which more than 4,000 people died and 70,000 were left homeless; Speke is an area on the southern out-skirts of the city – in 1930 its population was about 400 but urban redevelopment saw the figure rise to 25,000 by 1960; 'nits' are head lice; the 'Green' and the 'Orange' are Catholics and Protestants; 'the green card' was the union card at Fords car plant at Halewood (steady work and a pension made it a desirable place to be employed); the 'accent exceedingly rare' was of course Scouse; the 'exceedingly bare' statue was Epstein's 'Liverpool Resurgent' (1956), a sculpture of a naked man standing on the prow of a ship placed on Lewis's department store; the statue was known to all Liverpudlians as 'Dickie Lewis' (for an obvious reason); Liverpool has the distinc-tion of having two major cathedrals – one Anglican and one Catholic.

39 Questions included: 'What shop would you go to for (a) Wet Nellers, (b) Kecks, (c) Conny-onny'?'; 'What is the schoolboy word for (a) to play truant, (b) to tell tales, (c) the library, (d) the baths?'; 'In what district was "Her Benny" mainly set?'; 'Name five famous comics born in Liverpool'; 'Translate into Standard English: (a) our kid went to the cokes but I went for a bevy; (b) Meladdo marmalised him in the jowler (c) I was skint so cooden take the judy to no 'op'. Shaw turned Scouse culture into an object of knowledge in another way: together with Glyn Hughes he set up the short-lived 'Scouse Museum' (Shaw 1969: 72).

40 Hodgkinson made the same point in 'Save Our Scouse – The Dying Language of Liverpool': 'without a phonetic script, how does one show these refinements of pro-nunciation […] the Fazakerly "KH", the Garston "Ahr"?)' (1960: 11).

41 A review in the *Daily Post* praised *Lern Yerself Scouse* as 'outrageously funny and impressively erudite' and noted that it offered useful phrases for the World Cup visitor covering various situations – an encounter with the law, a fight, the football games at Goodison, dining out, a visit to the doctor and a dance. The terms offered for the dance hall included 'she's got up-de-entry eyes' and 'yer not on, la!' – trans-lated respectively as 'she has a come hither look' and 'you shall not have your way, young man'. Like all of the *Lern Yerself Scouse* books, the first was evidently skewed towards men and their behaviour ('Postman' 1966a: 6).

42 *Lern Yerself Scouse* was not, however, Shaw's final contribution. In 1966 he published *The Oxtail Book of Verse* and in 1967 the much more successful *The Gospels in Scouse* (co-written with the Revd Dick Williams). The latter text was originally conceived by Williams who, after reading *Lern Yerself Scouse*, claimed that Scouse 'hits the jackpot of human understanding' and that therefore 'the Church shouldn't wince away from Scouse into the splendid twilight of Elizabethan English' ('Postman' 1966b: 6). *The Gospels in Scouse* was published shortly after the consecration of the Catholic cathedral (the Metropolitan Cathedral of Christ the King) and was an ecumenical effort subtitled 'The Gear Story in Liverpoolese, the Language of the

Beatles'. It didn't, in fact, render the biblical text in full in Scouse, but presented selections. The opening of Genesis reads: 'Before God did owt else e ad summat ter say. It wus is last werd. Ony it come first. And it summed up is ole attitude to everythink. Now dis werd was wid God. Fact it wus part'n parcel uv im. So at start uv everythink an a long time fore man was akshully made, God's werd to men wus ready an waitin' (Shaw and Williams 1967: 1).

5

What is 'Scouse'?
Historical and theoretical issues

Liverpool is rich in natural traditions. (Fritz Spiegl, *Scouser Songs*, 1962)[1]

In a clear piece of codology, Shaw reported a claim by Farrell that there was 'evidence that Scouse was spoken hereabout at least 900 years ago' from a scroll found in a cave by the Cast Iron Shore. The text reported an exchange between two archers: 'I think our bows should be made with oak', one declared; 'Why, what's the matter wid yew?' said the other (Shaw 1963b: 6). In fact, as the last two chapters have demonstrated, 'Scouse' emerged as a category used to name the language of Liverpool at a very recent date. Skeat has no entry for the term with this meaning in his *Etymological Dictionary of the English Language* (1882), nor does Wright in his *English Dialect Dictionary* (1898–1905), and there is nothing in the first five editions of Partridge's slang dictionary (1937–1961). The 1989 edition of the *OED* does include the term in this sense, with the definition: 'the dialect of English spoken in Liverpool. Also, the manner of pronunciation or accent typical to the "scouse".' Symptomatically, the first supporting quote (1963) refers to the Beatles and the second is to the *ABZ of Scouse* (1966), volume two of the *Lern Yerself Scouse* series.[2] And yet as was shown in chapter three, the *OED* record is wanting since there were earlier and more illustrative examples of the use of 'Scouse' to refer to language, with perhaps the earliest featuring in the title of Shaw's 'Scouse Lingo – How It All Began' (Shaw 1950c: 4). Interestingly, given the modernity of 'Scouse' in this sense, it is notable (and indicative of what was to come later) that the first attributive use of the term was recorded in the dictionary as pejorative and journalistic: the *OED* cites reference by a contributor to the *Spectator* in 1960 referred to 'a horrifyingly plausible spiv, even down to that awful "scouse" accent'. But if the recent nature of 'Scouse' is worthy of note, there is another intriguing factor that is perhaps more important. Put simply it is this: what exactly *is* 'Scouse'? Does it mean a variety of English that has a distinctive vocabulary, that is, one that contains items not found anywhere else? Or is it a form of English that is grammatically different from other forms? Or a particular way of pronouncing a form of English? All three perhaps? A combination of any two? One way of addressing this issue in terms of the available categories of linguistic study is to ask whether the language of Liverpool is a dialect or an accent. Yet significantly, answers to this question have often been conceptually confused or simply unclear, and not just in the type of non-professional research that appeared in local newspapers. As will become clear, Farrell was neither the first nor the last to hedge his bets when he penned that first important article, 'About that Liverpool Accent (or Dialect)' (Farrell 1950a).

Classifying the language of Liverpool

One example of the sort of confusion that has surrounded Scouse is evinced by the poorly worded *OED* definition of the term cited above: 'the dialect of English spoken in Liverpool. Also, the manner of pronunciation or accent typical to the "scouse". In this instance, apart from the fact that the dictionary cannot decide on the capitalization of the term (noting just that it is used 'often with capital initial'), does 'Scouse' refer to a dialect, or is it simply a 'manner of pronunciation' that is 'typical' of 'the "scouse"'? And does the second phrase mean that Scouse is both ('also') a dialect and an accent? Or is the implication that the term refers to either a dialect or an accent? And is 'the "scouse"' in question a form of language or an inhabitant of Liverpool (the *OED* citation for 'scouse' as someone from Liverpool dates from 1945, which is earlier than the linguistic reference)?[3] Such questions are complex and will be taken up again in a later chapter, but before attempting to deal with some of the difficulties that surround the concept of 'Scouse', it may be helpful to take note of the ways in which a range of commentators – both professional linguists and amateur observers – have explicitly approached the topic of language in Liverpool. Again, it will be seen that the accounts are variable, often confused, and sometimes contradictory.

A.J. Ellis, one of the founding fathers of British dialectology in the nineteenth century, presented what at first sight appears to be a puzzling assessment of the language of Liverpool. In *On Early English Pronunciation,* Part V (1889), Ellis included Liverpool within the Western North Midland dialect area, but rather than discussing any features of its speech, he not only excluded it from consideration, he also implied that it had no dialect of its own. Thus when discussing the area north of Bebington on the eastern Wirral peninsula, Ellis commented that it was not considered in his analysis because it 'is affected by Liverpool and Birkenhead influence, that is, it has no dialect proper'. Likewise, when discussing the dialectal speech of Prescot, he noted that it has certain features that are unusual in the North Midland dialect, 'probably through the influence of Liverpool' (Ellis 1889: 409, 342). The apparent contradiction, however, between the idea that Liverpool did not have a distinctive pronunciation system (which was the primary basis of Ellis's determination of dialects in his important and influential history) and the fact that Liverpool speech exerted an influence on the surrounding districts is easily explained.[4] For Ellis, Liverpool did not have a dialect because by definition it couldn't have one.

Dialects were to be found in 'the mouths of uneducated people, speaking an inherited language, in all parts of Great Britain where English is the ordinary language of communication between peasant and peasant'; dialects were not to be found in cities (1889: 1). In this respect what applied to London also applied to Liverpool: 'the enormous congeries of persons from different parts of the kingdom, and from different countries, and the generality of school education, render dialect nearly impossible' (1889: 225). It wasn't that Liverpool didn't have a particular form of language, at least at the level of pronunciation, it was just that it didn't have a dialect according to the standards of the day, which privileged the rural over the urban areas. Such a view was not confined to professional linguists and another example demonstrates its cultural prevalence in the late nineteenth century. Leo Grindon's *Lancashire: Brief Historical and Descriptive Notes* (1892) commented that 'the modern slang of great towns is of course a different thing from the ancient dialect of a rural population'. It warned that 'affected mis-spellings, as of "kuntry" for country, are also to be distinguished *in toto* from the phonetic representation of sounds purely dialectical' (Grindon 1892: 177). Strikingly, this emphasis on the rural was to persist in British dialectology until the late twentieth century.[5]

If Ellis's treatment of the language of Liverpool required interpretation, it was at least consistent in its adherence to a theoretical principle. Later versions were not quite so rigorous. The position of a social commentator such as Whittington-Egan, for example, writing after the publication of Farrell's pioneering essays, is made clear in his 'Is Liverpool Dialect Dying Out?' The essay opened with an attempted transcription (of the type Grindon cautioned against) of 'the rich vein of Liverpool dialect': 'De quare-fellow in de green gansey got lushed-up an wen in de cokes fer a wet neller, but e' wooden cod on wen I wanned mugging, aldo I wus skint' (Whittington-Egan 1955c: 216). The aim was to convey both the phonetic and the lexical peculiarities of Liverpool speech, which Whittington-Egan calls 'scouse', or 'scouse lingo'.[6] Noting that the dialect was in danger (a recurrent trope as noted in chapter three) from 'pseudo-American jargon' and the effects of National Service, slum-clearance, secondary education, popular films and TV, Whittington-Egan observed that 'it is the poorer districts of Liverpool, and particularly the dock areas, where, incidentally, the docker has a rich additional dialect of his own, that constitute the last vanishing strongholds of our vanishing dialect' (1955c: 220). Such an observation (essentially lifted from Shaw) was interesting in its specification of the geographic and social location of linguistic difference. Yet it was combined with the type of aesthetic evaluation that has been so frequently attached to the language of Liverpool: 'that the vernacular of Liverpool, spoken as it is with adenoidal intonation and narrow epiglottal distribution of vowel sounds, is rather ugly, is undeniable. But this is to a great extent compensated for by its picturesque phraseology and imagery' (1955c: 216). In other words, the language of Liverpool has a quaint turn of phrase but it sounds awful. Somewhat disconcertingly, however, Whittington-Egan also went on to declare that 'actually, there is no Liverpool accent at all, in the sense that there is a Cockney, Devon or Gloucestershire accent. It would be truer to say that there is a characteristic intonation…' (1955c: 217).[7] Ellis, then, had effectively rendered Liverpool speech phonetically distinct but not dialectal; Whittington-Egan made it dialectal but lacking an accent (though with a dreadful 'intonation'). But in the city-sponsored history to commemorate the 750th anniversary of the granting of the Charter to Liverpool, the official historian and City Librarian went one better. For George Chandler, Liverpool apparently had neither dialect nor accent, at least in the traditional senses of the terms:

> Nor has Liverpool's subsequent speech become a distinct provincial dialect. The broad accents of the Lancashire man are not spoken there. In fact, the Liverpool dialect has no strong regional feature at all. It tends, as befits a cosmopolitan town with many Irish, Welsh and Scots, to be neutral phonetically; and the most characteristic feature is its monotonous pitch rather than vowel impurities, such as fer for for. (Chandler 1957: 423)

The confusion of social observers such as Whittington-Egan and Chandler is interesting, but it may simply reflect what amounts to no more than the influence of common folk-linguistic beliefs. It might be expected, however, that answers from modern professional historians or linguists to the question of whether 'Liverpool English' is an accent or dialect would be based on a sounder footing. After all dialectology is now (and has been for a long time) an established branch of linguistic study. But in fact contemporary professional commentators on language in Liverpool repeat the misconceptions of an earlier age. Belchem, for example, asserts that Scouse is 'an accent not a dialect', since lacking 'a distinctive grammar or extensive vocabulary, the peculiarities of scouse are almost entirely phonological' (Belchem 2000b: 32). His judgement is reinforced by Andrew Hamer, from the English department at Liverpool University, in his assertion that Scouse is 'an accent really'.[8] This was a categorization that was probably first recorded by a professional linguist in Gerry Knowles' doctoral dissertation on Scouse – the first extended study of Liverpool speech – in which he devotes the important introductory section to the analysis of grammatical features and vocabulary. His conclusion is that 'the very paucity of the material confirms the argument that Scouse is not a "dialect proper" but a variant of standard English. The grammatical peculiarities of Scouse amount to a few minor details, and local words number but a few dozen in a vocabulary of many thousand' (Knowles 1973: 48). For Knowles, displaying a stance that he shared with his nineteenth-century predecessor Ellis, Liverpool's status as a major port and centre of communication meant that 'no peculiar local dialect has developed' since 'the place to look for really localized speech is in isolated hamlets five miles from the nearest road, not in a centre of world trade'. His argument, taken as given by many later writers, is that 'the peculiarities of Scouse are almost entirely phonological' and that the 'main task will therefore be to compare Scouse phonologically with other varieties of standard English' (1973: 50). Indeed because of the difficulties of comparing the pronunciation of working-class men and women with Received Pronunciation ('the speech of public schoolboys from the South of England'),

Knowles took as his focus the investigation of the standardizing influence of 'General British', 'the most general type of educated pronunciation', on Scouse (1973: 50).

Given the centrality of Knowles' account to the story of Liverpool speech, it is worth considering the problems that it raises in specific and general terms. The fieldwork, conducted in the early 1970s, consisted of a series of interviews with native informants from Vauxhall (a working-class area in the north end of the city) and Aigburth (a largely middle-class suburb in the south). It is open to question whether a survey of 47 respondents should bear quite the weight that has been placed upon it since, but be that as it may, the work raises difficult theoretical and categorical questions. For example, as noted above, Knowles argues that the language of Liverpool is not a dialect because effectively, given the small number of grammatical features and the relatively few words that are local to Liverpool, it is simply a 'variant of standard English' (1973: 48). But this is a contentious claim for a number of reasons. First, as a matter of empirical fact, there are many words that appear to be 'local' to Liverpool – at least in the sense of being used there. Examples were cited in previous chapters, though many more could be furnished from the numerous glossaries of such terms that have been produced over the past fifty years or so.[9] Second, from a theoretical point of view, given that at least in terms of traditional, structural linguistic study the identity of a language or linguistic form depends on its nature as a systematic set of items and relations (words and the rules that govern them), then it follows that *any* variation in terms of lexis or grammar is sufficient to establish a distinct form of language.[10] If this were not the case, then in relation to any differences that do exist (lexical, grammatical or phonological), a number of problematic questions arise. For example, who would decide how many terms or grammatical characteristics are required before a 'variant' (to use Knowles' term) can be classified as 'dialect' (or indeed even a 'language')? Who would judge which differences should count and which are to be regarded as insignificant? And on what basis could such decisions be taken? The third issue that Knowles' assertion raises is that of the concept of 'standard English', meaning a standard, central *spoken* form of the English language, against which variants can be measured. As was noted earlier, Williams had contested this notion in the early 1960s, but the radical nature of his insight was not taken up until the 1980s and 90s. Thus, given that Knowles' work was published before the idea of standard spoken English was brought into question in any general sense, it can hardly be held against him that he followed the prevailing model. But it is now the case that this concept, simply taken for granted in the great bulk of linguistic description of English in the twentieth century, has been contested from a number of critical perspectives.[11] And in light of the challenges to the assumptions on which Knowles based his work, it is clear that many of his judgements are dubious – not least the idea that the language of Liverpool is simply a 'variant' of this 'standard' form, and that Liverpool speech is therefore to be considered an accent rather than a dialect.

It may well be that the conceptual difficulties of the accent–dialect debate simply derive from the unclear and often confusing ways in which these terms are used even by professional linguists. One example of such practice is evinced in Honeybone's discussion of the history of Scouse, specifically his observation that the accent–dialect distinction 'relies on a convention that some linguists adopt' (Honeybone 2007: 107). As evidence he cites Hughes and Trudgill's *English Accents and Dialects* (1996), in which the authors 'use DIALECT to refer to varieties distinguished from each other by differences of grammar and vocabulary', whereas 'ACCENT on the other hand, will refer to varieties of pronunciation' (Hughes and Trudgill 1996: 3). In this case the basis of the distinction is evident: grammatical forms and words rather than sounds. But as Honeybone notes, Trudgill claims elsewhere that 'when we talk about dialect we are referring not only to pronunciation but also to the words and grammar people use' (Trudgill 1999: 2). In this instance a dialect appears to be a combination of grammar, vocabulary *and* pronunciation. Yet the distinction between these two accounts raises a serious and significant problem. If Scouse is a dialect in the first sense of the term – a form distinguished by grammar and vocabulary – then it raises the possibility that it could be spoken with *any* accent. But is it possible to imagine Scouse enunciated in Received Pronunciation? Or to conceive of someone speaking Scouse with a Geordie accent? There is, however, a more important issue that pertains to both of Trudgill's accounts and that was mentioned in earlier chapters in relation to claims that specific words were 'unique' to Liverpool. That is, how are the lexical and grammatical forms that specifically belong to Scouse to be determined? Are they just those features that are distinguishable from the vocabulary and grammar of 'standard spoken English'? But this would call for an account of the grammar and vocabulary of standard spoken English, and it is far from clear how such an entity could be constituted (except as some sort of idealized, abstract construct of a particular type of linguistics perhaps).[12] Moreover, given that no such entity has as yet been determined (notwithstanding the loose use of the term in such a way as to suggest that it has), it is difficult to see how Scouse could be distinguished from it. There is, however, a more fundamental issue. If Scouse is in itself a dialect (a systematic structure of words, grammar and pronunciation), then why are those features that it shares with another form of English deemed in some sense not to 'belong' properly to Scouse but to the other form (in this case the 'standard')? That is to say, if Scouse, like other 'varieties' of English, is a linguistic form in its own right, then why should its lexical, grammatical and phonological features not be described holistically? Why should it be treated as a form which is a 'variant' of a 'standard' that is claimed to exist but that no one has as yet managed to describe?

It is worth reiterating that the difficulties and confusions that surround language in Liverpool may well ultimately derive not so much from particular words, forms of grammar and modes of pronunciation as from the theoretical principles and institutionalized methods within the formal study of language that are used to categorize specific forms of linguistic difference. In one sense, of course, this is no more than an observation on the constitution of a disciplinary field of knowledge (that is to say, the way in which an object of knowledge is ascertained and the establishment of the modes through which it is studied);

in this respect linguistics is like any other discipline. But it is necessary to be self-reflexive about disciplinary procedures and their effects – a point emphasized by the founding father of modern linguistics, Ferdinand de Saussure, when he noted that in the study of language 'it is the viewpoint adopted which creates the object' (Saussure 1983: 8). And it is particularly important not to conflate the result of methodological analysis with the social practice from which it is abstracted. In this regard, J.C. Wells makes a significant comment in his *Accents of English* (1982):

> in recognising […] varieties or tendencies within RP [Received Pronunciation], one must remember that they – like RP itself – are abstractions, not objectifiable entities […] The frontiers we may attempt to set up between them may well correspond to our perceptions of social reality rather than to exclusively linguistic and phonetic considerations. (Wells 1982: II, 280)

To extend the point, speech can indeed be considered in terms of pronunciation, grammar and lexis, but this depends in the first instance on the operation of a set of procedures whose function is precisely to produce a stable, analysable 'objectifiable entity' (in this case a dialect or accent of English). But it does not follow that the object of disciplinary investigation – the 'language', 'dialect' or 'accent' – corresponds to the social production, reception and perception of language. It might be, for example, that categories such as 'Liverpool English,' 'the Liverpool dialect' or 'the Liverpool accent' (to say nothing of 'Scouse') are already abstractions that can only be produced by discounting all sorts of linguistic differences that exist in practice in the social, cultural and geographic space of Liverpool. Of course this might not matter much once the (necessary) methodological fictionality of categories such as Liverpool English and so on is recognized. Perhaps it is simply the case that linguistics, like other branches of knowledge, has to produce such categories in order to maintain its disciplinary status (not to mention its standing as a 'science'). But what happens when the object of knowledge under consideration has an uncertain status, or when the construction of the category is unacknowledged? Another way of putting that is to say that if dialectologists decide, using the categories and methods of dialectology, that there is a dialect called 'Liverpool English', then it ought to be relatively simple to ascertain what they mean by this and to go about studying it (although as we saw earlier, this might not be quite as easy as it seems since at least some of the leading dialectologists don't appear to be quite sure what 'dialect' means). A problem arises, however, when the object under consideration appears to be not quite ascertained or fixed by the disciplinary categories and the boundaries that are used to police them. Thus, it may be that Liverpool English is, given the strictures just mentioned, an 'objectifiable entity' of linguistic knowledge – describable in certain ways according to accepted methods. But what about Scouse? Is Scouse an 'objectifiable entity' – a dialect, accent or perhaps just another term for Liverpool English? Does it refer to a specific type of Liverpool English? Is it limited in terms of class (a working-class form)? Or in relation to gender – is Scouse the prerogative of men? Is there a women's version? Is it restricted to particular areas of the city – the 'inner city' or the outlying estates? Or is Scouse a much more complex term altogether, one that appears to refer to a form of language but that in effect encompasses a variety of features to produce a mode of cultural value and social distinction?

Indexicality and enregisterment: theory

Research in cultural theory and (more recently) linguistic anthropology has offered a suggestive way of thinking about these questions by avoiding the sort of essentialist definitions that linguists have traditionally produced in relation to dialects (that is to say, 'X is a dialect because it has Y grammatical/lexical features'). In cultural theory, for example, the work of Mikhail Bakhtin has been influential in the developing understanding of the 'language-making' process. Indeed one of his assertions has become almost commonplace:

> unitary language constitutes the theoretical expression of the historical processes of linguistic unification and centralization, an expression of the centripetal forces of language. A unitary language is not something given [*dan*] but is always in essence posited [*zadan*] – and at every moment of its linguistic life it is opposed to the realities of heteroglossia. (Bakhtin 1981: 270)

Though Bakhtin's concern was primarily with the history of the novel, his particular focus in this regard was on the ways in which the modern European languages were given discursive stability and standardized (for example through developments in printing, lexicography, grammatical and orthographical pre-scriptivism and the stylistics of the novel itself). His central point was that 'language-making' is an ongoing, historically specific and inventive activity. Thus rather than being a quasi-natural 'fact', the 'unitary language' – which can be any form that is posited as having a static, 'real' existence ('language', 'dialect', 'variety', 'accent', 'idiom', 'slang' and so on) – is a product of abstraction, a category constructed over and against the realities of everyday differential practice. In other words, what is called 'a language', 'a dialect', 'an accent' or 'slang' is the creation of a meta-discourse that highlights certain features, ignores others, ranks them according to specific (if often unclear) criteria, and serves to produce the stable, commonsensical categories that are current in contemporary thinking about language.[13]

Another way of putting this argument is to say that the commonplace pre-supposition that linguistic 'facts' are found rather than made is a misconception that operates simply to mask the work that goes into the production of precisely such categories as 'language', 'dialect', 'accent' and 'slang' (not to mention the fact that these concepts are historically and culturally specific).[14] Of course such a contention is at odds with the dominant nineteenth- and twentieth-century accounts of language, whether they be positivist, quasi-naturalist or struc-turalist, but it is one that has recently been utilized by practitioners across a variety of fields – historians, discourse theorists, ethnographers of communica-tion, urban anthropologists and sociolinguists included.[15] And yet in point of fact, scepticism towards the ontological status of languages and dialects has been a long-standing though unacknowledged feature of the modern study of language. Hugo Schuchardt, for example, made 'the social character of a language, [and] the fluid borders of its spatial and temporal variations' one of the central aspects of his 'On Sound Laws' (1885), an important critique of the late nineteenth-century neo-grammarians (Schuchardt 1972: 62). A similar stance became influential among at least some of the early twentieth-century linguistic geographers, notably the 'neo-linguist' Bàrtoli and his followers.[16] And later, in one of the classic essays on the topic, 'Dialect, Language and Nation' (1966), Einar Haugen reflected on the difficulty of addressing questions such as 'how many languages are there in the world?' or 'how many dialects are there in [X] country?' because of 'the simple truth [...] that there is no answer to these questions, or at least none that will stand up to closer scrutiny' (Haugen 1966: 922). Perhaps the most succinct summation of the argument is made in the claim that 'a language is a dialect with an army and a navy'. For, as the adage implies, there is nothing intrinsic to any set of linguistic features or practices that makes them either a language or a dialect.[17]

Recent research in linguistic anthropology has made explicit the argument that with regard to particular forms of language-making, the conferral of the status of language or dialect (or accent, idiom, slang and so on) is rendered by social forces that are external to the practices themselves (Gal and Irvine 1995: 969–70). On occasion the forces that create static, stable, even reified conceptions of language are overtly political (as indicated by the identification of military power as a significant factor in the language/dialect distinction cited above). A good illustration of this process would be the role of the State in the imposition of a language in a colonial context, for example the punitive language policies put into place in Tudor and Jacobean Ireland. The importance of this example lies not simply with the way in which linguistic colonialism sought to alter linguistic practice within Ireland as part of the project of cultural Anglicization, but perhaps more significantly for present purposes, with the way in which colonial policies gave impetus to the conception of '*the* English language' and '*the* Irish language' (in the senses of those phrases that are easily recognizable today). More often than not, however, centripetal forces work at a less obvious level through specific discursive procedures, practices and forms that can be relatively elusive and difficult to identify. And it is in this regard that the work of linguists and anthropologists such as Michael Silverstein, Asif Agha and Barbara Johnstone is significant and particularly relevant to the present study. For their research has been concerned with, to use the technical terms, 'indexicality' and 'enregisterment', that is to say, the complex processes by which specific features of language are made to bear 'social meaning' of various sorts (including modes of identity attached to place, class, gender and ethnicity) (Johnstone et al. 2006: 81). Given the pertinence of their findings for understanding the relation between the construction of specific forms of language and the socio-cultural values associated with them, it will be useful to set out the major features of their approach (even though there are differences of emphasis between these thinkers).

In 'Contemporary Transformations of Local Linguistic Communities' (1998), Silverstein observed that 'within the various processes of communicative regularities, users of language in essence construct culturally particular concepts of denotational normativity that bind subsets of them into "language"-bearing groups' (Silverstein 1998: 407–08). In other words, by means of regular use of linguistic features and normative practices related to the use of such features, two cultural constructs are produced: a group identified in terms of the use of a specific language or dialect, *and* the language or dialect itself. Thus the use of a specific pronunciation or lexical item, together with various practices of normativity (even just talk about talk) form part of the process by which both group-formation and the 'identification' of a language or dialect take place. Needless to say, the idea that language has been used ideologically to 'imagine' communities is now, after Benedict Anderson's pioneering work on the formation of nationalism, relatively commonplace (Anderson 1991). But one of the interesting features of the voluminous literature on this topic is that despite Anderson's pointing to the New World origins of nationalism, research in the area has tended to focus on the European philosophical underpinning of this development (the influence of the German idealist tradition in particular) and/or on the construction of national communities (or communities asserting a claim to national status).[18] In contrast, it is striking how little research has been undertaken on the imagining of communities at the sub-national level, though recent work in a number of fields has attempted to correct that discrepancy. Thus Silverstein's focus on the relationship between what he calls 'groupness' and language as a 'site of struggle' (specifically its contemporary 'essentialized [role] as a necessary condition of ethnocultural identity') is a useful and productive development in this area (Silverstein 1998: 415). Of particular interest is his discussion of the discursive construction of 'cultural locality', a practice that has the effect of creating 'particular, geopolitically conceptualized, bounded swatches of the earth attached to particular labels for "languages" – and their bearers' (1998: 405). Or as Johnstone, Andrus and Danielson put it, in somewhat more comprehensible terms, what the research of Silverstein and others has demonstrated is the process by which 'places and ways of speaking' are connected; in other words, how the sense of 'being from' a particular place is created and marked linguistically (Johnstone et al. 2006: 79).

Silverstein's rather technical account focuses on linguistic 'indexicality', a term developed from the work of the semiotician Charles Sanders Peirce to refer to signs whose meaning is context-dependent. Examples in English would include signs that signal person, place and time, as in 'I am here now', in which the meaning of 'I', 'here' and 'now' is dependent on who the subject is, where they are and when they are speaking. More interestingly, Silverstein drew attention to the encoding of non-referential indexicality, in which 'features of speech […] independent of any referential speech events that may be occurring, signal some particular value of one or more contextual variables' (Silverstein 1995: 201). The significant issue here is the transmission of 'value', or 'social meaning', that is to say, meaning that depends not simply on the variables of immediate context, but on the interaction between those variables and a discursive order that allows for the establishment of forms of evaluation. A standard example, no longer applicable to English but common in other modern European languages, is the signalling (or not) of deference through the use of 'the pronouns of power and solidarity' (Brown and Gilman 1960). Embodied in the T/V distinction ('tu' and 'vous' in French), this usage, which appears in different forms in many languages, conveys not simply contextual meaning (depending on who the 'tu' and 'vous' are), but a recognition of the relative status of speakers such that the 'improper' use of 'tu' when 'vous' is required entails either a failure of recognition or an offence against the order of social value. Other forms of non-referential indexicality, occurring in a variety of languages, include sex/gender, class, ethnicity and affect or attitudinal stance (among others). The important point for Silverstein is that the discursively produced correlation between linguistic form and social meaning (or evaluation) can be plotted against what he describes as 'orders of indexicality' such that the deployment of any indexical 'presupposes that the context in which it is normatively used has a schematization of some particular sort, relative to which we can model the "appropriateness" of its usage in that context' (Silverstein 2003: 193). In other words, the successful use of a linguistic marker of masculinity, to take one example, will depend on the discursive limits that govern the particular social index that constructs what counts as 'masculinity'.

Silverstein's aim was at least in part to give a more complex account of the 'ethno-pragmatically mediated orderliness of sociolinguistic variability over populations of users' (the relation between linguistic forms and social meaning in a given speech-community) than that provided by pioneers in the field such as John J. Gumperz and William Labov (Silverstein 2003: 217). Thus Silverstein's 'orders of indexicality' can be read as a way of reconfiguring the dualistic model of 'dialectal' and 'superposed' variability offered by Gumperz, and Labov's trichotomy of sociolinguistic 'indicators', 'markers' and 'stereotypes' (Gumperz 2009: 69–70; Labov 1972: 178–80). In the relatively simple account proposed by Gumperz, for example, linguistic variation delineated forms of inter- and intra-communal relations and identities: 'dialectal variation' 'set off the vernaculars of local groups (for example, the language of home and family) from those of other groups within the same, broader culture', whereas 'superposed variation' 'refers to distinctions between different types of activities carried on within the same group' (Gumperz 2009: 69–70). For Labov, however, in a study whose primary concern was with the 'mechanism of linguistic change', variation took tripartite form. 'Indicators' are variable features that manifest no pattern of stylistic variation in the usage of the members of a speech community and are thus, in effect, 'a function of group membership'. 'Markers' are variable features that evince socially meaningful stylistic variation to which speech community members react uniformly (though not necessarily consciously); markers thus become 'norms which define the speech community'. And finally, 'stereotypes' are variable features that, 'under extreme stigmatization […] become the overt topic of social comment and may eventually disappear'; 'stereotypes' are thus often 'divorced from the forms which are actually used in speech' (Labov 1972: 178–80).

Silverstein's account offers a more nuanced reading of the relationship between linguistic variation and social meaning than those offered by his predecessors. Thus, roughly corresponding to Labov's 'indicator', Silverstein described an 'n-th-order indexical', which involves a feature whose use is correlated with a specific form of identity – that of a region or social class for example. In this instance of 'first-order indexicality', the feature may be identifiable by an outsider such as a linguist even though it is unremarked by members of the speech community itself (since it is uniformly used), and the form's indexicality 'presupposes' an already existing categorization of social space such as regionality or class.[19] Likewise, Labov's 'marker' is conceived as a 'n+1-th-order indexical', that is, a feature that has been given 'an ethno-meta-pragmatically driven native interpretation' – or a meaning constructed by an ideological formation within the speech community (correctness, or 'sounding common', for example) (Silverstein 2003: 212). At this level of 'second-order lexicality', the feature has already become 'enregistered' or linked to a mode of speech and can be used to signal the use of that mode (hence its indexicality is 'entailing'). And finally, Labov's 'stereotype' is displaced by a form of 'third-order indexicality' that 'presupposes' 'second-level indexicality' but reflects consciously upon it. What Labov calls 'stereotypes' are thus markers that 'have tilted in the direction of ideological transparency, the stuff of conscious, value-laden imitational inhabitance – consciously speaking "like" some social type or personified image' (Silverstein 2003: 220).

As is evident, Silverstein's style is rather opaque and a clearer account of how different types of indexical meaning can function is provided in a study of the production of 'Pittsburghese' conducted by Johnstone, Andrus and Danielson. Taking as their starting point the fact that 'a set of linguistic features that were once not noticed at all, [were] then used and heard primarily as markers of socioeconomic class, [and] have come to be linked increasingly to place and "enregistered" as a dialect called "Pittsburghese"', the authors adopt Silverstein's model in order to understand the historical and ideological processes that underpin this development (Johnstone et al. 2006: 77). Thus at the level of first-order indexicality there is a correlation between regional linguistic variants and 'being from' south-western Pennsylvania, especially Pittsburgh (together with being working class and male). Though they may be easily identifiable by outsiders, such correlations are unnoticed by insiders in a relatively stable speech community because 'everyone speaks that way'. With second-order indexicality, however, 'regional features become available for social work'; speakers notice them and attribute meaning to them on the basis of ideologies related, for example, to class identity, doctrines of correctness or 'localness'. Finally, third-order indexicality is evinced by people noticing the existence of second-order stylistic variation in Pittsburgh and linking this with a Pittsburgh identity (on the basis of the commonplace belief that place, dialect and identity are in some sense essentially conjoined). At this level, both the inhabitants of Pittsburgh and non-Pittsburghers are able to draw on a store of materials to construct particular types of representation related to locale and/or class. Or as the authors of the study put it, they 'use regional forms drawn from highly codified lists to perform local identity, often in ironic, semiserious ways' (Johnstone et al. 2006: 82–83).

The implications of this schema for understanding the development of Scouse will be examined in the next section. But it is necessary first to outline the concept of 'enregisterment', a term borrowed from Silverstein by Agha and explicated in an important essay 'The Social Life of Cultural Value' (2003). As indicated by the title of the piece, Agha's concern in this essay is with the formation and transmission of cultural value (or social meaning) and it is worth beginning with an extended statement of the theoretical position from which his analysis starts. His grounding principle is that 'cultural value is not a static property of things or people but a precipitate of sociohistorically locatable practices, including discursive practices, which imbue cultural forms with recognizable sign-values and bring these values into circulation along identifiable trajectories in social space'. Given this, he argues, his purpose

> is to draw attention to a series of social processes – processes of value production, maintenance and transformation – through which the scheme of cultural values has a social life, as it were, a processual and dynamic existence that depends on the activities of social persons, linked to each other through discursive inter-actions and institutions. (Agha 2003: 231–32)

In short, the aim is to trace the means by which cultural value is constructed, deployed and becomes socially effective, bearing in mind the nature of such value as open, contested and discursively fixed (rather than in some sense inherent). With specific regard to language, Agha's concern is with 'the processes through which a linguistic repertoire becomes differentiable within a language as a socially recognized register of forms', and the register itself develops into 'an emblem of speaker status linked to a specific scheme of cultural values' (2003: 231). Or as he put it later in slightly modified form, his interest lies with the means by which 'distinct forms of speech come to be socially recognized (or enregistered) as indexical of speaker attributes by a population of language users' (Agha 2005: 38). Thus the concept of 'enregisterment' can be considered to refer to the means by which second-order indexicality is achieved – the manner in which ideological or social beliefs of various kinds are encoded and transmitted. And an important exemplification of this process is given in Agha's study of the construction and dissemination of Received Pronunciation (RP) (and the values associated with it) from the eighteenth century to the present. His method in the piece is to specify precisely the historical deter-minants by which a particular mode of pronunciation becomes delimited as a recognizable linguistic register and invested with social value such that its speakers are linked with high status.[20]

Before presenting his historical account, however, Agha makes a number of significant points about what he calls the 'folk-concept' of 'accent' which are pertinent to the study of language in Liverpool. First, he notes that 'everyday talk of accents implicitly presupposes a baseline against which some sound patterns – but not others – are focally perceived as deviant, foregrounded accents' (Agha 2003: 232). This is evident in the common belief that some people have an accent and others don't (though contrary to what Agha appears to think, the 'norm' in Britain is not so much a specifiable mode of pronunciation such as RP but vague yet ideologically powerful concepts such as 'talking posh', 'talking proper' or even 'talking with a BBC accent'). Second, as a consequence, 'accent contrasts are an inherently relational phenomena [*sic*] but are often grasped as monadic facts about a sound pattern' (2003: 232). Which is to say that accents are often considered in and of themselves, as though they were self-standing entities rather than knowable precisely by the fact that they do not conform to the 'norm'. Third, '"accent" does not name a sound pattern alone, but a sound pattern linked to a framework of social identities', identities that are, indexically, transferred to the speaker and that are recognizable through a set of meta-discursive labels ('Scouse', 'Geordie', 'northerner', 'working class' and so on) (2003: 232–33). And finally, 'accents are often described as if they operated in an all-or-nothing way: people either have accents or don't, either have certain identities or don't', whereas in fact, 'the recognition of speaker type by the hearer of an utterance operates relative to certain contextual pre-requisites' (2003: 233). Indeed, as Agha points out, it isn't variable linguistic features that produce differences in the recognition of accents, it is acquaintance with linguistic repertoires on the part of the hearer that determines the social (rather than purely linguistic) identification. An example from Wells illustrates the issue:

> a Liverpool working-class accent will strike a Chicagoan primarily as being British, a Glaswegian as being English, an English southerner as being northern, an English northerner as being Liverpudlian, and a Liverpudlian as being working class. The closer we get to home, the more refined are our perceptions. (Wells 1982: I, 33)

Agha's comment on this is that '*all* of these characterizations are correct' – which in a sense they are, though the more interesting and common case (and one that in fact reinforces Agha's general claim) is the common misidentification of any (and all) Liverpool accent(s) as 'working class'.

Having made a number of important general and theoretical points, Agha turns to the material means by which 'the accent called RP is enregistered in cultural awareness as part of a system of stratified speech levels linked to an ideology of speaker rank' (Agha 2003: 242). Building in effect on work by Crowley (1989), Honey (1989) and Mugglestone (2003) – each working from a different perspective – Agha traces the development of meta-discourses on English speech and accent that were disseminated primarily through the medium of print (and, though he focuses on this to a lesser extent, through the formal education system). Thus, addressing 'the mechanism of social transmission' of linguistic values, he considers the means by which 'a social regularity of recognition' was forged and consolidated (2003: 245–46). He begins with a brief analysis of the work of prescriptivists such as Thomas Sheridan and John Walker in the late eighteenth century, particularly their construction of 'characterological figures linking differences of accent to matters of social identity' (2003: 251). In fact such figuration was part of a more general development in eighteenth-century Britain. V.J. Peyton, for example, in his *History of the English Language* (1771), associated national languages with national identities:

> The Italian is pleasant, but without sinews, like a still fleeting water; the French delicate, but even nice as a woman scarce daring to open her lips for fear of spoiling her countenance; the Spanish is majestical, but runs too much on the *o*, and is therefore very guttural and not very pleasant; the Dutch manlike, but withal very harsh, as one ready at every word to pick a quarrel. (Peyton 1771: 29)

And while Peyton claimed that the English language borrowed the 'good properties' from other languages, leaving them with the 'dregs', Sheridan's *Dissertation on the Causes of the Difficulties, Which Occur, in Learning the English Tongue* (1762) nonetheless characterized the English as a 'amongst the more rude, and scarcely civilized nations of the North' on the basis of the 'neglect of regulating and polishing our speech' (Sheridan 1762: 1). Characteristics were also ascribed at the sub-national level, with a key distinction made between 'provincialisms' (spoken by 'all British subjects, whether inhabitants of Scotland, Ireland, Wales, the several counties of England, or the city of London, who speak a corrupt dialect of the English tongue') and the usage of the 'polite' (Sheridan 1762: 2). George Campbell expressed the point succinctly:

> In the generality of provincial idioms, there is, it must be acknowledged, a pretty considerable concurrence both of the lower and middle ranks. But still this use is bounded by the province and always ridiculous. But the language properly so-called is found in the upper and middle ranks, over the whole British Empire. Thus though in every province they ridicule the idioms of every other province, they all vail to the English idiom and scruple not to acknowledge its superiority over them. (Campbell 1776: I, 353–54)

There are two important features to note here. The first is the ascription of characteristics to a form of language that is taken to be national ('the English idiom' or 'the language properly so-called'), which is both a linguistic and a political contribution to nationalist ideology. The second is a significant change in the social meanings attached to dialect and accent embodied in a shift away from variation as a marker of geographic identity and towards its role as a signifier of social status; what Agha calls the transformation of 'a system of dialect differences into a system of status-differentiating registers' (Agha 2003: 252).

Needless to say, against the tendency of a certain type of culturalist history of the language, the work of the eighteenth-century prescriptivists could not alone have brought about this change since, as Watts has demonstrated, their influence was limited to a relatively small discursive group (Watts 1999).[21] To explain the shift, Agha also explores the significance of the emergence of a genre of works on speech and accent in particular in the mid nineteenth century – etiquette manuals, elocution handbooks, pronunciation guides and grammar books. Such texts helped to shape the perceptions around language that became associated with the complex evolving class structure of Britain and on occasion conveyed the anxiety related to the establishment of a 'proper' linguistic identity. In *A Plea for the Queen's English*, for example, Henry Alford drew attention to 'the worst of all faults':

> The leaving out of the aspirate where it ought to be, and putting it in where it ought not to be. This is a vulgarism not confined to this or that province of England, nor especially prevalent in one county or another, but common throughout England to persons of low breeding and inferior education, particularly to those among the inhabitants of towns. (Alford 1864: 40)

Such examples demonstrate the enregisterment of a specific linguistic feature (the dropping or insertion of 'h') as an index whose social effects were consequential. Thus in a literary representation of a spoken utterance such as 'an 'orse, an 'orse, my kingdom for an 'orse', the depiction of such 'vulgar' pronunciation might well have indexed, to use Alford's terms, 'low breeding' and 'inferior education', and placed the speaker as a city dweller (or, to play on different senses of the term, it could have bespoken 'urbanity' without 'urbanity').

Another factor in the generation of a meta-discourse around speech that Agha notes is the deployment of linguistic variables in literary texts, a process that does not so much reflect linguistic facts as 'amplify and transform them into more memorable, figuratively rendered forms' (Agha 2003: 255). Again this was a long-established practice, ranging from Chaucer's representation of 'Northern' English in *The Reeve's Tale* to late eighteenth-century comedy of manners.[22] Thus, to take an example from the later period, the character of Mrs Malaprop, in Richard Brinsley Sheridan's *The Rivals* (1775), unwittingly articulates anxieties about class status and education through her mis-uses of words.[23] In this comic instance, the effect is achieved by distancing the audience from the character in a 'knowing' way, although there must have been at least a few uncomfortable members of the contemporary audience who wondered why their neighbours were laughing when Mrs Malaprop said 'progeny' (for 'prodigy'), 'supercilious' (for 'superficial') and 'orthodoxy' (for 'orthography') (Sheridan 1975: 21). Yet while this sort of thing became commonplace in the revealingly entitled 'comedy of manners' of the late eighteenth century, it was in the novelistic discourse of the nineteenth century that the linguistic indexing of social class became almost a reflex. And if, as Mugglestone notes, there is evidence that some of the late Victorians (George Gissing and Thomas Hardy for example) were familiar with the sort of manuals and textbooks cited in the previous paragraph, it is nonetheless evidently the case that the figurations were derived not so much from direct sources as from the growing tendency within British society to index language to class (a tendency to which literary representation of course made its own contribution) (Mugglestone 2003: 1).[24] For as Agha notes, works of literature 'do not describe the value of accent, they dramatize its uses', and so for the literate at least, specifically the novel-reading public, the message was conveyed so frequently as to become commonsensical: linguistic differences signal social distinction (Agha 2003: 257). Instances abound in the major literary texts (Dickens being perhaps the most influential contributor to the process), but more pertinent examples for the purposes of this study can be found in the 'lost' literature of Liverpool. Thus in *The Melvilles* (1852), a novel purportedly written by William Wilson but in all likelihood authored by Mrs Oliphant, the heroic protagonist Hugh, a trainee doctor, is addressed by the sister of a working-class woman dying of cholera:

> She's very bad, Sir, awful bad; she wouldn't look at the tea after I took it to her… I've been obliged to lay her down on the old sofa in the back kitchen, for there isn't a place in the house but what we need ourselves… poor thing, she lives no place regular. She's like a lost creature, my poor sister; many's the sore heart we've had with her, and I doubt it's coming to an end. (Wilson 1852: 119–20)

Likewise Hocking's *Her Benny* (1879) represents a form of Liverpool working-class speech, as does Tirebuck's *Dorrie* (1891) in a scene in which Dorrie, having been kidnapped, pretends to be dead and becomes the subject of a conversation among her captors:

> 'We've been too long over her!' growled the husky voice. 'She's clemmed her – that's it.'
> 'She hasn't!' said the young woman ascending the stairs with two bottles and a jug. 'You can't keep anyone going as *won't* go! She spilt what *I* gave her. She's had her chance and hasn't took it. I suppose if she'd tried it on with *your* throat, you'd have fed her with a spoon – wouldn't you?'
> 'Well, if the blue Peters scent it, this catch isn't mine – that's all.' (Tirebuck 1891: 266)

Such literary representations were reinforced by the efforts of the penny weekly journals, the most famous of which (the *Family Herald* and *London Journal*) achieved sales figures for which even the most established authors could only hope. Perhaps the most significant aspect of their contribution to the process of indexation was in relation to the audience that they reached. The extent of the readership was one factor (Agha cites a claim that the *Family Herald* and *London Journal* were read by one in three of the literate), but potentially more important was the fact that their readers were predominantly 'lower middle and upper working class' (key social groups in terms of social and linguistic anxiety) (Agha 2003: 257, 259).

Again, however, even if accounts of the extent and composition of the readership are accurate, it is still doubtful whether the combination of the use of these texts, the influence of literary representations and earlier efforts at prescriptivism did any more than create 'a widespread awareness in the reading public of the social value of accent, including an awareness of the social value of the most prestigious accent' (Agha 2003: 260). In other words, such factors may explain in part what Agha calls 'the competence to recognise' accent contrasts and values but not 'the competence to speak the most prestigious accent' (2003: 260). In order to account for that development, Agha, following Honey (1989) and Mugglestone (2003), turns to the history of the major public schools and the teaching of RP. Yet such a focus needs to be treated with caution since, although a concern with the public schools and RP may help explain how a very small number of people (relative to the general population) ended up speaking in a specific, socially distinctive way, that is hardly the most important point. What really matters in terms of the effect of educational practices is precisely the inculcation of an ideology of correctness ('the best speakers', 'proper English' and so on) among the vast majority of the population. For although it is a seriously under-researched topic, what we do know about the teaching of English language in schools following the extension of education in 1870 and thereafter is that many children, working-class children included, were indeed taught elocution and pronunciation (Crowley 2003: 174–216) . But the net effect was not the competence to speak RP, since for many children that would have been not only a difficult but also a remarkably self-alienating feat. The more significant consequence was the inculcation of the ability to recognize the values associated with specific forms of linguistic variation, including that of accent. No less an aim was expressed – at least implicitly – in *The Newbolt Report* (1921), the account of an influential governmental commission on 'The Teaching of English in England': 'It is emphatically the business of the Elementary School to teach all its pupils who either speak a definite dialect or whose speech is disfigured by vulgarisms, to speak standard English' (Newbolt 1921: 65). Despite the frequent exhortations, what most children were taught in their English-language instruction was not in reality the specifics of standard English or Received Pronunciation, but the crucial lesson that their own language was in some sense inferior. Detailed linguistic knowledge was in fact unnecessary, a point made clear by George Sampson, a key figure in early twentieth-century education debates (and Newbolt Commissioner), in his *English for the English. A Chapter on National Education* (1925):

> there is no need to define standard English speech. We know what it is, and there's an end on't… We know standard English when we hear it just as we know a dog when we see it, without the aid of definition. Or, to put it another way, we know what is *not* standard English, and that is a sufficiently practical guide. If anyone wants a definite example of standard English we can tell him that it is the kind of English spoken by a simple, unaffected young Englishman like the Prince of Wales. (Sampson 1925: 41)

The real lesson was social rather than phonetic. For working-class children especially, gaining 'competence' in RP was highly unlikely, particularly given the fact that they would have had little access to it outside the school in the pre-broadcasting area (it would have been utterly foreign to their homes and neighbourhoods). But such competence was in any case beside the point. What mattered was that partly through the symbolic violence of the education system, they came to recognize the 'legitimate' language of authority (which may have been spoken in RP but probably wasn't). More importantly perhaps, they were brought to understand their own way of speaking as sub-standard, defective and of course, anything but well 'received'.

Be that as it may, Agha's concern in his study is to identify not so much a 'metaphysics of shared belief' but 'certain regularities of *evaluative behaviour*' which can be found with regard to linguistic phenomena (Agha 2003: 242). This is an important point for two reasons. First, it allows for contradictory beliefs and indeed patterns of evaluation. For example, it may be that RP is treated both as the voice of power and authority, and as a symbol of class identity that causes its speakers to be regarded with contempt. Or a speaker of Scouse may be proud of speaking in a way associated with Liverpool and yet also express the belief that their speech is in some sense sub-standard.[25] Second, Agha's emphasis is on social activity expressed in specific forms:

> The *dissemination* or spread of a register depends on the circulation of messages typifying speech. Such messages are borne by physical artifacts: in the case of face-to-face communication, by acoustical artifacts, i.e. 'utterances'; in the mass-mediated cases by more perduring text-artifacts – books, magazines, cartoons, musical scores – that are physical objects conveying information about cultural forms […] Each event in this complex cultural process is a metadiscursive semiotic event with its own forms of recruitment to *roles of communicative participants* (senders and receivers of messages); its own *genre* characteristics; its own *referents*, and in particular, a set of depicted *characterological figures*, or 'social personae' linked to speech. (Agha 2003: 243)

The significance of this approach is its emphasis on the modes of dissemination – literary texts, mass broadcasting, individual speech acts – and on the agential nature of the process. That is to say, and this reflects back to the issue of contradictory evaluations, although some of the forms by which speech is characterized are institutionally weighted (in the education system for example), it is nonetheless the case that the messages passed across the speech-chain are transmitted by agents who can modify them in various ways. This has the advantage of making clear that the process of enregisterment is both structural and yet open to change. It also allows for an understanding of why particular perceptions, once encoded, perdure. The significance of this is that the historicity of social forms whose transmission involves each and all of us is often hard to recognize and thus, for that very reason, difficult to change.

Indexicality and enregisterment: 'Scouse'

The theoretical framework outlined in the previous section is a useful way of thinking about the historical material presented earlier in this book, particularly in chapters three and four. For as noted earlier, what the insights forged in the recent work in linguistic anthropology facilitate is a critical understanding of the ways in which the language of Liverpool has been conceptualized over the past century or so. This has the advantage of avoiding essentialist questions such as 'Is there really a Liverpool dialect if it only has a small number of lexical/grammatical features?', or 'Does Liverpool have an accent which can be specified according to phonological criteria?' Instead the analysis can focus on another set of questions altogether. For example, with regard to the linguistic, cultural and indeed social category of 'Scouse', there are a number of important issues that would need to be addressed. These include: when did the category of 'Scouse' appear? What were the means by which it was created, and who was involved in the process? What was the goal behind the project to establish Scouse? And what effects did the appearance and dissemination of this category bring about? Of course none of this is to suggest that empirical research on grammatical forms, lexical items and phonological patterns used by people from Liverpool is insignificant or redundant, since such work may produce interesting and revealing results. It is to claim, however, that it would be useful and potentially illuminating if such investigations were self-reflexively aware of the historical and discursive constructedness of the phenomenon that is the subject of their research. The challenge then is to see whether the approach outlined in the previous section can explain 'Scouse' in such a way as to open up a fresh set of perspectives on this peculiarly productive cultural and linguistic category.

As noted above, the study by Johnstone, Andrus and Danielson of the way in which a number of once-unnoticed linguistic features, which became markers of social class and then of place in the form of a dialect called 'Pittsburghese', is a useful model for considering how language in Liverpool was framed discursively in the twentieth century. And yet their framework, while helpful, needs to be treated with caution in several respects. For example, there is something strikingly odd in the claim that a community can exist in which the linguistic features it uses are 'not noticed at all'; in which, in other words, there is no reflexivity about its words, grammar or pronunciation. Thus while it is asserted that until the Second World War in Pittsburgh, 'working-class Pittsburghers had little contact with anyone who spoke English differently than they did', and that they 'lived in insular neighborhoods within walking distance of the steel mills and other factories where their parents worked, and they went to school and church with their neighbors', such an account is open to serious doubt (Johnstone et al. 2006: 87, 88). Did working-class Pittsburghers never come into contact with figures of authority (a factory manager or a school teacher) whose own education and/or class background gave them access to a distinct linguistic repertoire (and whose linguistic usage thus stood in marked contrast to that of Pittsburgh working-class speakers)? Did they not watch films or listen to radio? Did the usage of migrants from other parts of the USA (Pittsburgh was a large steel town) not create linguistic reflexivity? And, given that a number of immigrant languages were spoken in the city, did that not lead to a sense that the language of Pittsburgh was distinctive? This is an important theoretical point since it challenges the idea within the theoretical model used by both Silverstein and the authors of the Pittsburgh study that there is a chronological progression effectively from ignorance through to the different levels of indexicality. A more nuanced account might argue instead that rather than beginning with an initial state in which 'insiders', in what amounts to what was elsewhere called a 'completely homogeneous speech community', do not reflect upon their own linguistic usage, it is much more likely that such reflexivity is present but that it only operates at the level of first-order indexicality when both insiders and outsiders associate linguistic features with a specific identity (that of belonging to a particular place for example).[26] In this respect the case of Liverpool is instructive, since evidence presented earlier suggests that not only were there literary representations of Liverpool speech from the eighteenth century on, but that there was also a long-standing sense that the language of Liverpool was distinctive. Examples include the representations of heteroglossia in Liverpool in Boulton's *The Sailor's Farewell*, the dispute about Gladstone's accent, and Dixon Scott's claim that working-class Liverpudlians in a particular area of the city spoke 'a bastard brogue: a shambling, degenerate speech of slip-shod vowels and muddied consonants' (Scott 1907: 144). Of course none of this material demonstrates that working-class Liverpudlians were reflexively aware of the distinctiveness of their own speech, but then the question arises as to where evidence of such reflexivity could be found. For given the practical restrictions on working-class self-expression (access to literacy, time to write, rooms of their own), it is hardly surprising that there is little material evidence of how working-class Liverpudlians thought about the language they used. It would be odd, however, to presuppose that they were not aware of the distinctiveness of the language they used, not least in view of the fact that they must have encountered linguistic difference constantly given the city's status as a major port and the movement of people (from elsewhere in Britain, Europe and the Empire) that this brought with it. Just to speculate on one example of linguistic sensitivity that must in all likelihood have existed: is it really plausible, given the sectarian animosities that scarred Liverpool in the nineteenth century, that attention was not paid to speakers who bore traces of forms of Irish English, Ulster English or Scots (not least because the use of such might have been taken to indicate religious affiliation)?

It is certainly the case that notwithstanding the history of literary (and other) representations, there is a shift to the level of first-order indexicality with regard to Liverpool speech in the early to mid twentieth century. As noted in chapter three, there is clear evidence that words and sounds were postulated (often incorrectly) as belonging uniquely to Liverpool. Thus for the majority of correspondents on this subject to the local newspapers (both 'insiders' and 'outsiders' – many of whom were exiled Liverpudlians), the point was to establish a link between the city and a form of language. From accounts of 'nix', 'jigger' and 'jowler', to speculation on the origins of Liverpool speech and attempts to represent specific words and phrases – 'wassemarrewichew', 'isavvy', 'Aagho whacker' – features of Liverpool speech became associated with the place itself and a linguistic identity was born. Once this had happened, it is also evident from the material presented earlier that second-order indexicality took the form of the characterization of the language of Liverpool as 'Scouse' (a significant re-appropriation of a name that had previously been used with negative overtones and an allusion to an older feature of Liverpool culture – the dish associated with the town from the late eighteenth century). In this modulation, and Frank Shaw's work was particularly significant in this regard, an association was forged between Scouse, a specific mode of class identity and a sense of what might be called 'authentic localism'. That is to say, Scouse became the index not simply of Liverpool identity, but of Liverpool working-class identity (embodied in the figure of the dockworker) and of the 'real' Liverpudlian (notably distinguished by Shaw from the middle-class Mossley Hill 'Liverpolitans'). From this it was but a short step to third-order indexicality, in which second-order variation became codified to the extent that it was almost automatically connected to the socio-cultural identity known as the Scouser.[27] And once this had taken place, the material was available for both 'insiders' and 'outsiders' to 'perform' the identity, for purposes ranging from self-identification, to solidarity, irony or even ridicule. As noted in chapter four, such performativity could be realized in various forms: from the staging of Scouse concerts, to representations of the Beatles as 'typical' Scousers, to Liverpool comics producing (and re-producing) Scouse humour, to the images of the 'Scally Scousers', and so on.

It is important to note, however, that there were those who resisted this development and who saw it as retrogressive. In 'Scouse Not So Exclusive', for example, 'Rancid Ronald' dismissed the contention that many words in Liverpool were unique to the city as 'a myth carefully fostered by Mr. [Frank] Shaw and the "Ekker"'. If, he argued, 'one eliminates all words and phrases of outside origin, what is left as attributable wholly to Merseyside is so little that the Scouse language can hardly be said to exist – except, perhaps, as an adenoidal exhibition of appalling illiteracy'; he signed off 'Ta-ra well', 'as they say in Chorley and Cheadle Hulme' (Rancid Ronald 1963: 8).[28] Slightly less provocative was Len Rush's 'Let's Give the Cult a Rest', in which he observed that the Liverpool accent served 'to identify you, to stick you with a label that was as distinctive as the Sikh's turban or the Scotsman's kilt'. And, he noted, as soon as the 'catarrhal strains' were heard in particular circumstances, they evoked a response:

> Let the exiled Scouser hear them, wherever he may be and the effect is astonish-
> ing. Hard-headed engineers become as little boys as they ply you with questions
> about ferry boats, green-goddesses and the Overhead Railway. Tough bosuns on
> the North Sea run are almost in tears as they plead for news of Norris Green.
> (Rush 1966: 6)

A distinction was to be made, however, between these pathetic creatures and the 'other breed of exile [...] rather less deserving of sympathy'. These were the Liverpudlians who had spent years 'carefully covering up' their accents, only to change now that 'it's quite all right to be a Scouser. It's *in*. It's *gear*.' An encounter with one of these ne'er-do-wells, with his 'phoney reminiscences', could only evoke condescension since 'it would be cruel to disillusion him; to point out that the Rotunda stood in Scotland Road, not Lodge Lane; that Ted Ray's birthplace was nearer Wigan than Wavertree; that the Cast Iron Shore was nowhere near Gladstone Dock'. And when he 'discurses nostalgically on "the old salt fish" – just as though it had gone out with dodo-soup', and breaks into 'Maggie May' it could only be 'time to murmur "ta-ra well" and make for the door'. All of which was enough to make Rush 'feel we have had a little too much of the Liverpool cult' and so to reject it by embarking on a new diet – 'no scouse for a year' (Rush 1966: 6). It was a sentiment echoed by one Mr Milligan, a correspondent to the *Daily Post*, who described Scouse as a 'nitwick gimmick' and the first *Lern Yerself Scouse* book as 'an unsavoury jumble of incoherent noises' (Shaw 1966d: 6). And yet even such negative sentiments make the general point about third-order indexicality and the 'performativity' it facilitated. For by the mid 1960s, 'Scouseness' (the 'Liverpool cult') was well enough established that it could allow for dissidents to react against it, even if they were patronized for their trouble. Thus noting that Milligan wrote from the new town of Kirkby (populated mainly by inner-city Liverpudlians whose housing had been condemned), Shaw cited 'rumours of a unilateral declaration of independence by that pure-spoken garden city' and observed sardonically that 'the Knotty Ash Infantry (2nd Battalion Diddy Men) are manning the boundary' (Shaw 1966d: 6).[29]

If the treatment of language in Liverpool, and specifically the emergence of Scouse, broadly fits Silverstein's indexicality schema (though with the caveats mentioned above), what of Agha's notion of enregisterment? Again it is clear that the evidence presented in previous chapters can be considered in terms of Agha's model of the discursive and meta-discursive processes by which specific figurations of language (in this case that of Liverpool) were created, disseminated and sustained in order to construct forms of social value. Examples of the construction of Liverpool language included literary representation, journalistic correspondence and feature articles, celebrations of Scouse culture (folk songs, ballads, stories and dialogues), and the prescriptivist *Lern Yerself* series (five volumes from 1966–2000). There were of course other cultural media that served to convey representations of Liverpool language to 'internal' and 'external' audiences. The older tradition of music hall was one important location (featuring Liverpool comics such as Robb Wilton, Arthur Askey and Ted Ray).[30] But in terms of national reach, the more telling development was the appearance during the Second World War of Liverpool comedian Tommy Handley's BBC radio series *ITMA* (*It's That Man Again*), featuring one Liverpool character, Frisby Dyke, and Handley's 'unmistakable, unashamedly Scouse voice' (Shaw 1971: 161).[31] Viewed historically, however, both music hall and radio were simply the precursors for the decisive development that saw Liverpool appear as the focus of a variety of programmes that were not only crucial in the enregisterment of Scouse, but also central to the formation of popular culture itself on British television. For as noted in the previous chapter, an important early example of this process was the BBC TV documentary *Morning in the Streets*, the Liverpool component of which (researched by Shaw) featured a fascinating set of interviews with working-class men and women in the Dingle, Scotland Road and Everton. More significant perhaps was the appearance from the early 1960s of a number of TV series that were located in Liverpool and that brought aspects of the city's culture to a national audience: from *Z-Cars*, through *The Liver Birds*, *A Family at War*, *The Wackers*, *Boys from the Blackstuff*, *Bread*, *Liverpool 1*, *Merseybeat* and, for twenty-one years, *Brookside*. It is worth noting that the dominant style of these works was social realism: three were police/crime series, one dealt with Liverpool at war, four dealt with the daily realities of working-class life (three in comic fashion), and one was a soap opera. Given their form, of course, it was inevitable that such programmes would enregister Scouse as the language of Liverpool (working-class Liverpool in particular).

There were, of course, other means than those of popular drama by which Liverpool speech was represented to the nation (and beyond). They included the continuing vitality of the Mersey pop music scene – the Beatles and Mersey Beat being the most prominent early examples, though there has been a complete span, from Billy Fury to the Zutons.[32] Likewise the sustained success of the city's football clubs (with Liverpool FC's numerous triumphs in Europe being a key element) has led to repeated – and often repetitious – representations of particular aspects of Liverpool culture. The national standing of Liverpool comedians, particularly in the 1960s–80s, has also been an important factor in this tendency – though again it is important to emphasize the range (from Alexei Sayle to Jimmy Tarbuck). In this regard it is interesting to compare the sustained depiction of Liverpool in television series noted above with the work of a number of the comedians. For whatever their faults, several of the programmes that focused on Liverpool advanced radical innovations and perspectives in British television, ranging from the representation of policing as socially complex, to the problems and pleasures of young single women, a focus on civilians in wartime, working-class poverty and fierce criticism of the social effects of mass unemployment. In that respect at least their dramatic integrity marks a sharp contrast with the use of Liverpool for the production of the glib and often pernicious stereotypes produced by a number of successful comics both from within the city and elsewhere. Such negative representations also found their way into the British media as Liverpool took a prime role in the British news media as the site where the social price of the Thatcherite policies of de-regulation, de-industrialization and economic decline was both brought into focus and contested.[33] Overall, then, it can be argued that broadcasting in its most popular modes – drama, comedy, sport and news – was a crucial site for the enregisterment of Scouse in the national and local imaginary. Over a fifty-year period and through a variety of media, Scouse indexed Liverpool as a physical place, a site of cultural production and the location of a particular form of identity. Originally enregistered as the linguistic marker of a geographic region, the language of Liverpool, latterly Scouse, became an expansive cultural repository for the generation of images of a specific type of contemporary urban working-class life.

Conclusion

The aim of this chapter has been to consider how the language of Liverpool has been treated from historical and theoretical perspectives and to suggest an alternative way of thinking about the phenomenon of Scouse in particular. Central to this analysis has been the important insight that one of the most important elements in the construction of languages or dialects is the practice of 'a group of people using, or orienting to and/or talking about, a particular set of linguistic features, *in a process that also constructs the group itself*' (Johnstone et al. 2006: 79, emphasis added). That is to say, the sort of 'talk about talk' (or more precisely, letters, feature articles, performances and so on) that formed the focus of earlier chapters of this work was the means by which both a form of language and a cultural identity was forged. Another way of putting that is to say that Scouse was and is a construct generated by specific forces for particular purposes with discursive and thus material effects. Its power as a cultural form lies in part with the fact that its historical origins and development are largely obscure; it is, to adapt Spiegl's beautifully oxymoronic phrase, a prime example of a 'naturalized tradition'.

Notes

1   Fritz Spiegl, *Scouser Songs* (1962), 18.
2   *Oxford English Dictionary*, 2nd edn (Oxford, 1989), *s.v. scouse n 2b.*
3   As will be illustrated later in the Appendix, this dating of 'Scouse', in the sense of an inhabitant of Liverpool, is also very late – it appears to be an early twentieth-century term, probably military (services' slang) in origin.
4   Ellis used the 'dialect test' to determine the boundaries of English dialects (though it was in fact the invention of Joseph Wright, editor of the *English Dialect Dictionary*). The test consisted of seven specimen phrases that were to be spoken by informants: 'So I say, mates, you see now that I am right about that little girl coming from the school yonder; She is going down the road there through the red gate on the left hand side of the way; Sure enough, the child has gone straight up to the door of the wrong house; where she will chance to find that drunken deaf shrivelled fellow of the name of Thomas; We all know him very well; Won't the old chap soon teach her not to do it again, poor thing!; Look! Isn't it true?' Ellis's instructions to the dialect gatherers (contained in 76 notes) were almost exclusively concerned with the recording of pronunciation, with only a few references to lexical or grammatical variation (Ellis 1889: 8–16).
5   The persistence of this stance is evinced by the fact that one of the major linguistic undertakings in Britain in the twentieth century, Harold Orton's *Survey of English Dialects* (1950–1961), focused primarily on rural areas with stable populations. The survey took material from 313 localities, but with the exception of Hackney, Sheffield, York and Leeds (where the project was based), urban areas did not form part of the analysis. The nearest the survey came to Liverpool was Halewood (a township that remained primarily agricultural until it was finally swallowed up into Liverpool's outermost suburbs in the 1960s).
6   As noted in previous chapters, Whittington-Egan's essay was heavily indebted to, not to say plagiarized from, the writings of Frank Shaw, whose work was in turn heavily influenced by Farrell's important essays.
7   This is another likely example of Whittington-Egan's 'borrowing' of material. This claim was probably taken from H.R. Shaw's 'Liverpool Accent' in the *Liverpool Echo*, 4 August 1950: 'there is no Liverpool accent in the sense that there is a Cockney and Somerset, but there is a Liverpool intonation' (H.R. Shaw 1950: 2).
8   See Andrew Hamer, http://www.bbc.co.uk/liverpool/content/articles/2005/01/14/ voices_linguist_feature.shtml.
9   Apart from the *Lern Yerself Scouse* series, which were published between 1966 and 2000, other Scouse glossaries included Diana Briscoe, *Wicked Scouse English* (2003); Ron Freethy, *Made Up Wi' Liverpool: A Salute to the Scouse Dialect* (2007); and Peter Grant, *Talk Like the Scousers* (2008). Susie Dent's *How to Talk Like a Local: From Cockney to Geordie* (2010), also includes Scouse words and phrases.

10 This is a point made by Saussure in the founding text of the structural study of language in the twentieth century, *The Course in General Linguistics* (1916). For Saussure, the distinction between the language system (*langue*) and how it is used in practice (*parole*) means that there can be variation at the level of speech that does not affect the system in the slightest. Once a change takes place within the language itself, however, in particular lexical or grammatical innovation, then the system itself is disturbed and thus a new 'state' of language is brought about. In this sense languages don't evolve organically, since what is called '*a language*' is no more than a succession of distinct historical (or more accurately, time-related) states. Of course this principle does raise both theoretical and practical difficulties for the structural study of language. For example, if *any* change means that a new form has been created, then at what level of language is stability to be found (how is it known when a change has taken place)? For a related discussion of theoretical aspects of Saussure's account in this regard, see 'For and against Saussure' in Crowley 1996. For a practical example of the difficulties of accounting for variation, or at least categorizing it, see the fact that in the latest edition of *Language in the British Isles*, the following 'varieties' of English are mentioned: Estuary English; the working-class dialect of Milton Keynes; Scottish Standard English; 'Basic' Scottish Standard English; Highland and Hebridean English; (London) Derry English; North West Welsh English; Mid South Welsh English; West English English; Port Talbot English; Rhondda Valleys English; South West(ern) English English; general English English; Gower English; traditional Manx English; Channel Island English; London Jamaican; British English and London English (Britain 2007). There are two questions that this list might prompt, depending on the perspective taken: why is it so long, or why is it so short?

11 See Bex and Watts 1999 for a collection of critical essays on the concept of 'standard English'.

12 For a discussion of the problematic status of spoken standard English, see Jenny Cheshire, 'Spoken Standard English' (1999).

13 In a perceptive comment, Rumsey has suggested that linguistic categorization and linguistic ideologies (defined as 'shared bodies of commonsense notions about the nature of language in the world') are often closely related (Rumsey 1990: 346).

14 As an example, Asif Agha makes the point that 'the term "accent" itself constitutes a highly culture-specific framework for characterising and discussing contrasts of phonolexical register' (Agha 2003: 235).

15 For a discussion of recent developments in the study of language in history, see 'Prologue: communities and domains', in Peter Burke, *Languages and Communities in Early Modern Europe* (2004).

16 A critical view of such developments is offered in Robert Hall, *Idealism in Romance Linguistics* (1963); Bàrtoli's thought had a significant impact on the social theory of Antonio Gramsci, particularly his account of hegemony.

17 It is not clear who first used this expression, though it appears to have been either the linguist Max Weinreich or his student, the sociolinguist Joshua Fishman. For a discussion of the coinage, see the note by William Bright (Bright 1997: 469).

18 For a brief account of the history of the putative relation between language and nation, one that conforms to the Eurocentric model, see John E. Joseph, '"The grammatical being called the nation": History and the Construction of Political and Linguistic Nationalism' (2006). Crowley challenges the idea that linguistic nationalism was necessarily a product of the influence of the German Romantic tradition, and Anderson's claim that nationalism was pioneered in the New World, by identifying an earlier development of this political and cultural formation in the colonial history of early modern Ireland (Crowley 2005: chs. 2–3).

19   First-order indexicality can 'presuppose' a division of social space (class or region-
     ality for example) or a semantic function (such as number-marking); the focus here
     is with the first of these possibilities.
20   As Agha points out, the goal of his study is not so much to provide a history of RP as
     to illustrate the socially constructed, active and continuing nature of cultural evalu-
     ation. He could equally well have taken another mode of pronunciation and shown
     through a similar analysis how it is enregistered as a culturally devalued form with
     its speakers given low status.
21   In fact Watts' own essay is an example of culturalist history in that it claims great
     influence for the work of the prescriptivists (while at the same time indicating that
     they were a relatively small group who mostly addressed each other).
22   For an interesting discussion of *The Reeve Tale's* construction of 'Northernness', and
     the role language plays in it, see Joseph Taylor, 'Chaucer's Uncanny Regionalism:
     Rereading the North in *The Reeve's Tale*' (2010).
23   R.B. Sheridan was Thomas Sheridan's son; the son did indeed 'dramatize' the
     relationship between language and 'vulgarity' upon which his father pronounced.
24   Mugglestone also notes that George Bernard Shaw (a passionate advocate of spelling
     reform) studied works on elocution in the British Library (Mugglestone 2003: 1). He
     may have been gathering material for *Pygmalion* (1912), perhaps the twentieth cen-
     tury's sharpest example of the comedy of (linguistic) manners; in the preface, Shaw
     noted that 'it is impossible for an Englishman to open his mouth without making
     some other Englishman hate or despise him' (Shaw 1957: 5).
25   Both examples are cited on the basis of personal experience. First, as an academic
     teaching in an English department in a large northern university in Britain
     (Manchester), my observation was that in a large student body, the students who
     spoke what was understood as RP attracted most hostility on the basis of their way
     of speaking. And second, growing up in Liverpool, it was common to hear both
     pride in Scouse and a ready acknowledgment that it was 'poor' English. As noted
     in chapter four, Shaw's work is scored through with this ambivalence.
26   The notorious phrase, 'a completely homogeneous speech community', is taken
     from Noam Chomsky's *Aspects of the Theory of Syntax* (1965). Such a conception
     has been anathema to sociolinguists, discourse theorists and linguistic anthropo-
     logists (anthropology being, if nothing else, the study of difference in and between
     human groups). Suffice it to say that the influence of the idea that languages and
     communities are wedded to each other is a deeply embedded one.
27   One of the difficulties with the model, which has hardly been avoided here, is the
     idea that the different levels of indexicality form a sort of progression: from lack of
     awareness through steps one, two and three. It seems more likely that the phases
     overlap and that in fact there are elements of the different modes of indexicality at
     each level.
28   The reference to Cheadle Hulme was particularly provocative since it is an affluent
     suburb of Manchester; Chorley is a town in Lancashire, approximately twenty-five
     miles north of Manchester.
29   The historical reference is to Rhodesia's Unilateral Declaration of Independence
     from the United Kingdom in 1965.
30   Ted Ray was indeed, as Len Rush points out, born in Wigan, though his family
     moved to Liverpool a few days after his birth.
31   One of Britain's most successful radio comedians (as performer and scriptwriter),
     Tommy Handley was born in Threlfall Street, Toxteth Park (now the Dingle);
     Handley's Liverpudlian character was often played off against a cockney char, Mona
     Lott. Frisby Dyke was played by another Liverpudlian actor, Deryck Guyler; the
     character's name was taken from a furniture store on Lord Street.

32 See Paul Du Noyer, *Liverpool: Wondrous Place. Music from the Cavern to the Capital of Culture* (2007), for a detailed history of the Liverpool music scene during this period.

33 In 1993 the disastrous effects of economic re-structuring were recognized in the European Union's designation of Liverpool as an 'Objective One Priority Status' area (the status was renewed in 1999); this meant in effect that Liverpool was deemed to be one of the poorest places in the European Union (one of the criteria for the designation was that Liverpool had less than 75% of the EU GDP average).

6

Liverpools: places, histories, differences

I didn't choose you, nor did you choose me.
I was born into a version called Accent,
I haven't lost it, nor could it lose me –
I own it; it owns me, with my consent.
(Douglas Dunn, '*English*. A Scottish Essay', 2008)[1]

In this final chapter I want to present a personal account of how I came to reflect on many of the issues addressed in this book: the dominant historical and theoretical narrative concerning language in Liverpool; possible alternatives to the prevailing story; interest in 'local' language; the creation and forging of Scouse; the ways in which Scouse has been used within popular culture; and the creation of a cultural identity around Scouse. There are two dangers in this approach. The first is that my own experience will be presented or taken as typical, and the second is that of nostalgia. In the first regard, I hope it will be clear that my account is designed simply to present a journey to a number of questions that I think are of more than personal significance. People move, but they do so in space and history; if that were not the case, then much of the following chapter would be neither more nor less interesting than a snippet of memoir, but I think that the personal presentation helps to explain how a number of issues that I consider in the book arose. With regard to nostalgia, it's fair to say that there is a lot of it about in relation to Liverpool, and some of its results are pretty awful: rose-tinted recollections of organic communities in which Scousers stood together against the world and its evils, or ahistorical accounts of the glories of 'our Liverpool' and its achievements. Such narratives retain a sense of the past only by eliding history itself, and their flaws are evident. But as the *OED* entry indicates, 'nostalgia' is a nuanced word that has two main senses which don't always complement each other. The older sense of the term dates from the mid eighteenth century and relates to a sense of place, specifically home (the Greek root νόστος meant 'return home'): 'acute longing for familiar surroundings, esp. regarded as a medical condition; homesickness'. The more modern, twentieth-century sense, however, which is now the dominant meaning, refers to time: 'sentimental longing for or regretful memory of a period of the past, esp. one in an individual's own lifetime; (also) sentimental imagining or evocation of a period of the past'.[2] This is a semantic complexity that Carol Ann Duffy's poem 'Liverpool Echo' plays on nicely as it warns against the dangers of the emptiness of longing for, and lingering in, the past: 'as though nostalgia means you cannot die'. It is an admonition that appears to be repeated in the assertion that Liverpool is a city that 'cannot say goodbye' (Duffy 1994: 19). Yet in this phrase there is also a hint of the pull of the place since it is hard to say goodbye to a city that will not, or cannot, say goodbye to you. In any case, in so far as there is nostalgia in what follows, the intention is that it will be confined to the places and the imagined (rather than imaginary) linguistic and cultural communities in which I grew up. That said, one of the aims of this chapter is to suggest that imagined communities are themselves made up of imagined communities (hence 'Liverpools'), and that social acts of imagining occur under particular circumstances to produce specific effects.

Toxteth, Dingle

One of the oldest areas now included within the city of Liverpool is Toxteth, a name that appeared in the Domesday Book as 'Stochestede' (with later variations including 'Tokestath', 'Toxtathe', 'Toxstath', 'Tocstath' and 'Tokstaffe'), but whose origin is disputed. In his *Memorials of Liverpool*, Picton cited the etymology given in Baines' *History of the County Palatine and Duchy of Lancaster* (1836) – 'the woody place', from 'stoc', 'wood' and 'stoethe, stathe, sted', 'station, place'. And he noted Joseph Boult's account, given to the Archaeological Society of Liverpool in 1867, in which he proposed 'stoc', 'stem or trunk', and 'stoedth', 'shore, river bank', and hence 'the wooded shore'. Rejecting both, however, Picton argued for 'stoc' as 'log of wood' and 'stede' as 'clearing, station', and thus 'the wooden station' (Picton 1875: II, 451). This was more or less reaffirmed by Harrison's *Place-Names of the Liverpool District*, in which he gave 'stockade or enclosed place', on the basis of Anglo-Saxon 'stocc' (German 'stock'), 'stake', and A-S 'stede' (German 'stadt'), 'place, stead' (Harrison 1898: 67).[3] Yet an entirely different account was provided by Wyld and Oakes Hirst in their *Place Names of Lancashire* since they argued that the name 'may mean "the landing place (or the homestead) of *Tōki*," from: *Tōki*, a chiefly E. Scand[inavian] pers[onal] n[ame], and O[ld] N[orse] *stoð* "landing place"' (Wyld and Oakes Hirst 1911: 115).[4] Whatever its origins, Toxteth attained contemporary national prominence as the site of major rioting in 1981, at which point it gained a novel pronunciation to go with its new-found notoriety (Liverpool people stress the first syllable, media visitors the second). In fact, like the derivation of its name, the area of Toxteth is somewhat nebulous (its boundaries often appear to be contextual – or perhaps indexical in the sense of the word discussed in the previous chapter – rather than geographically specific). For what others called Toxteth, and people from the city call, sometimes, Liverpool 8, constitutes a large expanse of the inner city, ranging roughly from Dingle Lane in the south to areas of the city centre itself in the north, and from Grafton Street on the dockside to the west, to Lodge Lane and Smithdown Road on the east. Moreover, encompassed by Liverpool 8, which is also at once geographically delimited and culturally complex, Toxteth consists in an overlapping patchwork of communities, marked off spatially by officially (and unofficially) named areas, streets and main roads: from Dingle Lane, Park Road, the Holy Land, High Park Street, Windsor Street, the Welsh streets, Warwick Street, Granby, Lodge Lane, Upper Parliament Street, through to the edge of the cathedrals area, back down to St James Place, Stanhope Street, Park Lane and Mill Street. It is an area of extreme contrasts: it includes some of the oldest buildings in Liverpool and some of the newest; some of the most lucrative real estate in the city and some of the poorest housing in Britain.

Within Toxteth there is another area of some historical standing: the Dingle. As with Toxteth, the origin of 'dingle' is obscure. It appears with the sense of 'deep hollow, abyss' in the late twelfth-century homily *Sawles Warde*, and as a family name (Richard Dingyl/Richard de Dingyll) in the Lancashire Assize Rolls in 1246. It then disappears from the record until included in John Ray's early dialectal *Collection of English Words not Generally Used* as 'a small Clough or Valley, between two steep Hills', though it became used as a literary term, with the sense of a wooded or shaded dell, in the seventeenth century and thereafter (notably in Milton's *Comus* [1634]: 'I know each lane, and every alley green,/Dingle, or bushy dell of this wild wood') (Ray 1674: 14; Milton 1998: 55). None of these references are to Liverpool (with the possible exception of the allusion to Richard Dingyl/de Dingyll), though the area was immortalized in an apostrophic poem by William Roscoe, the great abolitionist:

Stranger, who with careless feet,
Wanderest near this green retreat,
Where, through gently bending slopes,
Soft the distant prospect opes;

Where the fern in fringed pride
Decks the lonely valley's side;
Where the linnet chirps his song,
Flitting as thou tread'st along:

Know, where now thy footsteps pass
O'er the bending tufts of grass,
Bright gleaming through the encircling wood
—Once a Naiad rolled her flood

If her Urn, unknown to fame,
Poured no far extended stream,
Yet along its grassy side
Clear and constant flowed the tide.

Grateful for the tribute paid,
Lordly Mersey loved the maid:
Yonder rocks still mark the place
Where she met his stern embrace.

Stranger, curious wouldst thou learn
Why she mourns her wasted Urn?
Soon a short and simple verse
Shall her hapless fate rehearse.

Ere yon neighbouring spires arose,
That the upland prospect close;
Or ere along the startled shore
Echoed loud the cannon's roar;

Once the Maid, in summer's heat,
Careless left her cool retreat,
And, by sultry suns opprest,
Laid her weary limbs to rest;

Forgetful of her daily toil
To trace each tract of humid soil,
From dews and bounteous showers to bring
The limpid treasures of her spring.

Enfeebled by the scorching ray,
She slept the sultry hours away;
And when she oped her languid eye,
She found her silver Urn was dry

Heedless Stranger, who so long
Hast listened to an idle song,
Whilst trifles thus thy notice share,
Hast thou no Urn that asks thy care?
(Roscoe 1853: 79–81)

The poem was entitled simply 'Inscription', though a note by the publisher asserted that 'Mr. Roscoe resided for some time in the vicinity of "the Dingle" in Toxteth Park, belonging to Mr. Yates. Its delightful scenery suggested this poem' (Roscoe 1853: 79). On close reading it is clear that the poem – undated but from the early nineteenth century – is a lament for the fact that Dingle Brook (which began near what is now High Park Street and ran down to Dingle Vale before emptying into the Mersey) had long since dried up and that the tranquility of the Dingle itself was being threatened by the 'neighbouring spires' and 'loud cannon roar' associated with Liverpool. This was confirmed later in the century when Picton claimed that despite its proximity to 'the smoky town', it was still 'one of the most lovely bits of scenery in the neighbour-hood of Liverpool', although, he warned, 'by some unhappy fate a portion of the land has fallen into the hands of the property speculators' and thus would be destroyed 'for industrial purposes' (Dingle shore became the site of the Herculaneum Dock) (Picton 1875: II, 470–71).[5]

'Rural idyll' wouldn't be the first phrase that comes to mind when describing the area today (nor indeed for a long time since). But the vale does mark one of the limits of the contemporary Dingle (another of Liverpool's ill-defined areas) which is bounded, more or less – again it's a matter of local understanding – by Dingle Lane, Belvidere Road, Devonshire Road, Princes Road, Upper Warwick Street, Park Place, Hill Street, down to Grafton Street and then back up South Hill to Dingle Mount. Yet if the physical boundaries of the Dingle are not always clear, there is no doubt that it is culturally differentiated from other parts of Liverpool (not least in the sense that people describe themselves as coming from the Dingle and recognizing others as so doing – 'Dingle born and bred' – as opposed, say, to 'Cressington Park born and bred', which doesn't have quite the same resonance).[6] Of course the Dingle itself had, and in some instances continues to have, its own cultural demarcations and local traditions: the Welsh streets off High Park Street (currently slated for demolition) were, in their heyday, predominantly Chapel Protestant, while areas of Mill Street and Park Road were either staunchly loyal to the Orange Order or fiercely Catholic and Irish; a small area, consisting of a few streets, may have been named 'the Holy Land' by the original Nonconformist settlers in the seventeenth century; in a limited number of streets (not exclusively Catholic, even though the origins of the rite were) the ritual of Judas-burning on Good Friday morning was practised until relatively recently; November the Fifth bonfires were guardedly local – often street-specific; some locations were inhabited largely by millworkers (sometimes in the houses built specifically for them such as Yates Walk – flour-milling began in the eighteenth century on the Mill Street site) while the majority living in other streets worked on the docks or in 'town' – Park Road was a main route into the city; some pubs were music venues, while others were known for their lax attention to licensing regulations.[7] One way and another, the Dingle was – and remains – a distinctive locale (at least to people who are familiar with it, though presumably to others it looks much like other parts of Liverpool and, in all probability, to other areas of Britain too).

I was born in the Dingle in 1960 and within walking distance of the house (in Prophet Street, just off Northumberland Street, towards the north end of Park Road) the marks of history were evident.[8] At one end of Park Road stood the Ancient Chapel of Toxteth, originally built in 1618 as a place of Puritan worship and renovated in the late eighteenth century; its early congregation included Jeremiah Horrocks, the father of British astronomy (Horrocks was the first to predict and understand the consequences of the transit of Venus across the sun and his influence was acknowledged in Newton's *Principia*) ('M' 1874: 720). A mile or so away, at the other end of Park Road (Park Lane in fact), stands St Patrick's chapel, opened in 1823 to serve the needs of the predominantly Irish Catholic population. Dominated by a statue of St Patrick (which originally adorned the offices of the St Patrick's insurance company in Dublin) and what Picton called 'two absurd Greek Doric porticoes', the church was the site of both history and story (Picton 1875: II, 472).[9] Set in front of the church is a memorial, erected in 1898 in the form of a Celtic Cross, to 'the Famine Priests' (or 'Martyr Priests'), ten of whom died of typhoid contracted while ministering to the poor of the parish between March and September 1847. As children, however, we were more familiar with the stories of how the Orange Lodge repeatedly attempted to storm the chapel in order to bring down the statue of Patrick; look closely, we were told, and you'll see one of his fingers is missing (the rope caught on it but the finger miraculously broke and the statue was saved).[10]

From seventeenth-century Puritanism then to a church that became a focal point for refugees from the Irish Famine – the length of Park Road marks out one specific aspect of the history of Liverpool and, by extension, that of Britain and Ireland more generally. Things were, however, slightly more complicated in terms of local religious fidelities. In fact the nearest denominational institution to the house in which I was born was the black, forbidding and castellar Welsh Congregational church on the corner of Northumberland Street/Park Road, where services were regularly held in Welsh. And a couple of hundred yards away, between Dombey and Dorrit Streets, was the Toxteth Tabernacle, a Baptist church – bonnets, suits and smiles on Sunday evenings, with a congregation that included a good number of black faces (which was relatively unusual on Park Road at the time, though, such was the integrity of racial segregation, the reverse was true only half a mile away in Granby).[11] Of more immediate relevance to us were the various Catholic churches, which were differentiated by function: St Malachy's for school events; Mount Carmel for Christenings, marriages and funerals; the black wooden pews of plain St Patrick's (with the exception of the huge painting of the Crucifixion above the altar) for Sunday Mass.[12] There were other buildings, sights and sounds that also marked out the space in which we lived. Opposite 'the Welsh church' on Northumberland Street stood the enormous brick pile of Coleman's Fireproof Depository, an incongruous testament (given the poverty of its surroundings) to the wealth of the Liverpool bourgeoisie ('Separate Lock-Up Rooms. Strong Rooms for Deedboxes, Silver Etc. Special Room for Pianos and Musical Instruments of All Kinds' – 'Telegraphic Address: "Readiness" L.Pool'). And Northumberland Street itself ran down to the Mersey, which echoed at night to the noise of foghorns; if you lifted your head, walking on Park Road, or taking a bus, there it always was, a cold, grey, mysterious expanse. On the river itself great tankers were visible as they moved slowly towards or from Stanlow oil refinery, while on the other side the Cammell Laird shipyard loomed as a further reminder of Liverpool's past (more than a thousand ships were built there after its foundation by a Scottish engineer in 1824, a history epitomized in Chambré Hardman's iconic image of 'The Birth of the Ark Royal' in 1950). Needless to say, the area, particularly Park Road and Mill Street, were well supplied with pubs. Some of them were known by their real names: The Pineapple (dating from the eighteenth century), The Crown, The Eureka, The Mersey Beat, The Coburg, The Phoenix, The Mersey View, The Toxteth, The Globe, The Grapes. Others were given abbreviations: The Bleak [House], The [High] Park, The [Great] Eastern, The Farmer's [Arms], The Queen's [Head], The Poet's [Corner]. And still others were familiar by nicknames known only to locals: Peg Legs, Dirty Dick's, The Dead House, Blacks, The Wellie, The Nut House, The Sixie, The Volly. Such pubs, sometimes yards from each other, also often stood facing, in a defiant sort of way, the numerous churches and chapels, but they were not the only local amenities. At the bottom of Park Road there was a 'picture house', The Gaumont (later a bingo hall), while Mill Street housed 'The Florrie' (the Florence Institute for Boys) – an imposing Victorian (1890) building in which there was a boys' club (football and boxing mostly). For the purposes of public hygiene, since few of the older houses had bathrooms or inside toilets, the area also had Steble Street Wash-House and Baths, which was founded in 1874 (the street sign said – and still says – 'Steble Street To The Baths', which reads like an injunction). The public wash-house and private baths were invented in Liverpool – Kitty Wilkinson, a Derry woman who settled in the city, came up with the idea as a response to a cholera outbreak in 1832 that killed more than 1,500 people (a portent of things to come). In my childhood, as well as being a crucial amenity, the wash-house was also an important social location for women from around the area; they pushed prams piled high with washing to 'Stebbie' on their designated wash days (chosen carefully, not least as a way of meeting friends); during school holidays, kids went swimming (or at least running along the side of the baths and 'bombing' the water), ate at 'the toastie' (the tea-bar at the side of the wash-house) and helped with the 'folding-up'. Many of the same women bumped into each other on Park Road – the main shopping area in working-class south Liverpool at the time – on Saturdays. All the staples were there: clothes and shoe shops, hardware stores, newsagents, chippies and cafés, a food and general market and, pride of place, Rays (for china and glass – essential for the ornamental cabinets in the scarcely used 'sitting room').

Allerton, Garston

These then were some of what might be called the supports around which the imagined community of the Dingle of my early childhood was structured: churches, schools, pubs, workplaces, streets, buildings, the wash-house and baths, the health centre, the ever-present Mersey, being on a bus route to 'town'. Yet there were other features, just as real, that produced a sense of 'being from' and 'being part of' that particular place within a place: stories, myths, histories, ritual practices, communal traditions as well as communitarian fears, antagonisms and forms of solidarity (the Dingle was at once a 'close-knit' community and one that was riven by sectarianism and largely segregated in terms of race). Taken together they produced a feeling of 'identity' (that peculiar word that resonates with the contradictory senses of uniqueness and sameness), grounded in the local and particular and yet deeply rooted in historical events and processes about which as kids we knew nothing (and cared less) but that linked us anyway to distant places, histories, peoples. And then my family moved – we were 'housed', to use a word that accurately reflects the power relations involved in the process – on the basis that seven people couldn't live in a flat with no bathroom or inside toilet and two bedrooms in a rat-infested area (we were the exception – the street remained inhabited for almost another decade). The new place was a three-bedroomed house, garden front and back, on a large council estate ('Springwood' in its original planning department designation) which lay a mere five miles to the south, towards but well within the city boundary. There was a tangential link to the Dingle, since the estate was bounded on one side by Mather Avenue (Mather was the first tutor at the Ancient Chapel of Toxteth – he escaped persecution by the Established Church by fleeing to New England – Horrocks was one of his first pupils). But this seemed like a different world. The estate, built in the 1930s, was technically in Allerton (amusingly described by Whittington-Egan as a place 'where pert pebble-dash rubs shoulders with solid sandstone in a democratic design for living' – a description that combines an accurate sense of class distinction in housing with a woeful misunderstanding of the term 'democratic') (Whittington-Egan 1957: 103). This wasn't quite, however, the Allerton of Menlove Avenue's prehistoric burial ground, the Neolithic dolmen of the Calderstones, the thousand-year-old 'Allerton Oak', the birthplace of St John Almond, or All Hallows' church with its sapling from the Glastonbury Thorn (the staff of Joseph of Arimathea) and its Edward Burne-Jones windows (Lewis 2010: 28–35). That Allerton was a place of detached or semi-detached private houses, the demesne of the solid and respectable Liverpool middle class (we thought them rich, though they were probably mostly teachers, senior clerks and managers) who shopped in Allerton Road and the better department stores of the city centre.[13] The Allerton we moved to, though close and connected to its counterpart (it was walkable), was slightly different. There were of course tangible signs of the past all around, not least in the prodigious and pleasant public greenery and surviving mansions of Allerton Towers Park, Calderstones Park and Clarke Gardens (all of which were acquired by donation or purchase from the descendants of owners whose money was largely made in Liverpool's nineteenth-century mercantile trade). Allerton Hall – an example of English Palladianism completed by the abolitionist Roscoe (now the Pub in the Park) – was only a quarter of a mile away, while at the top of our road there was a seventeenth-century farmhouse whose stables and yard had been made into a corporation depot. That apart, however, the estate was pretty barren in many respects; it lacked amenities of course, apart from a small number of shops at either end, a couple of pubs on either side, a Catholic and Protestant church, a large cemetery and two (Protestant) schools. Though not unfriendly in some ways, and certainly respectful towards the basic rituals and courtesies associated with births, illnesses and death, it seemed to lack a sense of community, or at least any form of recognizable 'identity' (no one ever said that they came from 'the arse-end of Allerton', at least in my hearing). This perception may of course simply be a consequence of the fact that we 'came from' the Dingle, an area that many of its residents saw as a cut above places like the estate (despite the fact that the housing was in general far superior in the new location). Such local patterns of identification are common in Liverpool, and this would probably explain the feeling of dislocation from an area that, although it was divided from it by the local railway line to Crewe and the national line to London, belonged geographically and socially to Garston (a mile or so west on the river). In fact many of its older inhabitants had been re-housed from there and retained their affiliation with it; they were largely employed either in the Speke industries (Fords, British Leyland, Dunlop) or Garston docks and its related works.

The move from Dingle to Allerton/Garston certainly entailed a significant change in my life, but it was indicative of a larger development that occurred both in Liverpool and in many British towns in the twentieth century: that is, the demolition of much of the working-class housing in inner-city areas and the re-housing of the people in new-build estates on the outskirts of the city (a process that began after the First World War, was interrupted by the Second World War, and then began again in earnest in the post-war period). Actually, my family's re-location was distinctive in some ways since, given the specifics of the case, we were moved a good while before any of our neighbours and we were re-located to an estate that had been built in the 1930s rather than to one of the 'new town' estates (such as Kirkby, Skelmersdale and, slightly later, Netherley). So despite lacking some amenities, the estate was at least established and supported by certain facilities that others lacked – a frequent, regular and reliable public transport system for example (which made possible my attendance at a grammar school some seven miles across the city). But as noted above, this didn't prevent a sense (or firm conviction in my father's case) that we didn't 'belong' in this new place and that our roots were elsewhere (a feeling exacerbated by disruption within the family). Perhaps this was a form of nostalgia, one that conflated the sense of longing both for a lost place and a lost time, but it had clear material bases in the disturbance of patterns of (often intimate and long-term) friendship; of neighbourliness; of practising specific local traditions; of using spatial and cultural knowledge of an area; and of course, for children, of schooling (along with my sister I began my education in the same school my father attended). None of which is to excuse or even go along with the often tedious invocations of 'are street', as Shaw puts it in 'What Songs will be Sung about Speke and Kirkby?', an article that lamented the loss of 'a Liverpool of not so very long ago […] which is fast fading with the growth of the new housing estates' (Shaw 1957c: 6). Nor is it to indulge in the rose-tinted historical revisions of Harry and Gordon Dison's folk song of the 1960s, 'Back Buchanan Street', of which the first two and last verses typify the dominant sentiments:

This fella from the corpy, just out of planning school
Has told us that we're being moved right out of Liverpool
They're sending us to Kirkby, to Skelmersdale or Speke
Don't wanna go from all I know in Back Buchanan Street.

We'll miss a lot of small things like putting out the cat
There's no back door on the fourteenth floor of a corpy block of flats
Don't wanna go to Kirkby, to Skelmersdale or Speke
They'll need some clout to get us out of Back Buchanan Street.

From Bootle to the Dingle you'll hear the same old cry
Stop messing round with Liverpool at least until I die
Don't wanna go to Kirkby or to Skelmersdale or Speke
Don't wanna go from all I know in Back Buchanan Street.

The corpy's mad, and we're all sad
In Back Buchanan Street.

Such laments need to be put into perspective, since Back Buchanan Street, or streets like it, were often (though not always) lacking in the basic facilities of modern life – bathrooms, toilets, reliable gas and electricity supply to name but a few; they were easier to reminisce about than to live in. And yet the social, cultural and personal difficulties engendered by the mass demolition of housing were real enough. For among other things, communities are created and maintained by patterns of settlement within a specific location; displacement didn't so much destroy community as make it much harder to sustain in the ways that people knew, recognized, and reproduced.

In any case, we ended up in Garston (or Allerton cum Garston), a name derived from the Old English 'grēat stān' – 'great stone' or possibly 'gaers tūn' – 'grazing settlement' (Mills 1976: 86). Garston was another place altogether and was divided between the older, poorer area at the bottom of the hill – the closer to the docks the worse the conditions, particularly 'under the bridge' – and the better housing that was built in the 1930s to the east of St Mary's church. Originally a monastic settlement (though with some evidence of Roman occupation), Garston was largely a rural area, lightly populated and dominated mostly by farming, fishing and watermills until the mid to late nineteenth century. A poem of the period ('Garston's Wants') captured the misguided optimism engendered by the possibilities of incipient industrialization:

What Garston wants is Capital
    To set her Works in motion,
And working men well occupied,
    With wages in proportion.

A rise in rents for Landlords poor,
    By reason of depression;
And everyone, both great and small,
    Made happy in reaction. (Swift 1937: 119)

In fact there had been docks in Garston from the eighteenth century to service the coastal trade in Cheshire salt and Lancashire coal, but modern Garston was a product of the development of railways and the larger dock system in the 1850s (Lewis 2010: 26). Owned by the London and North-Western Railway system, and exempt from Liverpool dock rates, Garston port was a cheap and busy alternative to the main docks down the river; it was also a horribly dangerous place – the LNWR had its own mortuary on site (Saunders Jones 1919: 22; Lewis 2010: 26). Needless to say it was the docks and related industries that were responsible for the large influxes of workers from Wales, Ireland and the Lancashire hinterland in particular into Garston. Welsh workers often moved with particular skills and experience from the South Welsh industrial heartlands and were employed in the iron and copper works; workers from Ireland and the rest of Lancashire tended to find employment in the Woolton quarries and as labourers on the docks and in surrounding industries (railways, the gasworks, the bottle works, tanning, bobbin-making, match-manufacturing and the banana factory). In religious terms the area was overwhelmingly Anglican, with Catholicism being the second largest denomination followed by various modes of Nonconformism (Swift 1937: 138). Both the Irish and Welsh had their own places of worship; around the school I attended, attached to the Church of St Francis of Assisi in Earp Street, there were several Welsh chapels, including some in which preaching was in Welsh (Eglwys Y Methodistiaid Calfinaidd – the Welsh Calvinistic Methodists in Chapel Road), as well as a variety of other Protestant sects – Congregationalists, Methodists, Presbyterians, United Reformers, Unitarians, Baptists, English Calvinists (Mount Zion), the Salvation Army and Gospel Hall (affiliation undeclared). Given the tenor of the place, it is slightly surprising that Garston baths (attached to the wash-house) hosted extremely popular, not to say notorious, dances on Saturday nights in the 1950s and 60s, at one of which my father and mother met. Dingle meets Garston, Catholic encounters Protestant, the prospects were surely bleak; as my father once remarked sardonically, mixed marriages never work (though he was actually referring to those between men and women).

Dingle had Roscoe's encomium; Garston on the other hand suffered a rather snooty dismissal by Donald Davie in 'Winter's Talents', a poem about a winter's train journey through England in search of 'a feelingful voice':

> Dee-side and Mersey-side
> Lie up ahead, blocked off
> In freezing fog. To them
> The voice must speak. The rime
> Dies off in the chemical reek.
> Whose swag, whose chiseled cadence
> Crusts, or whose coral, in
> Garston, Halewood, Speke? (Davie 2002: 390)

The conflation of Garston, Halewood and Speke – three very different areas (even though geographically contiguous) – is telling. But Garston has been better served by its own bard, the contemporary poet Peter Robinson, whose 'Interrupted Views' rewrites Davie's voyage – this time over the Runcorn (rail) bridge and into Liverpool:

> A feeling for landscape
> we call it.
>
> But I didn't expect
> the river's inimical chill.
> The carriage window
> reflects me so.
> Then a latticework
> of girder, flickering,
> black on the water a long way beneath:
> the train is crossing the rail bridge;
> the view, interrupted,

of home, my old home –
a low shelf of alluvial deposit.
The airport control tower,
derelict gasworks,
these are the landmarks.
They put us in our place
and wanting it, I come
back to the ash heaps,
the car dumps, each graffito
taken as a welcome.

Mute welcomes proliferate.

Home is the view I appropriate. (Robinson 1996: 142–43)[14]

Robinson uses a quote from Adrian Stokes as the epigraph to this poem – 'The world is full of home' – and indeed it is (though it might be added that in Liverpool, as in many places, home is also full of the world). But as Robinson's writing indicates, home is also where your roots are (even if those roots end up sustaining a plant that grows a long way from where it was first grounded) and Garston/Allerton wasn't home to me, despite my spending most of my youth there. One of my schools was there, and for a number of reasons I spent a long time living in Stormont Road with my maternal grandmother, who, like others of her generation, had notable pronunciations – 'lurry' [lʊrɪ] for 'lorry' [lɔri:] and 'tong' [tɒŋ] for 'tongue' [tʌŋ]. Was this explained by the fact that her family was Welsh perhaps, or that her husband was from Widnes?[15] Was the Garston accent influenced by the fact that the distance between Garston and Widnes – where the accent was and is very distinct from that of Liverpool – is more or less the same distance as that between Garston and Liverpool city centre? (Garston was only incorporated into Liverpool in 1902 – against the wishes of the Garston Urban District Council.)[16] Linguistic differences notwithstanding, I have vivid memories of the area at the top of St Mary's Road: Binny's the general hardware store at one end of Stormont Road (which sold many things but only ever smelled of paraffin); Tushy's the grocer's at the other end (owned by the actress Rita Tushingham's dad – the Tushinghams were an old Garston family); Banks's on Garston Old Road, for when my nan had fallen out with old Tushy (to my mystification, Les Banks said, *every time*, in response to my grandma's order for 'a quarter of boiled ham and make it lean': 'which way?'). And many of my after-school hours were passed in the mock Tudor and beautifully wooden vaults of Garston Library, clutching those green, hard cardboard tickets (three maximum) that gave us the publicly entrusted right to take the world in books home. It was a Carnegie library in fact, established by the Andrew Carnegie foundation in 1909 at a cost of £8,000 (a lot of money in those days apparently, although it seemed to be the case that you could specify any amount and it would have been 'a lot of money in those days'). The Order of Ceremony for the opening noted that the 9,000 books included 'works of interest to the student, the artisan and mechanic and the general reader' and advised that 'the building will be suitably warmed in the winter time by a low pressure system of radiators'.[17] Perhaps it was the warmth of the place that attracted some of the local itinerants and older unemployed men who congregated in the newspaper reading area (either that or they wanted to read the papers). For some reason, the welcome afforded to them did not extend to facilitating their reading of the racing pages; results, runners and forecasts were all blacked out by a large ink roller kept at the front desk for this very purpose. They complained about it bitterly, and right they were. The library, though, was a highlight, well-set in the leafier end of the area and slightly but significantly removed from 'the working-class, dockside village slum of Garston [...] and, next door, the over-spill estates of Speke' (Robinson 1996: 140). It was both a crowded and an empty landscape, tiny streets, some of them with two-up/two downs (I remember later, at university, someone asking 'two what up and down?') and 'the wide, flat/arena of parkland/gathering to its piece of skyline,/empty but for someone in a sunburst' (Robinson 1996: 144). The allusion is to Garston park, a bare space denuded of its trees by the ravages of Dutch Elm disease (for which, we assumed, Holland was in some vague way responsible – I blamed Johan Cruyff):

> The white seagulls dip for scraps above
> Long Lane's central reservation; brittle leaves
> are ousted by heaped shreds of paper
> and, at a football pitch's edge,
> I'd watch a while the Sunday League game. (Robinson 1996: 152)

I did the same before rushing home for Sunday dinner and *The World At War* (narrated by Laurence Olivier). It was vivid and horrific enough to prompt 'ahs' and 'tuts' from the elders, though sometimes dull and abstract enough to a child to seem tame by comparison with some of the violence committed in the game I'd just been watching.

The park was also the scene of some linguistic exoticism when the 'Russians' (a term that covered any sailor off a ship that might have been from anywhere from Norway to Sakhalin) came to play football and left behind the posts that the ship's carpenter had evidently made (they were painted in black and white blocks). Those same Russians could also be seen in Garston market on Fridays, groups of them spending good cash, though only one held the money (to stop them running away we were told – to Garston? we wondered). They seemed to buy inordinate numbers of batteries and some dreadful clothes, but then dreadful clothes were the order of the day. Those moments of excitement apart, however, Garston seemed a dreary place to me – the British Legion, the Masonic Hall, the Cenotaph, the Orange Lodge marching, the bells of St Mary's on a Sunday evening – all were symbols of exclusion from a place that was never mine, all the more so since we lived on the peculiar side of a strange cultural boundary:

> Copper-oxide-coloured ledge
> slung between two brick supports,
>   the bridge

marks the line's trajectory,
bisected by the avenue. (Robinson 1996: 145–46)

The bridge stood over Mather Avenue, carrying the railway line south and effectively demarcating Garston from Allerton. On one side of that bridge was Holly Park, the ground of South Liverpool Football Club (The South) – a decent Northern Premier League outfit that had started life in Dingle Lane, migrated to Garston, and won the Welsh Cup in 1939 (fittingly given the area's Welsh connections, though it must have involved creative interpretation of the boundaries of Wales). On the other side of the bridge were Woolton Road, which led to what was by then the genteel old village of Woolton, nice pubs and all, and Mather Avenue itself, which was the route to the posher parts of Allerton (once it had scooted past the embarrassment of the Springwood estate).

School, University

There is a story, common enough in a period of history from the 1950s to the 1980s in Britain, of the working-class scholarship boy (it's a gendered tale more often than not).[18] Educated at a grammar school, sometimes at Oxbridge, he is often taken to typify, in his social and geographic mobility, his career, his cultural tastes and practices, his language even, a particular experience of the social history of his time. In a way it has become a classic narrative, pertinent examples of which are set out in the sociological work of Richard Hoggart (*The Uses of Literacy*, 1957), the novels and some of the criticism of Raymond Williams ('Culture is Ordinary', 1958; *Border Country*, 1960; *Second Generation*, 1964) and the poetry of Tony Harrison (*From the School of Eloquence*, 1981). There are other versions of the story of course, some of which are distinctively complex, at least in certain respects, because told from the perspective of a female subject – the essays by Valerie Walkerdine, Carolyn Steedman, Liz Heron and Sheila Rowbotham in Heron's pioneering *Truth, Dare or Promise* (1985), Steedman's *Landscape for a Good Woman* (1987), the autobiographical sections of Rowbotham's *Threads through Time* (1999). But though the genre has become recognizable, the individual cases are significantly different – not least in terms of generation and place. My own story is that I attended St Edwards College (1971–78), where I learnt a lot about language, one way and another (for which I am grateful), and a great deal about bullying, violence and the contemptible misuse of adult authority in relation to children (which I continue to despise). The formal study of language was pretty basic though rigorous – at least in the terms of English traditional grammar – though I was also introduced to the delights of studying, reading and speaking 'foreign languages' (French and Spanish). More significantly, because of the nature of the school (the city's premier Catholic grammar school, which drew pupils from all over Liverpool as well as St Helens and Widnes), I became familiar with the differential social composition of the city itself, and the cultural forms, identities and indeed aspects of language that went with it. The 'Widdy' or

'Saints' boys were markedly distinct in terms of speech and unintentionally drew attention to the fact that there was a clear boundary between forms of South Lancashire speech and those of Liverpool (it was the basis of constant mockery). But what I soon understood was that boys from within the city itself spoke differently too – kids from Bootle and the Dingle, for example, or kids from Garston and Sandfield Park (the private estate that surrounded the school).[19] The point was not lost on the poet Michael O'Neill (born elsewhere, and with a voice to match, but brought up in Liverpool and also educated at St Edwards):

> Our Liverpool Catholic background?
> We boast it like a badge, but
> Don't share the nasal twang which warms
> This pub to life. Just open your mouth
> And it's there, the spirit of a city.
> [...]
> And I still sit apart like a spy
> Whose cover's blown, fixated on a desk
> Where a boy gets by heart his latest
> Lesson: "you don't speak like us." (O'Neill 1990: 16)

Was this (is this) explicable by socially constituted spatial differences between the areas? Or was it (is it) a question of social class in a more direct sense? If it was a question of class, how finely was this graded? (In answer to the question 'What does your dad do?', I once heard a boy respond 'He's a stevedore', only to be met with 'You mean he's a docker' by a classmate.) Were the production and perception of such differences also related to the construction of a particular type of (class-related) masculinity? I am not wholly sure of the answers to these questions, but at school one thing was clear: however we spoke, the authorities thought our speech needed attention. And so, a generation after Shaw recalled that one of the aims of his school, St Francis Xavier's, was to produce 'an accent-less gentleman' (Shaw 1957b: 6), the classes of One Hope, One Domingo and One Mersey at St Edwards were subject to the gentle strictures of Miss Sarath and her 'speech-training' lessons. I suspect it was neither a happy nor successful experience for all concerned; to be sure, few of us ended up meriting either of the terms 'accentless' (if such a thing were possible) or indeed 'gentlemen' (though of course it depends what that history-laden term is taken to mean).

Did people in Liverpool speak in different ways? At one level of analysis the answer to that question is clearly yes – everyone speaks differently in some way, shape or form. But what form did the differences take? Were they empirically distinct in patterned ways, or were they 'indexical' and 'enregistered' in the way suggested in the previous chapter? (They could of course be both.) This remains a significant question, and it is addressed, at least indirectly, in Kevin Sampson's *Outlaws* (2001) (one of a number of contemporary texts written in a style that attempts to represent forms of Liverpool speech).[20] In the narrative, Ged, a professional robber from the Dingle (the novel has yet to be written about the honest, employed, working-class Dingleite) reflects:

People in the North End try to say the Dingle lads have our own way of talking, but that's shite, really. We do have sayings and that, to be fair – the lads at the match used to slaughter us for the way we'd say 'a accident' or 'a escort' and that. What we'd do to properly wind them up is we'd drop an aitch an all, too. A amburger and that. A atchet. But we don't talk no different to any other cunt, in fairness. That's the Tocky lads. It's the Granby firm's got the patter, all the black boys and that, all the lads with race, if you will. Now them lads have got their own thing going on. The black lads that we grew up with round the South End, once they got to a certain age they did all start talking that bit more Yardie, to be fair. They'd be saying 'I axed him' and that instead of 'I asked him'. Perfectly A-OK saying 'I asked him' the year before, but once they started getting older it was all the other thing. 'Ah axthed 'im for thum thkunk.' Putting on a lisp, by the way. Oh yis. *Pretending* to have a speech defect. That was just a handful of them, to be fair – Granby Street and round there. Lisps and Jamaican accents. (Sampson 2001: 24–25)

He continues, referring to people from the Dingle (in fact he specifies 'the Holylands', which 'was considered posh compared to the other side of Harlow Street' – a couple of hundred yards away):

We haven't really got an accent. We use a bit of backslang, to be fair, now and then and that, but we don't really talk different to the Scotty Road crew. 'Stotty Road', that's what they used to say up there. And 'the Stratford End'. Them North End beauts, always going on about taking the Stratford End, they were. You'd give up telling the cunts it weren't called that. (Sampson 2001: 24–25)

As noted previously, this was not the first novelistic attempt to represent Liverpool speech. Perhaps the first sustained effort is found in H.J. Cross's novel *No Language But A Cry* (1951), even though in this case the effect reads more like typical renderings of Cockney:

'Nah then, clever,' began the biggest tough, 'nah then, wot about it?'… 'Stamp on me bleedin' fingers, would yer?'[…]
'I ain't 'andin' over nothink' […]
'Wot's the trouble, Mick? These mokes pickin' on you?' (Cross 1951: 8–9).[21]

Other representations were made in Shaw's *The Scab* (1952) and, more importantly, in Alun Owen's work 'No Trams to Lime Street' (1959) – a play specifically written for television and thus influenced by the emerging conventions of television drama. But Sampson's text brings us back again to the significant issue of the perception of speech differences within Liverpool. For after denying that there are such differences, Ged then goes on to cite a number of notable distinctions: Dingle lads (according to his strict specification of that group) have 'sayings'; they use one form of the indefinite article – 'a' – in contexts where others expect 'an'; they don't use the 'Yardie' language of the black 'Tocky' (Toxteth) lads from Granby; they use backslang; their pronunciation of specific words differs from that of the 'Scotty Road crew' (Scotland Road) in the 'North End' and leads to prescriptivism – they constantly have to correct the pronunciation of 'Stratford' for 'Stretford'. And yet the point here is not the fact of difference, but the way in which it is framed and evaluated (this is a passage that starts with the declaration that it's 'shite' to say that Dingle lads have their 'own way of talking' and ends with a form of exasperated prescriptivism that unsuccessfully tries to correct a pronunciation of the name of one end of Manchester United's ground).[22]

My own experience of such framing and the patterns of evaluation associated with it has varied greatly. At St Edwards I became aware of speech differences and the social meanings attached to them (not least location in geographic and social space), but after leaving school I spent six years at Oxford University as an undergraduate and graduate student and tutorial fellow and learned another set of lessons entirely. In 1966 an article in the *Liverpool Echo* entitled 'That Scouser Accent… It's an Asset Now' argued that, whereas 'once upon a time the Liverpool accent was a liability',

> nowadays reaction to raw accents has changed. As the old school ties fade; as job mobility increases, the language barriers are dropping. The Tykes and Geordies may have some way to go, but the Scouser has arrived; the Liverpool accent is now an asset rather than a liability. They even try to ape it at fashionable parties – with disastrous results, for it is, in the most literal sense, inimitable […] A London firm of consultants told me: 'Nobody takes much notice of accents now, certainly not in senior executive positions. Experience and ability in the job are what matter. In certain fields a Liverpool accent could be a positive help, implying a toughness and determination to get on with the job.' (Frank 1962: 8)

The claim was supported by a cartoon featuring an office manager addressing a male clerk (in reference to a female secretary): 'Eh, La! Ask dat Judy out der to gerrus a cuppa tea, will yer?' Such sentiments were not uncommon. In 'We Owe these Wackers more than We Know', another correspondent argued that 'recent events have proved beyond all doubt that "Scouse" is by no means as unattractive as certain people make out. Millions of people in Europe and America are now using many of the "Scouse" idioms that were brought to them from Liverpool by the Beatles' (Welsh 1964: 8). Leaving aside the somewhat dubious assertion concerning the outbreak of meritocracy in Britain, there seems little doubt that the cultural and linguistic capital associated with Scouse was real enough. Welsh ascribes it to the Beatles, though the argument in the previous chapter proposed that there were a host of forces that combined to produce such an effect. In any case, there is no doubting that many of the post-war forms of cultural authoritarianism and social deference were indeed under threat at this time, and that, as Tony Lane puts it, in many of the representations of popular culture, 'Liverpool's irreverent and self-confident people seemed especially expressive of these new, subversively democratic sentiments' (Lane 1997: xv).

Yet if that was the case in the mid 1960s, things had changed by the time I arrived in Oxford in 1978. By that stage, having a Liverpool accent definitely was *not* an asset. In fact more often than not it was simply taken as a marker of class identity – working-class identity – and that wasn't entirely in vogue on The Broad at the time. In truth, apart from a few egregious instances, crude and unpleasant enough in their own way, I came across overt hostility towards my Liverpool voice relatively infrequently. It mostly took the form of the sort of ignorance that presumes to be able to place you, in any number of social and cultural ways, from your speech (but then ignorance is ignorance – it's why we have education). Such placement usually meant being treated as though you didn't quite belong, whatever you did, which wasn't altogether agreeable (though Oxford University was such a snooty, unfriendly place in those days that I imagine only a very small minority felt entirely at home there). Oxford the city of course was a different matter – there are probably more people of Irish descent in Oxford (many of them drawn to Cowley car works) than students and they produced an alternative scene that made the place bearable. And I was interested in my language studies (I entered to read French and Spanish and switched to English) and was able to pursue them with the help of superb opportunities in terms of tuition and resources (including studying later with an intellectually inspiring doctoral supervisor and a great cohort of graduate students). It was during my undergraduate degree, however, that I became interested in the field of the history of the language (and to a certain extent sociolinguistics), both of which allowed me a certain critical edge when it came to understanding the patterns of evaluation associated with forms of speech in Britain. And so I gradually became critically aware, or at least self-reflexively so, of the social roles of language; of the narratives that are told about its history; of the models that are used to frame and tame it; of issues of symbolic power and violence. Evidently one of the lessons I learned, by experience as well as theoretical analysis, was that articulated by Davie in 'Winter's Talents':

> I salute the
> Articulators of winter
> Wonderlands. Delamere Forest's
> Ramifications extort
> Arpeggio and cadenza,
> Too ornate for the *scouse* (Davie 2002: 391)[23]

Or as the poet Tony Harrison put more or less the same point in 'Them and [uz]':

> 'Poetry's the speech of kings. You're one of those
> Shakespeare gives comic bits to: prose!
> All poetry […] you see
> 's been dubbed by [Λs] into RP
> […]
> Your speech is in the hands of the Receivers.'
> 'We say [Λs] not [uz], T.W.!' That shut my trap.
> I doffed my flat a's (as in 'flat cap')
> My mouth all stuffed with glottals, great
> Lumps to hawk up and spit out … E-nun-ci-ate! (Harrison 2006: 122)

There were, I suppose, occasions when I paid the symbolic price of inclusion, or at least non-exclusion, but there were other lessons to learn in this regard too, particularly with reference to the relationship between 'standard English' (in the sense of the system of writing) and 'standard English' (when used to refer to a form of speech).[24] For example, there is the important question that arises whenever dialectal (or supposedly 'non-standard') speech is represented: in what sense do the non-standard spellings on the page 'reflect' the sounds that issue from people's mouths? Does the form 'wot', as used by Cross in the passage cited above, accurately reflect a (any?) Liverpool pronunciation of 'what'? Does a specific accent, or dialect, require a standardized way of representing just that form? Or can dialects only be rendered accurately if they are given phonetically (using the symbols of the International Phonetic Alphabet)? These are difficult questions to disentangle, and they are made more complex once the concepts of indexicality and enregisterment are taken into account, since they make clear that the role of a spelling such as 'wot' is not to represent speech but to index (and further enregister) class and regional identity. But then, as Williams noted in the early 1960s, the real issue that haunts all such representations does not concern 'non-standard' spellings and 'non-standard' speech at all. It is instead the implicit idea that the standard spellings of written English in some sense 'reflect' the speech of some group of English speakers ('the cultured', 'the educated', 'the literate', 'proper speakers', 'posh people' or even 'standard English speakers'). For it is a deeply rooted and powerful assumption, but a somewhat bizarre assumption nonetheless, that when standard English spellings are used in a word like 'laugh', the vowel should be taken to be pronounced in its lengthened form [lɑːf], whereas if 'laff' appears, it surely indicates the use of the short vowel [læf] (and thus dialectal or class-based speech). But in what sense can the orthographic sequence 'laugh' be taken to reflect anyone's speech?

It took me a while to realize the implications of this fundamental insight, and to recognize fully the force of Williams' summoning of a time 'when people will know enough about their own language to stop [repeating the mystification of non-standard orthography], so that naked prejudice no longer goes bowing graciously down the street' (Williams 1965: 245). I'd left Oxford by the time I understood his point, and it took a while longer to realize that linguistic prejudice really is one of the last socially respectable prejudices. But when it came, the clarification was a liberation of the sort described (in regard to a different though related context) in an imaginary exchange between the poet Seamus Heaney and the ghostly figure of James Joyce in the sequence 'Station Island'. Reflecting on Heaney's concern with the 'tundish' episode in Joyce's *Portrait of the Artist* (in which Stephen Dedalus is made to feel that his use of the word 'tundish' marks him out as someone who doesn't quite speak 'the best English'), Joyce answers:

> 'Who cares,'
> he jeered, 'any more? The English language
> belongs to us. You are raking at dead fires,
>
> a waste of time for somebody your age.
> That subject people stuff is a cod's game...' (Heaney 1984: 93)

What took longer to work out was the ability to separate out that sense of freedom and recognition – that the language in which I had been brought up was as good as any other (which is not to say that there aren't many other forms to learn) – from the critical stance required to start an enquiry into that language: into the received version of its history, the way in which it had been framed and theorized, the values and social meanings that went along with it. This book is, at least in part, a record of that working out, though of course it is a process that is never complete at either a personal or social level.

A view from elsewhere

Though I return to Liverpool regularly and frequently, I have not lived in the city on a permanent basis since I left when I was seventeen. I spent six years studying at Oxford, and then took up a series of academic posts: ten years at the University of Southampton, eleven at the University of Manchester, a year in New York, San Diego, and (best of all) at the University of California at Santa Cruz, and now the past five years just outside Los Angeles. Needless to say, the reception and evaluation of my voice and language has been different in all of these places. Being from Liverpool, and speaking in a way that makes that fact recognizable, evoked a whole variety of specific reactions (some predictable, some not) in Southampton, a poor and depressed city in the wealthy south that suffered the ravages of Thatcherism, and in Manchester, a lively and exciting place in the mid 1990s and after. In America, of course, once the Beatles question has been asked ('Isn't that where...?'), attitudes are a bit different. I treasure to this day the comment made by a student in San Diego who asked me to read a line from Shakespeare twice since the way I spoke was 'refined' and made it sound 'really authentic'. He looked bemused when I stopped laughing and told him that no one, but no one, had ever said anything like this about my voice ('the speech of kings' indeed). Of course, sad to say, all this shows (*all* this shows?) is the arbitrariness of evaluations of speech and their socially constructed basis; it made for a nice change though all the same.

Perceptions and evaluations differ according to place, history, context. In the preface to *Three TV Plays*, Alun Owen made an interesting and revealing comment which I have pondered often, both before and during the writing of this book:

> The town I was brought up in is an active part of these plays. I think it is highly individual, but then everyone's home town is, and Liverpool has the added advant-age of having a multi-racial population. It's a Celtic town set down in Lancashire. Its people have evolved an accent for themselves that they've borrowed from their Irish and Welsh grandfathers. The problem of Identity, which is to me one of the greatest the twentieth century has produced, is exaggerated in Liverpool, and the exaggeration makes it dramatic. (Owen 1961: 8)

There is much to consider here, a lot with which to agree and disagree. Liverpool is, of course, individual, and it has its own history (though whether its individuality deserves to be called 'exceptionalism' is open to debate, and to describe the place as 'isolationist', as one critic does while also hailing its cultural openness, seems somewhat confused) (Belchem 2000a; Griffiths 2008: 17). And it is indeed multiracial – though the historical variability of its racial make-up needs to be borne in mind when this claim is made. Yet does it make sense to describe it as a 'Celtic' town, given the mythifications that surround the term 'Celtic'?[25] And, as the work presented in previous chapters has suggested, is it really the case that its 'accent' (a term that already begs the question of the status of its language) is 'borrowed' from Irish and Welsh antecedents in the apparently simple way that Owen suggests? Moreover, on the question of 'Identity' (which may or may not have been one of the twentieth century's greatest problems – there were other contenders for that title), if it is true that the problem of identity is 'exaggerated' and 'dramatic' in Liverpool, then the question to ask is surely why that is – how was that effect produced, for what reasons, and by whom? For identity isn't a natural or ahistorical thing, but a social process from which emerge certain (precarious) modes of cultural stability and fixity that are posited over and against changing historical, political and ideological realities. In other words, identity is a battleground, a terrain on which competing discourses, and the interests they serve, struggle to achieve hegemony. That isn't to say that the effects of identity are illusory or not real, since that would be a bizarre claim in a world in which one of the bases on which people willingly go to war is that they are 'from' a certain place and 'have' a specific identity. (And there is nothing more tediously revealing in this respect than the petty forms of aggressive parochialism on display at times in characterizations of Liverpool in Manchester and Manchester in Liverpool.) But it is to say that identity is always the product of material forces combined in a particular way; it may appear monological and unchangeable, but then that is part of the trick of hegemony, and such an effect only lasts as long as the dialogism of social reality is suppressed. How is such hegemony achieved? As this book has attempted to demonstrate from a variety of perspectives, one of the ways this is done is by presenting an essentialized view of language and relating it to an essentialized view of a place and the people who live there. Such essentialism takes various forms. For example, consider this assertion in an interesting, sympathetic and often perceptive essay on Liverpool by Paul Morley, the music journalist and writer:

> Liverpool is not part of England in the way that New York is not part of America. It is more Welsh, more Irish, a shifty, shifting outpost of defiance and determination reluctantly connected to the English mainland, more an island set in a sea of dreams and nightmares that's forever taking shape in the imagination, more a mysterious place jutting out into time between the stabilizing pull of history and the sweeping, shuffling force of myth. (Morley 2007: 42)

This is a nice piece of rhetoric and it reinforces a number of mythical views that have in fact added weight to the stabilizing pull of a certain type of history and thus closed down the complex, dialogical openness that characterizes Liverpool in history and history in Liverpool. Take the claim that Liverpool is not part of England.[26] This is an assertion that allows the constructors of a certain type of exclusive, narrow Englishness to have it their own way. For England, like

Liverpool, is a complex, multicultural, multiracial place, and always has been. And part of England's awkward, difficult and uneven history has been made by Liverpool. So in whose interest is it exactly to assert that Liverpool is not part of England, that it is 'reluctantly' connected to the 'English mainland' (to 'real' England perhaps)? And 'more, Welsh, more Irish'? What do these terms mean precisely? More culturally, socially or politically Welsh? Or Irish? Perhaps the claim simply means that Liverpool is part of Welsh and Irish history, and of course it is. But then it is also part of Scottish history, and Atlantic history, and thus African and African-American history, and the history of many other places too (including, dare it be said, the history of England), since it has played an important role in the development of all of those places and cultural realms. An outpost of defiance and determination? At times Liverpool has been this, and on occasion gloriously so, but it has also been a location of conservatism, conformity and orthodoxy too (Roscoe the brave abolitionist was howled down by his fellow Liverpool merchants; the city was run for a long time by the Tory–Orange Order hegemons; and Liverpool's racial history has been and remains one of segregation and discrimination, despite all the consoling references to 'mixed-race' marriages). A place taking shape constantly in the imagination? Is this not simply another way of saying that, like all places, 'Liverpool' is a historical construct, an imagined location that is formed by the selection and narration of elements of lived experience? And is it not the case that the way in which that process and its results are evaluated really must depend on what stories are being chosen and told, how far they attempt to match up to the complications of reality and what their effects are? Now, are the myths, narratives and histories seductive? Let me give an example. At the Liverpool vs Chelsea game in the semi-final of the Champions League (1 May 2007), an important cultural as well as sporting event, a giant banner was held up on the Kop that read: 'We're Not English We Are Scouse'.[27] Need I say that I like the sentiment, revel in its performativity, enjoy its humour? And yet, ultimately, I can't agree with it. Why? Because in the end it chooses one categorical abstraction over another, which means that it is based on a refusal of the cultural particularity of Liverpool, its historical specificity, its unevenness and internal fragmentation, in the name of an 'identity', Scouse, that was manufactured at a given time for a combination of reasons, and that has now become in many contexts little more than a pernicious way of attacking Liverpool and its inhabitants, often in the guise of comedy. Of course that doesn't necessarily mean that the term and concept 'Scouse' (in any of its senses) has to be rejected, since it has its positive aspects too. But it should at least be understood as an historical and cultural construction whose utility has to be evaluated rather than taken for granted; in other words an abstraction whose cost should be carefully weighed. Another way of making the same point, from a more theoretical perspective, is to see this as part of a general problem of categorization that is often couched in diametrically opposed (rather than dialectical) terms. On the one hand there is the emphasis on difference – the refusal of any category because no category can do justice to the specificity of historical reality and the differences that constitute it. The danger of this view is that the insistence that there are only differences ends up in a curious reductiveness: asserting that that there is nothing more to say than that there are only differences is in the end a way of making everything the same (everything is an instance of difference). On the other hand, taking 'Scouse' – and its correlative, the 'Scouser' – as categories that denote some fixed essence is simply to elide the differences of history. For as I have attempted to show, 'Scouse', and by implication the 'Scouser', were categories whose beginnings were often slightly ambivalent, gendered, class- and racially specific instantiations of local pride, uniqueness and authenticity.[28] But they became, by a sort of looping effect, ways of being, thinking and representing what it meant to 'come from' Liverpool. And that – at least in part because of the reductions and abstractions involved – facilitated the sort of nasty and often vicious representations of Liverpool that have become familiar over the past forty years or so (one of which – 'the Liverpool kiss', meaning a head-butt – has been codified within the language itself).[29] Such representations were often dichotomous (two sides of the same bad penny would be another way of putting it): for every witty Scouser there was the lippy, aggressive Scally; for every friendly generous and good-hearted Scouser there was the self-privileging whiner; for every compassionate Scouser there was the self-pitying sentimentalist; for every Scouse challenger to the social order there was the petty robber; for every Scouse player with words there was the illiterate Malapudlian. The general point can be summed up this way: without categories it is difficult to engage with history in all its specificity; using categories that are essentialized leads to an engagement with history conducted necessarily on abstract and reductive terms. There is no disputing the fact that the categories 'Scouse' and 'Scouser' exist; perhaps it is just time to re-evaluate them in relation to their use in the present, past and future.

Let me return to language to conclude. As noted in the introduction to this book, my interest in this project was piqued, both as a professional linguist and as someone born and raised in Liverpool, by two passing comments that appeared to show some scepticism towards the history of Scouse. I thought I knew the story of language in Liverpool, even if my training had taught me to be dubious about some of the cruder, more populist versions. As it turns out, the history was much more intricate, and unravelling it was much more difficult, than I had expected, though that is perhaps simply a testament to the richness and depth of the history and the issues it raises. And so it has been a journey that began with a question – 'But what if…?' and that has ended with a series of other questions, some of which may be answerable by further research, many of which will not (for example, ascertaining the exact nature of Liverpool speech in periods before the advent of recording devices or in the absence or accurate, reliable evidence). The voyage took the form of an exploration of language, past and present, that sometimes delighted me (it was a pleasure to uncover some of the roots and routes of words), often amused me (some of the uses of language that I came across made me laugh out loud), and on occasion made me wonder (a few of the characterizations of language in Liverpool, including those of the professionals, were startling). At times too it annoyed me, never more than when a putative form of language, Scouse, was taken metonymically to represent a city, its inhabitants and their culture(s). In that respect, as should be clear from the argument made in the previous chapters, and with due respect to the folk song 'The Leaving of Liverpool', it really isn't the language of Liverpool that grieves me, though what its friends and enemies have made of it is enough to give anyone pause for thought.[30]

Conclusion

I am grateful that I was born and brought up in Liverpool. It was, and in many ways always will be, my home and it gave me a sense of place and a feeling of 'being from' somewhere ('cognitive mapping', to adapt a current phrase). Along with many other factors, it gave me the confidence to travel to other locations safe in the knowledge that I have a reference point – cultural, linguistic, historical, political if you like – that allows me to have some sense of where I am in the world. Of course it hasn't always felt like that since at times the pull of Liverpool has been a hindrance and some of the cultural evaluations that are sometimes associated with the place and its language have been a bit of a nuisance (even if treated with the contempt they deserve). But I am glad to have been formed in that city and as part of my debt to it I wanted to consider a number of questions about it – specifically about its language – that I thought ought to be addressed. I hope that I have set some of the more unlikely aspects of the standard history straight, and answered some of the more complex questions in a properly sceptical and critical way. Needless to say, there are many other issues that I have merely touched on or have failed to answer altogether. And then of course there is the matter of the literature of Liverpool, especially its 'lost' literature; but that, so to speak, is another story altogether…

Notes

1   Douglas Dunn, '*English*. A Scottish Essay' (2008), 25.
2   The full etymology of 'nostalgia' is the Greek νόστος, 'return home', and αλγία 'pain', combined in the post-classical Latin 'nostalgia'. *Oxford English Dictionary*, 2nd edn (Oxford, 1989), *s.v. nostalgia*.
3   If Harrison's account is correct, it would provide a possible explanation for the etymology of 'stockade', which the *OED* otherwise gives as a seventeenth-century import from French or possibly Spanish. *Oxford English Dictionary*, 2nd edn (Oxford, 1989), *s.v. stockade n*.
4   Wyld and Oakes Hirst's account was supported by Ekwall's *The Place-Names of Lancashire*; Ekwall also noted the use of the final element, 'staðr', 'teth', in the name of the local area of 'Croxteth' – 'Crōc' being the Old English form of the Old Norse personal name 'Krōkr' (Ekwall 1922: 114, 115).
5   The Herculaneum Dock was opened in 1866 and closed in 1972 (though there had been dock work at the site since the mid eighteenth century); the dock took its name from the Herculaneum Pottery (1794–1841), a successful ceramics business located in the same area which produced highly distinctive work. Interestingly, Picton asserted that many of the potters were brought from Staffordshire to settle in what

was (in the 1790s) a rural backwater: he also noted that 'the potters long continued a separate and isolated people, preserving their own manners and customs, and retaining their Mercian dialect' (Picton 1875: II, 466).

6 For a discussion of the views of Dingle residents on their area, see Ronaldo Munck (ed.), *Reinventing the City? Liverpool in Comparative Perspective* (2003), pp. 204–07.

7 The 'Welsh streets' – Voelas, Rhiwlas, Powis, Madryn, Kinmel, Gwydir – were so-called not simply because of their names, but also because they were originally built to house Welsh workers; there were in fact a good number of streets with Welsh names in the Dingle, such as Gwendoline, Geraint, Enid, Elaine, Merlin, Modred. For an informative account of the role of Welsh workers and building entrepreneurs in the construction of nineteenth-century Liverpool, see Thomas A. Roberts, 'The Welsh influence on the building industry in Victorian Liverpool' (1986). The Holy Land, towards the top of Park Road, consists of Moses Street, Isaac Street, Jacob Street and David Street, and may have been so-titled not, as is commonly supposed, because of the street names (the streets were built in the late nineteenth century), but because the first inhabitants of the place – early seventeenth-century Puritan refugees who were granted right of abode by the Catholic Sir Richard Molyneux – referred to the area in this way. Other biblical names were given to Jericho Farm, Jordan Stream, the rocks of David's Throne and the cave called Adam's Battery (Robberds 1862: 345). Despite protestations claiming that the practice died out in the 1950s, 'Judas burning' took place to my personal knowledge in the mid 1960s in the Dingle (in Prophet Street to be exact). For discussion of the social origins and history of 'Judas burning', see the references in chapter three n. 19.

8 I was born at home in Prophet Street, just off what was once the effective southern boundary of Liverpool, Northumberland Street. Picton describes the building of the area: 'a tract of land adjoining and extending from Mill Street to Park Road was laid out soon after [1826] by a Welsh physician, John Hughes, M.D., who made extensive purchases from the earl of Sefton. The present plot comprised Essex, Prophet, Hughes and Dooley Streets, which were speedily crowded with a dense mass of houses of a very low class' (Picton 1875: 465). A discussion about the morality of praising the Lord while simultaneously building slums can be found in 'Owen's father becomes a "Jerry builder" and an Elder of the Church', chapter xiv of Eleazar Roberts' *Owen Rees: A Story of Welsh Life and Thought* (1893), one of the 'lost' Liverpool novels.

9 In his *Catholic History of Liverpool*, Thomas Burke claimed that, according to 'a well-founded tradition', St Patrick stopped off in Liverpool to preach while on the way to the Isle of Man (Burke 1910: 9). In a journey that was the reverse of that taken by many later, Patrick, who was British (probably what we now call Welsh), was captured and taken to slavery in Ireland before his later journey to Liverpool.

10 Burke noted attacks on St Patrick's in 1841, 1844, and then during the year of the Fenian Rising in Ireland, 1848, when 'again and again, with ladders and ropes, the Orangemen of Toxteth sought to pull down the statue which stands outside the western wall' (Burke 1910: 92). This was the story that was passed on to us as children. One of the interesting architectural features of St Patrick's is its plain style – the *Pevsner Architectural Guide to Liverpool* notes that 'the body resembles a Nonconformist chapel' (Sharples 2004: 271). If, as some believed, the aim was to appease the local Protestant population, the effect may have been slightly marred by the positioning of the statue of Patrick in such a way as to dominate the entrance to Park Road.

11 The streets behind and adjacent to the chapel commemorated Dickens (an author who had a strong affinity with Liverpool): Pickwick, Dombey, Dorrit, Nickelby, Copperfield, Micawber, Pecksniff, Weller and Dickens.

12 One of the makers of Scouse – Peter Moloney – taught at St Malachy's in the late
    1950s and 1960s and his after-dinner repartee consisted in part of stories about the
    kids; Malachites (including my father) considered themselves a cut above their con-
    temporaries. The altar painting at St Patrick's is by Nicaise de Keyser of Antwerp.

13 That Allerton was the home of John Lennon (Menlove Avenue), though Paul
    McCartney lived nearer our end (Forthlin Road). It was a sign of the times that
    I had only a dim idea that they had been born in the area, despite the fact that
    I passed their houses (which are now National Trust 'heritage' properties) every
    schoolday. The bus to school also went past Quarry Bank school (the source of
    Lennon's Quarry Men) and through Penny Lane, which was known to us from the
    song, though there were no evident signs of Beatles tourist tat in those days; all
    that came a bit later.

14 Garston gained another literary reference in Malcolm Lowry's *Under the Volcano*
    (1947): one character 'presented himself at the Marine Superintendent's office in
    Garston' to sign on to the SS *Philoctetes* (Lowry 2000: 161). Lowry was born in New
    Brighton and, despite an upper-middle-class upbringing, persuaded his father to
    allow him to sign on as a deckhand on the SS *Pyrrhus*, which sailed from Liverpool
    in 1927.

15 In the course of researching this history I made an enlightening discovery. My
    grandmother's maiden name was Meredith and I had been told as a child that my
    grandmother's uncle had owned a vineyard in Speke – in fact on the site of the Speke
    tenements, just off the Speke Road. Give the likelihood of Speke grapes, I treated
    this nonsense with the scorn it deserved until I read the Revd J.M. Swift's *The Story
    of Garston and its Church*, in which he noted that 'industries began to appear in the
    early [eighteen] seventies. The vineyard owned by Mr. Joseph Meredith grew grapes
    which had a great reputation, but Vineyard Street is the only reminder of this once
    famous vineyard' (Swift 1937: 84). Historians have a duty to be sceptical, but it's hard
    to judge at times.

16 The case made on behalf of the Corporation of Liverpool rested mainly on the
    contention that 'Garston upon our borders is a serious menace to Liverpool. Its
    defects are our dangers' (by which was meant that the inadequacies of the sanitary
    and health provisions in Garston posed a threat to Liverpool in terms of contiguous
    contagion – fears of 'the plague' were deployed in the legal arguments) (Swift 1937:
    142–43).

17 The Order of Ceremony was displayed at the library for the Centenary celebrations
    in May 2009.

18 My dad was a 'scholarship boy', though for boys of his background that meant
    attendance at Toxteth Technical Institute for Boys ('Tocky Teck' or 'TTI' – 'Tommy
    Tucker's Idiots' – for short). Tocky Teck was originally the Matthew Arnold School,
    named after the poet, critic (author of *Culture and Anarchy*) and sometime school
    inspector. Arnold's sister married into the Cropper family, which owned the Dingle
    Estate; Arnold died on Dingle Lane in 1888 running to catch a tram. I've heard it
    said (by my father in fact) that, with all due respect, Tocky Teck was more anarchy
    than culture.

19 I was not the first to notice this point. In a letter to the *Liverpool Echo*, Edward
    Macklin asserted: 'something no one seems to have noticed, however, is that
    the Scouser accent varies from distict to district. That other Shaw's Professor
    Higgins could have had a Pygmalion field-day sorting out the Dingleites, the
    Scottie-Roaders, the Edge-Hillians, the Bull-Ringers, and perhaps the Swan-birds!'
    (Macklin 1963: 8).

20 The appearance of a number of contemporary Liverpool novels that are largely
    written in Scouse is an important and as yet un-analysed development. They include

Sampson's *Awaydays* (1998), *Outlaws* (2001), *Clubland* (2002) and *Stars are Stars* (2006); Niall Griffiths' *Kelly + Victor* (2002), *Stump* (2003) and *Wreckage* (2005); and Helen Walsh's *Brass* (2004).

21 Cross's story is a moralistic account, as the cover has it, built around 'one family – a dock-labourer, black-haired giant of a man, to whom his army service has opened up a new world of cleanliness and cynical selfishness; his wife, well-meaning but degenerated into a slut, and their twelve-year-old son Mickey – a child of the gutter with a natural talent for drawing' (Cross 1951). There is no reason to suppose it was the case, but if it wasn't then Cross's novel should have been the text that prompted Shaw's (slightly cheeky) comment that 'the attempt to reprint in print a local accent or the use of expressions peculiar to a district bores the average reader' (Shaw 1955c: 5).

22 Another significant example of such discursive framing occurs in the *Lern Yerself Scouse* books, which also recognized a distinction between 'Dingle Scouse, from the South End' (covered in volume one), and 'north end dialect, or Bootle Scouse' (volume two) (Spiegl 2000: n.p. – foreword).

23 Davie's attitude to Liverpool, as opposed to Scouse, seems ambivalent. In 'A Liverpool Epistle', the poetic persona asserts: 'This is/Liverpool, one enormous/ Image of dereliction.' Later in the same piece, however, the persona proclaims that 'More/Human warmth, it follows,/Is possible or common/In Liverpool than in/ Some spick-and-span, intact,/Still affluent city' (Davie 2002: 394, 395).

24 See chapter three.

25 For a useful historical account of the development of the term 'Celt' and its historical uses, see Malcolm Chapman, *The Celts: Construction of a Myth* (1992).

26 Morley was not original in his claim. In an essay in the *Liverpool Echo* cited earlier ('It's an Asset Now'), Frank reported a comment by a London taxi-driver: '"Scousers, they're all right, but I must say I prefer the English"' (Frank 1966: 8).

27 http://www.lfcpicturestore.tv/were_not_english_were_scouse/print/4533477.html (accessed 23 October 2011).

28 For important critical discussions of the way in which Scouse identity was racialized, see M. Christian, 'Black Struggle for Historical Recognition in Liverpool' (1995); Diane Frost, 'Ambiguous Identities: Constructing and De-constructing Black and White "Scouse" Identities in Twentieth Century Liverpool' (2000); and Jacqueline Nassy Brown, *Dropping Anchor, Setting Sail: Geographies of Race in Black Liverpool* (2005).

29 *Oxford English Dictionary*, 2nd edn (Oxford, 1989), *s.v. Liverpool* n^3. The somewhat tedious history of vicious representations of Liverpool and Scousers is recounted in Philip Boland's article, 'The Construction of Images of People and Place: Labelling Liverpool and Stereotyping Scousers' (2008). The historical low point of this process (as yet) was surely the false smears printed by the *Sun* newspaper after the criminal events that caused the Hillsborough disaster. Rather than focusing on the police negligence and incompetence that led to the tragedy, the *Sun* saw fit to print anonymous claims that Liverpool fans had stolen from the dead and urinated on their bodies. One consequence of this was the refusal of Liverpool people to buy the *Sun* thereafter, though one question to be asked in this regard is why it took a disaster of such proportions for people to reject the cruel and nasty nonsense that this paper propagated as its staple diet. The Hillsborough coverage was exceptionally offensive and unfair, but this wasn't the first time that the *Sun* had portrayed Liverpool and its inhabitants (along with many other people) in stereotyped, crude and malicious ways.

30 'The Leaving of Liverpool' is a nineteenth-century sailor's lament. The apt first verse (at least in my case) and chorus are:

Farewell to Prince's Landing Stage
River Mersey, fare thee well
I am bound for California
A place I know right well.

Chorus:
So fare thee well, my own true love
When I return united we will be
It's not the leaving of Liverpool that's grieving me
But my darling when I think of thee.

APPENDIX

Stories of words: naming the place, naming the people

The whole subject is very mysterious and well worthy of research. (Stephan Jack, 'Dialect Expert', 1945)[1]

Despite its significance, the received version of Liverpool's linguistic history is not the only narrative told about language in Liverpool. For on a more specific level, there are word-stories that have been woven about both the name of the place itself and the terms used to refer to the people who live in it. The purpose of this appendix, then, will be to explore the ways in which 'Liverpool', 'Liverpolitan', 'Liverpudlian', 'Dicky Sam', 'Whacker', 'Scouse' and 'Scouser' have been explained and made the subject of particular types of narration. As will become clear, the stories of these words have been spun by various types of cultural and linguistic analysts, both professional and amateur: etymologists, onomasticians, historians, social observers, journalists, folklorists and practitioners of popular culture have all had their say. Sometimes 'scientific', sometimes highly speculative, sometimes pointed, sometimes comic, the narratives are united only by the underlying sense that the terms under review are worthy of attention – a proper subject of analysis and therefore in need of investigation. Thus, given that all stories in one way and another are posited on a necessary confidence in the significance of their subject matter, the narratives to be analysed in this chapter play an important role in the formation of the notion that the language of Liverpool is a discursive object in its own right. That is, they contribute to the idea that this is a form of language that is specific to a particular place and a given set of people. As with the Irish *dinnseanchas* tradition (the lore of place names, including events and characters associated with a particular location), the histories of the terms considered below are themselves texts that make a contribution to the cultural history of Liverpool; they are in a sense part of the place. For these, if no other reasons, it is worth considering the stories told about the past and present terms used to name Liverpool and its population.

Naming the place: 'Liverpool'

Though there has been long-standing interest in tracing its origins and development, the name of the city of Liverpool has been shrouded in confusion.[2] The first recorded attempt to explain the name was rendered in Camden's *Britannia* – 'ubi Litherpoole floret, Saxonicè Lyferpole, vulgò Lirpoole, a diffusa paludis in modum aqua, vt opinio est, nominatus' (Camden 1590: 614) – which Holland translated as 'where *Litherpoole*, called in the elder ages Lifer-pole, commonly *Lirpoole*, is seated, so named, as it is thought, of the water spreading itselfe in maner of a Poole' (Holland 1610: 748). More than a century later, William Baxter's *Glossarium Antiquitatum Britannicarum* (1719) asserted confidently that 'hodiernum verò loco nomen Lither-pool est, sive *Pigra palus*' [the present name in truth is taken from the location – Lither-pool or *sluggish swamp*] (Baxter 1719: 213),[3] while another eighteenth-century effort to elucidate the name appeared in Enfield's *History of Leverpool* (1773), in which he noted the problem of orthographical instability:

> concerning the name in question, we find it spelt in ancient records and books in a great variety of ways. In Cambden's Britannia it is called *Litherpoole*; in Leland's Itinerary, *Lyrpole*, alias *Lyverpoole*; in Morery's Dictionary, *Lerpoole*, or *Leerpool*; in some ancient writings, *Livrepol*, *Lyverpol*, and *Leverpole*. (Enfield 1773: 2)

Despite this, however, and on the basis of an analysis of the original letters patent of King John (and Henry III's charter in 1229), and supported by a further text from 1524, Enfield claimed that the early forms were properly 'Leverpoole' or 'Leverpole'. Using documents in the Harleian collection in the British Museum, he went on to argue that by the Elizabethan period the established spelling was 'Leverpoole' (contracted to 'Lerpoole') and that

> the modern manner of spelling the name with an *i* in the first syllable, appears to be without sufficient foundation; and we may fairly conclude the original orthography of the name to have been *Leverpoole*; which, by dropping the final *e*, has been customary with respect to all English words, where it is not necessary to render the vowel long, makes *Leverpool*. (1773: 3)

Yet if Enfield thought that he had the evidence to ascertain the proper orthography, he was clear that the etymology of the name was uncertain:

> Some suppose that the former part of the name is derived from a bird which used to be found in this place, and was called the *Liver*; but this bird does not appear to have had any existence except in fabulous tradition and in the herald's office. Others imagine that it might have been taken from a seaweed, now known by the name of Liver in the West of England, or from a species of the *Hepatica*, vulgarly called Liverwort, often found on the sea coast: and others who favour the orthography above established, suppose that it might be derived from the *Lever* family, which is of ancient date in this county […] With respect to the latter part of the name, it seems generally agreed that it took its rise from a body of water formerly spread there like a pool. (1773: 3)

In his *Liverpool Guide* (1796), Moss agreed that 'pool' referred to the pool that 'wound round and extended the whole length of the old and high part of the town' and maintained that 'tradition says, that a singular bird, called a Liver, formerly frequented this pool; hence the place was called Liverpool; and the Liver, adopted as its Crest' (Moss 1796: 15). But in Troughton's *History of Liverpool* (1810), a more detailed view of the origins of the 'liver' bird was presented. Noting that the 'lever' bird was a common heraldic device among the Lancashire gentry, Troughton cited Holmes's *The Academie of Armorie* (1688), which referred to various attempts to identify the bird: 'denominated by Conradus Gessner, in Latin, Platea, which he conceives to be the Water Pelican, or Shoveller (Anglice); but in the Dutch it is called Lepler, or Lepelar, or Leefler; in the German, Lefler, or Lever; and it is supposed to be the Spoonbill of Mr Ray, and the Pelican of Onocrotalus' (Troughton 1810: 17). And on the basis of the representation of the bird on the borough seal, he argued somewhat sceptically that 'if such a bird really exists in nature', it is 'no other than the blue duck, which sometimes frequents our coast, and is also found in the river Ribble, known at present by the name of the *Blue Shoveller* (the *Anas Clypeata of Linnaeus*)' (1810: 17).[4]

As part of his account of the etymology of 'Liverpool', Troughton listed the historical variants of the name: Lyrpul, Litherpul, Ly'rpole, Lyverpool, Livrepol, Lyverpol and Liverpole, together with Lerpoole, Leerpool, Leverpole and Leverpool.[5] Yet unlike Moss, Troughton argued that the name had nothing to do with the 'liver' or 'lever' bird and cited in evidence a purported charter of Henry II in 1173 in which the town was described as a place 'quod homines de Lyrpul quondam vocant Litherpul' ('which the Lyrpul men call Litherpul').[6] On this basis, and his knowledge of 'the provincial dialect used in this part of Lancashire', Troughton concluded that in the original form of 'Litherpool'

> The word *lither* signifies *lower*, so that Lither-pool means simply the *lower pool.* Hence the name of the village of Litherland, or lower land; and of a passage, yet called Litherland Alley, in the neighborhood of Pool-lane, corroborates our assertion, that the foregoing is the original derivation of the name of the town. (Troughton 1810: 20)

Other commentators of the same period were not so sure. The anonymous *The Stranger in Liverpool* (1812) noted that on the topic of the etymology of 'Liverpool', 'little can be advanced with certainty' given the passage of time, 'the corruptness of provincial pronunciation, and the orthographical varieties in writing in different periods' (Anon 1812: 4). Nonetheless the author shared Troughton's scepticism towards the ornithological explanation, noting that even if the existence of the 'species of water-fowl' called the Liver bird were granted, 'that they were found in the pool in question in sufficient numbers to denominate it Liver's-pool, or Liverpool, (as some have contended,) is merely a hypothetical question' (Anon 1812: 4). Yet while Troughton's identification of 'Litherland' as the original form from which 'Liverpool' was derived was admitted as a possibility, the later text also raised the question of whether the best explanation was simply that the name was taken from the Lever family, 'which is certainly of great antiquity in this country' (Anon 1812: 6).

In an essay entitled 'On the Etymology of the Word *Liverpool*' in the *Gentleman's Magazine* (1817), W.R. Whatton argued against Camden's early account on the basis of linguistic evidence found in Lye's *Dictionarium Saxonico et Gothico-Latinum* (1772). Noting the declension of the Anglo-Saxon adjective 'lið, liða, liðe, tener, mollis, lenis' (soft or gentle, calm, slow or mild), his supposition was that by 'joining the adjective Liðe with the Saxon substantive word pol, or more properly pul, lacus, we have Liðepul, a still or quiet lake'. 'Nothing', he added, 'can be more beautiful or expressive than this simple term when applied to the harbour of Liverpool as it must have appeared during the Saxon æra, with its fenny banks, and quiet waters, as yet undisturbed by the busy hum of men' (Whatton 1817: 508). Whatton's conclusion, 'that Litherpul was the original epithet bestowed by the Anglo-Saxons, and it is from this that we derive our word Liverpool', was taken up in Edward Baines' *The History of the County Palatine and Duchy of Lancaster* (1836). In that text, Baines acknowledged that 'the name of this place has given rise to much discussion', though he rejected both 'the fanciful derivation from the heraldic bird called the Lever' and Camden's account of 'Lyferpole': 'as this name *Lyferpole* does not rest upon any Saxon authority, its correctness may be questioned. An ingenious derivation has been proposed, which will account for the more ancient orthography Litherpool; liðe pol, or the gentle lake, on which it is situated' (Baines 1836: 55).[7] Baines explained the shift from 'th' to 'v' in the name with the breezy comment that 'those who are conversant in the commutations of similarly formed letters in early times, know how easily the þ of the Saxons would give way to the Longobardic v' (1836: 58). And he gave even shorter shrift to the ornithological account of the name's origin by referring back to the image of the bird inscribed on the first corporation seal:

> The head of this bird seems to be the head of a dove; but the eagle of Tarbock has been mistaken for a dove, and recently for a green parrot. The eagle of the Stanley crest has the neck of a stork or goose. In deriving the name of the town from this imaginary bird, which was unknown long after the town had a common seal, we have a remarkable instance of […] putting the cart before the horse. (1836: 58)

This version was disputed in *The History of the Commerce and Town of Liverpool and of the Rise of Manufacturing Industry in the Adjoining Counties* (1852) by Thomas Baines (Edward's son), the most distinguished nineteenth-century contribution to the history of Liverpool. Noting that 'attempts hitherto made to explain the meaning of the first part of the word Liverpool have been very unsuccessful', Baines junior claimed that he did not intend to add to the list but simply to 'point out the one which seems to me to be the most probable'. Thus after reviewing a number of variants of the first element of 'Liverpool' from different historical sources, he asserted:

> I am inclined to think that the Lider and Liter of Domesday Book; the Liver of the reign of Richard the First, the Lither of Testa de Neville, and the Lithe of the

sheriff's accounts, are all originally the same word, and that they are derived, as has been suggested, from an old Gothic word Lide or Lithe, the Sea, or from some of the words formed from it, as Lid and Liter, a ship; Lithe, a fleet of ships; Lithesman, a seaman. (T. Baines 1852: 58)[8]

And so the controversy continued down the generations. In Picton's *Memorials of Liverpool* (1875) he commented that 'the name of Liverpool is even more enigmatical [...] and has hitherto baffled all investigators in endeavouring satisfactorily to account for its origin'. Noting that 'liver' was generally agreed to refer to the river or water of the area, and having dismissed the bird-based explanation, he nonetheless concluded that 'many conjectures and etymologies have been hazarded, but none has hitherto been found which meets with general acceptation' (Picton 1875: I, 17). This did not, however, prevent him from returning to the subject in 1884 in response to a query – 'Can anyone give me an account of the liver, the eponymous bird of Liverpool' – posted in the journal *Notes and Queries*. Picton's answer clarified the status of the 'liver' bird (and contradicted his earlier account) in that he pointed out that on the incorporation of Liverpool in 1222, a common seal was adopted featuring a bird with elevated wings and a sprig in its beak – the bird being the symbolic eagle of St John the Evangelist. At the end of the eighteenth century, however, application was made for the granting of a heraldic device for the town, the central element of which was described as: 'argent, a cormorant, in the beak a branch of seaweed called laver, all proper, and for the crest on a wreath of the colours a cormorant, the wings elevated, in the beak a branch of laver proper' (Picton 1884: 350).[9] Asserting that 'the *liver* was a foolish invention to account for the name' (based on the fact that if 'pool' referred to the water, then 'liver' must refer to the bird on the medieval common seal), Picton proposed the simple explanation that as the heraldic grant makes clear, 'the term *laver* is applied to the sprig' which the bird holds in its beak rather than to the bird itself (1884: 350).[10]

As the study of language entered the latter stages of its first scientific period towards the end of the nineteenth century, explanations of 'Liverpool' became more confident, if no less contentious. For example, in an article in *Notes and Queries* in 1896, one of the period's leading experts on English etymology and dialectology, W.W. Skeat, pronounced on the origin of 'Liverpool'. Noting that the term was still in doubt, Skeat observed that 'a great deal has been written on it, mostly of a very careless sort', but in support of Picton's account, he asserted that the key issue was why the spring in the heraldic arms was called a 'laver', since 'the answer to this question solves the whole enigma' (Skeat 1896: 173). His explanation lay with the Anglo-Saxon word 'læfer' (pronounced 'lavver'), given in Oswald Cockayne's *Leechdoms, Wortcunning, and Starcraft of Early England* (1886) as 'gladiolus' or 'bull-rush', and the related terms 'lĕver' or 'liver', defined in Britten and Holland's *English Plant-Names* (1866) as 'any sword-bladed plant' such as the iris, bur-reed or gladiolus. Skeat's conclusion was:

putting all this together, we see that the name liver was certainly applied to some kinds of the iris and the bulrush which grew in pools. When it appears that *liver*-pool, originally, meant more nor less than 'a pool in which livers grew,' meaning by liver some kind of water-flag or bulrush. And this is all! (Skeat 1896: 174)

The one thing 'liver' did not mean was a type of bird: 'all things considered, the liver, interpreted as "a bird," is a considerable myth'.

Perhaps predictably, Skeat's authoritative explanation turned out to be not quite definitive. In a later edition of *Notes and Queries*, Canon Taylor challenged Skeat's account on the basis that the 'pool' in 'Liverpool' referred to a body of sea-water (rather than fresh water), in which gladioli, bullrushes and so on would not have grown. His suggestion was that 'we have to discover the meaning of Lither-landt, which would determine the meaning of the later derived names of Litherpul and Liverpool' (Taylor 1896: 233). It was an objection that Skeat had pre-empted in private correspondence with Henry Harrison, author of *The Place-Names of the Liverpool District* (1898), in which Skeat admitted the possibility that 'Liverpool' was derived from 'lither-pool' – 'lither' being the common Old English word for 'bad', 'dirty' or 'disagreeable' which had passed into later usage (Shakespeare uses it to mean 'sluggish').[11] Harrison, however, found Skeat's explanation implausible since if 'lither' meant 'bad', and thus 'lither-pool' was 'bad pool', then what of 'Litherland'? Would that have to be rendered as 'bad land' (rather than the more plausible 'lower-land')? Harrison dismissed this possibility, as well as the idea that 'Liverpool' was a derivation from a 'hypothetical Celtic' root: '*Llyrpwll* (Welsh *llyr*, "brink," "shore," "sea")' and 'Cymric *pwll*' (Harrison 1898: 28–29).[12] Instead, he adopted another suggestion, also made in response to Skeat's *Notes and Queries* piece, formulated by H.A. Strong, Professor of Latin at Liverpool University (and translator of Hermann Paul's *Principles of the History of Language*). Strong's argument was that 'Liverpool' was indeed derived from 'Litherpool', and that this was

> like so many others in its vicinity, a Norse name, meaning, 'pool of the slope or brow,' O[ld] N[orse] *hliþ* = a slope; cf. Litherland, a suburb of Liverpool, near Crosby, and a numerous list of place-names similarly formed in Vigfusson's 'Dictionary'. The Norse word is connected with the Lat[in] *clivus*. (Strong 1896: 233)

As part of a fuller explanation, Harrison noted that the genitive singular of Old Norse *hlíth* is *hlíthar* and thus,

> In Old Norse we find *hlíthar-brún*, 'the edge of a slope,' *hlíthar-fótr*, 'the foot of the slope,' so that there would not be too much difficulty about *hlíthar-land*, 'the land of the slope' or 'the slope land,' and *hlíthar-pollr*, 'the pool of the slope' [...] It is scarcely necessary to point out that the Norse element in the vicinity of Liverpool was very strong; and the appropriation of creeks and sea-pools, and of land adjacent to the coast, was a well-known characteristic of the ancient Norwegians and Danes, as indeed, the name *Vik*-ing implies. (Harrison 1898: 30)[13]

Addressing the question of why the 'th' of 'Litherland' transitioned to the 'v' of 'Liverpool', Harrison cites language contact (though he doesn't use the expression): Litherland was 'a remote and secluded village', whereas Liverpool was a seaport that was increasingly 'subject to extraneous and distracting influences' and thus the influence of various forms of language (Harrison 1898: 31).

It was an ingenious account, but twentieth-century scholarship rejected it. In Wyld and Oakes Hirst's *The Place Names of Lancashire* (1911), 'Liver' was explained as a derivation of the Old English personal name 'Lēōfhere', and so 'Liverpool' meant 'Lēōfhere's pool' (compare 'Otterspool' from 'the pool of Ohthere' – rather than the commonly supposed pool of the otters). Harrison's suggestion was relegated to the status of an exercise in folk-etymology, an example of the tendency 'to alter [an apparently meaningless form] to something else which does mean something'. Thus, in face of the seemingly inexplicable 'Lēōfhere's pool', Wyld and Oakes Hirst claimed, 'people said "What, Liverpul? What does that mean? It must be Litherpul, of course, the pool by the slope, like Litherland, a few miles down the river"' (1911: 179–80). But scepticism towards this version was expressed by Ekwall in another text also, and somewhat confusingly, entitled *The Place-Names of Lancashire*, published in 1922. Rejecting the thesis of Wyld and Oakes Hirst on phonological and morphological grounds, Ekwall argued instead that 'Liver- is to be compared with O[ld] E[nglish] *lifrig* (in *lifrig blod*), M[iddle] E[nglish] *livered*, "coagulated, clotted."' Citing the *OED*, he noted the use of 'liver-sea' (1600) 'an imaginary sea in which the water is "livered" or "thick"' and concluded that '*Liverpul* may mean "the pool with the thick water"'.[14] Unfortunately, however, Ekwall rather undermined the argument by adding as a side-note that '*Liver* may have been the name of one of the streams that fell into the pool' (Ekwall 1922: 117).

Ekwall's version is but the latest to join the list of contending etymological accounts about 'Liverpool'. What then is the explanation? Is the Liver Bird a pelican, a spoonbill or a duck? Was 'Liver' originally 'Lever'? And did it refer to the Lever family? Was 'Liver' the name of a type of sea-weed, or plant (hepatica)? Or an altered form of 'lither', meaning lower (or perhaps bad, sluggish, or even slope)? Was the name actually 'Liðepul', hence a still or quiet lake? Or did it derive from the Gothic 'lide' – sea? Was 'Liver' properly 'laver' – a sprig, from the Anglo-Saxon 'læfer', a bladed plant? Was the origin Celtic – from the Welsh 'Llyrpwll', pool on the sea? Is 'Liver' a corruption of the name of a person, 'Lēōfhere'? But then who was Lēōfhere and why was the pool named after him? Did 'liver' mean thick or clotted as Baxter had speculated in the eighteenth century and Skeat had scientifically pronounced in the nineteenth? The short (and long) answer to these questions is that we don't know. The *OED* notes simply that the phonology of 'Liverpool' is 'difficult to explain' and the etymological origin is 'uncertain'. As for 'Liver Bird', it was nothing more than 'a name arbitrarily given to the bird (heraldically identified as a cormorant) represented in the arms of the City of Liverpool'. The *OED* explanation, apparently based on Picton's account in his *Memorials of Liverpool* (1875), cited above, gives the origin thus:

> A 14th-cent. seal from Liverpool shows a bird apparently intended to represent an eagle (symbolizing St. John the Evangelist). Legend has it that poor draughtsmanship led to the bird being variously identified as (amongst others) a spoonbill, a

glossy ibis, and a pelican. Since the late 18th cent. the bird represented on modern grants of arms, etc., has been identified with the cormorant.

In other words, somewhat ignominiously, the most authoritative source on the English language has it that the Liver Bird was a badly drawn eagle that morphed into a bird often known as the common shag.

Naming the natives (i): 'Liverpolitans', 'Liverpudlians' and 'Dicky Sam'

Of course the etymological mystery surrounding 'Liverpool' (even the *OED* account says 'legend has it') may simply be one of those puzzles that the history of language presents. There are after all many words whose origin is simply unclear. And yet it is interesting to note that a similar obscurity affects a number of important terms in the Liverpool lexicon. Another example is the set of words used to denote the inhabitants of the city, of which the most straightforward are 'Liverpolitan' and 'Liverpudlian', though there were other possibilities at earlier points in history. For example the highly contentious election in the town in 1670 produced 'Liverpoldon' (used by Sir Gilbert Ireland, the sitting MP) and 'Leeirpooltonians' (in the phrase, 'those infidell Leeirpooltonians', deployed by Roger Bradshaigh, an unsuccessful candidate).[15] In 1788 the novelist and letter-writer Catherine Hutton commented: 'the general observations I have been enabled to make on the Lancastrians are that the Boltoners are sincere, good-humoured, and noisy; the Manchestrians reserved and purse-proud; the Liverpoolians free and open as the ocean on which they get their riches' (Hutton 1891: 57). For better or worse, 'Liverpoldon', 'Leeirpooltonian' and 'Liverpoolians' never caught on. But 'Liverpolitan' was used as a slightly formal term throughout the nineteenth century, and was possibly formed by analogy with 'metropolitan' (from the Greek roots μᾱτέρ-, μάτηρ 'mother' and πόλις, 'city') to give a classical-sounding adjective befitting the constant comparisons between the city and its ancient forbear of Tyre (the 'Venice of the North' was the other common nineteenth-century analogy). Strikingly, however, the term is not recognized at all in the *OED*, a fact that is all the more surprising given the use of the term throughout Chandler's monumental mid-twentieth-century history of Liverpool, as for example when he asks: 'is it not a political example for all the world that the descendants of the Normans, Anglo-Saxons, Irish, Welsh, Scots and Vikings who have peopled Liverpool are now united in a common pride in being Liverpolitans?' (Chandler 1957: 9). 'Liverpudlian', on the other hand, despite the fact that it is described by the dictionary as possibly derived by 'jocular substitution of *puddle* for pool', fares slightly better in terms of textual support.[16] An anonymous satirical short story entitled 'A Trip to Paris with Mr. Jorrocks' (by a 'Yorkshireman') in the *New Sporting Magazine* (1833) provides the earliest record: 'and he stalked into the hotel with all the dignity becoming a compatriot of Wellington's, and one of that nation whose firmness and perseverance had humbled France, as Mr. Canning said to the Liverpudlians' (Anon 1833: 40). And the term was often deployed as a pseudonym when writing to journals or newspapers, as in a letter to the *Liverpool Mercury* in 1845 complaining about the punctuality of the trains between Liverpool and Manchester signed by 'A Liverpudlian' (Anon 1845: 7). Its use as a noun was clearly established by the mid century – a rather barbed example being a comment by Arthur Hugh Clough that somewhat belied his status as a native son of the city. Writing from Liverpool to Thomas Arnold in 1849, Clough opined that 'I like the Manchester people, of whom I have been seeing a little, better than the Liverpudlians. They are more provincial perhaps, but have more character; are less men of the world, but more men of themselves' (Clough 1888: 143). It is also evident, however, that 'Liverpudlian' was used adjectivally in the mid nineteenth century. In the notices for 'the amusements at Liverpool' in the *Era* newspaper in 1854, the writer observed that 'the recent performances of the French company have proved beyond the bounds of Liverpudlian comprehension [...] their very excellence has produced the strange fit of absence that has kept Dicky-Sam out of doors during the brief visit of his too clever allies' (Anon 1854: 11).[17]

The debate over these rival terms continued in the twentieth century. A letter to 'Postman' requested the 'correct form' of the 'term given to an inhabitant of Liverpool'. The verdict was:

> Liverpudlian means an inhabitant of the pool of Liver, which, of course, is Liverpool. Liverpolitan, on the other hand, means an inhabitant of the city of Liver, or Liverpolis, which does not exist. Whether euphemistically or not, therefore, Liverpool people are Liverpudlians. ('Postman' 1950: 4)

This definition was, however, superseded by Frank Shaw's use of the terms to differentiate between different categories of Liverpool's population along class lines.[18] Yet in point of fact, neither 'Liverpolitan' nor 'Liverpudlian' was the most popular usage to refer to the citizens of Liverpool in the nineteenth century. The term in common use was 'Dicky Sam', a phrase defined by Picton when referring to himself as 'a Liverpool man, or Dicky Sam, as we love to call our native-born inhabitants' (Picton 1888: 210).[19] Early uses of the term indicate that, like 'A Liverpudlian', it was used frequently as a journalistic pen-name. A letter of complaint to the *Liverpool Mercury* in 1820 for example (about obstructions around St George's market) was signed 'A Dicky Sam', while 'Dicky Sam' also took responsibility for 'A Conundrum' in the *Liverpool Mercury* in 1827:

Said Dick to Will, who lov'd a pun,
'Why is the Duke of Wellington
Like somebody standing on one leg?
Come, give an answer soon, I beg.'
'It is,' cried Will, with all submission,
'Because he's in the HOP POSITION!'*
*Opposition (Anon 1827: 302)

The pseudonymous practice continued till late in the century, as in the important treatise *Liverpool and Slavery: An Historical Account of the Liverpool-African*

Slave Trade, By a Genuine 'Dicky Sam' (1884).[20] Like 'Liverpudlian', then, it is clear that 'Dicky Sam' was well established by the mid nineteenth century. *Punch*, for example, used the term as an adjective as well as a noun in an article that reported the response of the *Liverpool Mercury* to a reader's query as to the meaning of the letters SPQR on the doors of St George's Hall. The answer given by the *Mercury* was that the letters stood for *'salus populi qui Romanum* – the welfare of the people of Rome' (instead of the historically accurate 'Senatus Populusque Romanus' – 'the Roman Senate and People'), which prompted *Punch* to deride 'Dickey-Sam Latin' and to argue sarcastically that the translator should be employed by the Classical Dictionary, since 'so profound a scholar should not be lost among the Dickey-Sams' (*Punch* 1864: 186).[21]

The evidence suggests that 'Dicky Sam' entered the language in the late eighteenth or early nineteenth century, but its coinage was and remains something of an enigma. In 1821 a query to *The Kaleidoscope; or, Literary and Scientific Mirror* (possibly the first easily available weekly miscellany in Britain, published by the Liverpool Liberal Egerton Smith) asked about the origin of the term and was met with an editorial admission of ignorance and appeal for information:

> D.S. [Dicky Sam] is informed, that we are not sufficiently skilled in Etymological Antiquity, to explain to him the derivation of the term DICKY SAM, as applied to the good people of Liverpool, of which we are proud to rank amongst the natives, although we should thereby be comprehended amongst the DICKY SAM tribe. If any of our readers can throw any light upon this singular appellative, we shall be obliged; although the explanation may probably be as little satisfactory and as whimsical as that of the term COCKNEY. (Anon 1821: 96)

There seems to have been no response to the request but in 1855 the question was taken up again in a note to *Notes and Queries*: "'*Dickey Sam*". Whence this expression as applied to the inhabitants of the great commercial port of Liverpool?' (W.T.M. 1855: 226). And a month or so after the satirical *Punch* piece appeared in November 1864, another query appeared in *Notes and Queries* asking: 'LIVERPOOL.—What is the origin and meaning of the motto of the town of Liverpool—the Great Pool? and why is the name Dicky Sam applied to a Liverpool man?' (M 1864: 473). For over a decade no answer was the firm reply to both questions, which prompted the original correspondent (W.T.M. of Hong Kong) to make his own suggestion:

> DICKEY SAM… More than a dozen years having passed since I queried in your pages this name for a Liverpool man, and no reply having been offered, I venture to suggest that it is an easy and natural corruption, or rather contraction of διχασάμευος, – *divided into two parts, or set at variance,* – in allusion to the political contests between Whig and Tory, Liberal and Conservative, that have so often agitated the town. Liverpool was famous for its party contests, and its inhabitants may well have been said to be διχασάμενοι (participle, 1st aorist, med. voc. διχάζω). (W.T.M. 1868a: 493)

This was somewhat sniffily dismissed by T. Austin Junior as 'very far-fetched' and grammatically mistaken on the grounds that the etymology 'used the aorist middle διχασάμενος in a passive sense!' (Austin 1868: 546). To which came an even sniffier reply from W.T.M. that admitted the error, noted that the correction strengthened the case (διχασάμενοι 'having divided themselves into two parts'), and in view of the other 'wild plunges' into etymology on the part of correspondents, asserted the right 'to look to the Greek for the fancied origin of a slang term' (W.T.M. 1868b: 570). Picton later noted, slightly drily, that 'it must materially increase our admiration for the attainments of young Liverpool, to be assured that even its nicknames were derived from classical sources' (Picton 1875: II, 101).

The origin of 'Dicky Sam', then, was the subject of much speculation in the period but it remained (and remains) unclear. The evidential quotation in the *OED* cites a reference in the *Athenaeum* (1870), but the quotation is somewhat incomplete ('we cannot even guess why a Liverpool man is called a Dickey Sam'). The full citation (from a report on a meeting of the British Association for the Advancement of Science in Liverpool) is slightly more revealing, in that it suggests that the origin of the term might lie in a type of criminal argot current in the late eighteenth century. Referring to the disorderly activities of groups of men frightening women in the streets in the late eighteenth century (an observation first made in Troughton's *History*), the journal noted that 'from men and manners of this quality has sprung a slang which would fill a dictionary of its own. We do not profess any intimate acquaintance with it; we cannot even guess why a Liverpool man is called a *Dickey-Sam*' (Anon 1870: 328). A confident answer to the problem appeared in the *Proceedings of the Liverpool Literary and Philosophical Society* in 1871. Noting that 'a writer in the *Athenaeum* recently expressed surprise that the name of Dicky Sam should be retained', and that 'he, like many others, seems at a loss to explain its significance', Joseph Boult offered to clear the matter up:

> On a former occasion I suggested an A.-S. origin, namely *dic*, a dike or ditch, and *samnung*, an assembly; but these words apparently are derived from the Celts, with whom *dig*, genitive *dighe*, signified a pit, a dike, a ditch; and *samhadh* men, people; these two words then, *dighe samhadh*, signifying the people of the fens, would soon pass through Dicky Sammy into Dicky Sam, especially as the aspirated d is mute. The Celts appear to have been a people partial to equivocal language, such as admitted of a play, closely resembling that object of Dr. Johnson's aversion, a pun; and I suspect that the name Dicky Sam is an illustration. *Samh* signifies as a substantive rest, ease; as an adjective pleasant, still, calm; *Samachan* denoted a soft quiet person; the similarity of the meanings of this word with those of the English word *soft* and its congeners, leads me to suppose that in its uncomplimentary sense, Dicky Sam was equivalent to softy, or 'sawfty,' to give it the true Lancashire breadth of sound; to this day the word Sammy is still used in an uncomplimentary sense. (Boult 1871: 37)[22]

Other accounts moved away from such bold etymologizing in favour of more a localized derivation. Picton noted that 'Dicky Sam' was 'the local appellation for one born within the sounds of the parish bells' (of the church of Our Lady and St Nicholas) (Picton 1875: II, 1).[23] And this account clearly owes something to the popular derivation of the term 'Cockney', which first appeared in the early seventeenth century (as in the comment of Fynes Moryson, colonialist and English adventurer, in his *Itinerary* [1617]: 'Londiners, and all within the sound of Bow-Bell, are in reproch called Cocknies, and eaters of buttered tostes' [Moryson 1908: 463]).[24] Picton's own explanation was that the phrase 'originated from [the natives'] familiar style of addressing each other as Bill, and Tom, Jack, Dicky, and Sam, which to southern ears sounded somewhat uncouth' (Picton 1875: II, 101). This possibility was considered 'doubtful or far-fetched' by another correspondent to *Notes and Queries* (though he or she admits the Liverpudlian 'habit of abbreviating all Christian names'), and was rejected in favour of an explanation that was evidently considered more plausible:

> just as a 'dickey' is a substitute (or make-believe over a dirty one) for a clean shirt front, so the Liverpudlian, from his close business and social associations with our friends over the water, has, in many of his ways and much of his talk, become semi-Americanized, or, in other words, become a 'Dickey' (make-believe, second-hand, or counterfeit) 'Uncle Sam'. (Hackwood 1889: 332)[25]

In the same vein, though much later, Belchem asserted that the term 'hints at the growing import of American influences in the town' (Belchem 2000b: 34). The basis for this claim is unclear, since there is no record of 'Sam' in any American connection with Liverpool in any of the editions of Webster's dictionary until the heavily revised 1884 version, in which 'Dicky Sam' is defined as 'a cant name applied to the inhabitants of Liverpool'.[26] Moreover Frank Shaw, who noted that 'Dicky Sam' was still used in his childhood in the early twentieth century, rejected the idea that it meant 'a Little Yank (citizen of US)' on the basis of '"dicky" being an old slang, indeed dialect, word for "small"' (Shaw 1971: 21).[27]

The *OED*, somewhat elliptically, proposes that the term may be a corruption of 'Dick O'Sam's, an example of the Lancashire form of patronymic'. This possibility is at least partly supported by the inclusion of 'Dickey Sam' in the third edition of Hotten's *Slang Dictionary* (1869), in which it is identified as a colloquialism in Lancashire dialect. Partridge's *Dictionary of Slang and Unconventional English*, however, renders 'Sam' as pre-dating 'Dicky Sam' as the term for a Liverpudlian (from around 1840), though there is no corroboration for the claim. The same text derives 'Sam' from 'Sammy', meaning 'a fool', from the 1830s, a usage confirmed in the *English Dialect Dictionary* and the *OED* – although the term 'sam' in the sense of 'foolish empty fellow' was recorded in Potter's *New Dictionary of all the Cant and Flash Languages* in 1795.[28] 'Dicky' too has a variety of possible meanings. The *OED* gives the nominal sense of naval officer, whereas Green's *Dictionary of Slang* (2010) has 'a dandy or swell' and, perhaps relatedly, 'smart, fashionable' when used as an adjective. But in contrast, James Hardy Vaux's *New and Comprehensive Vocabulary of the Flash Slang* suggests 'very bad or paltry; anything of an inferior quality' (Vaux 1819: 166). There was also a verbal sense – to mess or fool around (now usually in the form 'to dick around'), nicely illustrated by a response in the *Era* to 'Dicky Sam', a correspondent: 'DICKY SAM is anything but a Sammy, though he would play Dicky with us were we to follow ALL his suggestions' (Anon 1841: 164).[29] How then did 'Dicky Sam' originate, and what did it mean? Was it the Liverpudlian equivalent of 'Cockney'? A misconstrual of the Greek διχασάμενοι (having divided into two)? A derivation of the 'Celtic' *dighe samhadh* (people of the fens)? Or a term meaning an American wannabe? It may be that the phrase started as an insult – 'Dicky Sam' meaning a foolish dandy or swell; perhaps it was a Lancastrian slur directed towards the inhabitants of the big city. The truth is, however, that though the stories are interesting in themselves, none of the explanations establish definitively why or how people from Liverpool became known by this epithet, nor indeed why it stopped being applied to them.

Naming the natives (ii): 'Whacker,' 'Scouse' and 'Scouser'

Even though it was used as the title of a TV series in the 1970s that featured a Liverpool family, little is known of the more modern term 'whacker' – also 'wacker', or, in its shortened form, 'wack' – common names for Liverpool people until the 1960s. In *Liverpool in the 1930s and the Blitz*, Ron Garnett describes how the term was used in contradistinction to 'scouse' in the 1920s and 30s: 'scouse' was 'a generic term applied to Liverpool seamen or members of H.M. forces. Whacker is used mainly as a form of greeting between fellow scousers' (Garnett 1995: 124). Evidence to support his claim is found in a biography of Tommy Handley (born in the Dingle and the first Liverpool comedian to achieve national pop cultural fame). Visiting a naval station during the Second World War, Handley found that a number of sailors hailed from Liverpool: '"Hey, Whacker!" they said as he passed. No other introduction was needed' (Kavanagh 1949: 179). The point was reinforced by Richard Whittington-Egan in his 1955 essay, 'Is Liverpool Dialect Dying Out?', when he asserted that Deryck Guyler's character in Handley's *ITMA*, Frisby Dyke, was 'the Liverpool whacker who brought us some much needed laughter' during the war. He also notes that '"Ello, la" and "Aago, whack?"' are greetings 'familiar to all' Liverpudlians (Whittington-Egan 1955c: 216, 220). As to the origin of the phrase, however, the situation is again somewhat opaque. The *OED* declares simply that 'wacker', when referring to a Liverpudlian, belongs to 'Liverpool dialect' and that its origin is unknown. The dictionary account includes one reference to 'wacker' in the eighteenth century and two modern citations to works dating from the 1960s and 70s. The related term 'wack' ('a familiar term of address; "pal", "mate"'), gained four citations from the 1960s and 70s; one to the Beatles, one each to Fritz Spiegl and Peter Moloney (both important figures in the Scouse industry, as noted earlier), and one to music journalism.[30] As the dictionary makes clear, suggestions as to the derivation of these terms are no more than speculative. Whittington-Egan claimed that 'whacker' derives from 'the fact that you share or whack out things with your friend or partner' (Whittington-Egan 1955c: 220), a sense that Belchem identifies with army slang (Belchem 2000b: 35). But the origin is more likely to have been criminal slang, as attested in Vaux's *New and Comprehensive Vocabulary of the Flash Slang*, in which he gives a nominal and verbal use of the word: 'WACK, to divide or share anything equally, as *wack the blunt*, share the money, &c' and 'WACK, a share or equal proportion, as give me my *wack*, that is, my due part' (Vaux 1819: 223).

In the first volume of the *Lern Yerself Scouse* series, 'How To Talk Proper in Liverpool', Spiegl proposed that 'wack' might originate with 'pea-wack', which he glossed as 'pea soup'. And this is a possibility confirmed in *Green's Dictionary of Slang*, in which 'whack' is given as Anglo-Irish or Scottish 'food, sustenance'. More significantly, Spiegl indirectly suggests a possible alternative, which is perhaps the most plausible, though he doesn't follow it through. Citing *The Sailor's Farewell; Or, The Guinea Outfit* (1768), the comedy set, published and performed in Liverpool that was discussed in chapter two, Spiegl drew attention to the use of 'wacker' by Bob Bluff, the clown who is recruited by the mate. Rehearsing the benefits of joining a slaver (as noted earlier, crews were hard to find given the atrocious conditions on slave ships both for the crew and the human cargo), the mate alludes to the opportunities for sexual predation: 'nothing to do there, but to lay your head on the knee of a delicate soft wench, while she plays with your hair'. Bluff in turn asks what sort of a place Guinea is, since, he says,

> I've heard folks say, it's wickeder place than Lunnen, and that every Blackamoor has as many wives as he pleases; nay I was toud for certain, that th' king o'th blacks had as mony wenches as wou'd stond I'th cumpus of seven acres a graund; and if it be true, he must be a wacker e'cod. (Boulton 1768: 31)[31]

Another text, published not long after Boulton's play, Francis Grose's *Classical Dictionary of the Vulgar Tongue* (1785) gives 'whack' as 'a share of a booty obtained by fraud' – the sense confirmed by Vaux. More interestingly, however, Grose also suggests that 'whack' is short for 'a paddy whack, a stout brawny Irishman' (Grose 1785: n.p.). The sense of 'paddywhack' as a derogatory term for an Irishman developed over the nineteenth century, but at least in Bluff's use, 'wacker' has a more approbatory connotation – the black king as an epitome of masculinity. It may therefore be the case that the two different eighteenth-century meanings combined in the twentieth-century Liverpudlian 'w(h)acker': a friend or partner with whom things are shared and a strong man ('w(h)acker' is clearly gendered) of Irish descent.[32]

The established etymological account of 'scouse' and 'scouser' also raises problematic questions. The origin of these terms lies with 'lobscouse', a word categorized by the *OED* as nautical and dialectal and defined as 'a sailor's dish consisting of meat stewed with vegetables and ship's biscuit, or the like'. The first citation refers to Ned Ward's satire on the English navy, *The Wooden World Dissected* (1708), specifically his treatment of the 'sea-cook': 'He has sent the Fellow a thousand times to the Devil, that first invented Lobscouse; but, for that Lewd way of wasting Grease, he had grown as fat in Purse, as a *Portsmouth* alderman, and made his Son seven Years ago, a down-right Gentleman' (Ward 1708: 83). The word was evidently current in the eighteenth century, since it also appears in a poem that depicts the forbearance of sailors through an allusion to the poverty of the dish: 'Some are rolling in riches, some's not worth a souse/

Today we eat beef, and tomorrow lob's scouse' (Dibdin 1781: 194). The origin of the term 'lobscouse', however, is not quite clear. The *OED* notes that the root is obscure, although it draws a comparison with 'loblolly' – 'thick gruel or spoon-meat, freq. referred to as a rustic or nautical dish or simple medicinal remedy; burgoo'. This use was first recorded in the late sixteenth century, though the word (or one of the forms of the word) appears in Robert Burton's *Anatomy of Melancholy* (1621) in a plaintive series of contrasts voiced by a malcontent: 'there is a difference, (he grumbles) between laplolly and pheasants, to tumble i'th' straw and lye in a down bed, betwixt wine and water, a cottage and a palace' (Burton 1806: 30). The *OED*'s suggested etymology for 'loblolly' is 'perhaps onomatopoeic: compare the dialectal *lob* "to bubble while in process of boiling, said esp. of porridge", also "to eat or drink up noisily" (*Eng. Dial. Dict.*), *lolly* (obsolete Devon), "broth, soup, or other food boiled in a pot" (*Eng. Dial. Dict.*).' But this seems unconvincing, not least in view of the fact that the *English Dialect Dictionary* references are either unreferenced or from the nineteenth century, and in any case the account does not explain 'lobscouse'. A description of a wedding supper in Smollett's *Adventures of Peregrine Pickle* (1751) suggests another possibility: 'This genial banquet was entirely composed of sea-dishes; a huge pillaw, consisting of a large piece of beef sliced, a couple of fowls, and half a peck of rice, smoked in the middle of the board: a dish of hard fish, swimming in oil, appeared at each end; the sides being furnished with a mess of that savoury composition known by the name of lob's-course, and a plate of salmagundy' (Smollett 1758: I, 66). In this example, 'lobscouse' appears to be a corruption of 'lob's course', an explanation followed by Dwight Whitney's great American *Century Dictionary* (from which the *OED* borrowed extensively): 'lobscouse (lob'skous), *n.* [Also *lobscourse*, *lapscourse* (the form *lobscourse* simulating *lob's course*, 'a lubber's dish'); prob. < *lob*, + *scouse*, a general name on shipboard for a stew. Cf. *Loblolly*, 2.] A dish made of pilot-biscuit, stewed in water with pieces of salt meat.' If 'lob's course' were the derivation, then the term would mean a meal served to a 'lob' – a sixteenth-century coinage meaning 'clumsy fellow, country bumpkin, clown or lout' (of which the nautical version was 'lubber' – hence the sailor's contemptuous word for a landsman, 'landlubber'). In which case the fact that a series of related terms for this type of stew exist in modern Norwegian – 'lapskaus', Swedish – 'lapskojs', Danish – 'skipperlabskovs', Dutch – 'lapskous' and German – 'labskaus' (the dish is a contemporary speciality in the northern ports of Bremen, Lübeck and Hamburg) suggests that the dish may have originated in England and spread through maritime trade with northern Europe.[33] In return for which the Teutonic languages provided the phonological alteration from [ɔ:] to [au]. Such an account seems to be supported by two *OED* references. James Fenimore Cooper's *The Pioneers* (1823) has: 'he acquired the art of making chowder, lobskous, and... other sea-dishes', while W.H. Smyth's *Sailor's Word Book* (1867) defines 'Lap's Course' as 'one of the oldest and most savoury of the regular forecastle dishes' (and cross-references it to 'Lobs-Scouse'). Further evidence appears in Kluge's *Etymologisches Wörterbuch der Deutschen Sprache* (1883), which notes that 'labskaus' first appears in German in a dictionary for seafarers published in 1878 and speculates that it was taken from low German as a borrowing from English.[34]

Given the commonality of the ingredients (various types of poor-quality meat, potatoes and vegetables), and the historical and geographical provenance of the usage, it seems likely that 'lobscouse' referred to a nautical dish eaten by seafarers that was spread through cultural contact along the northern seaboards.[35] 'Lobscouse', then, may just have been the term for a poor-quality stew that British sailors would have eaten along with their counterparts and that was established in the major ports. But then why would the terms 'scouse' and 'scouser' become attached to Liverpool in particular? Again, the answer is unknown, though it is perhaps significant that there was an established maritime trade between Liverpool and the North Sea, North Atlantic and Baltic ports in the eighteenth century. For as noted in chapter one, Defoe remarked on the fact that Liverpool sent ships 'to Norway, to Hamburg, and to the Baltick' (Defoe 2005: 541); while Troughton's figures for the mid to late eighteenth century show that the Nordic trade came third (behind the Irish and Atlantic operations) in terms of numbers of ships and tonnage (Troughton 1810: 261–66). It is therefore certainly not inconceivable that 'lobscouse' was standard fare on the northern voyages and that for unknown reasons the name of this stew became associated with ships that sailed to and from Liverpool and thus with those who sailed on them. But if this were the case, then it might be expected that 'lobscouse', or indeed the elided form 'scouse', would have been recorded in some form or another in Liverpool in this period. Yet 'scouse' is currently dated as emerging only in the mid nineteenth century; the *OED* cites Richard Henry Dana's *Two Years Before the Mast* (1840) in which he refers to a mealtime on a ship when 'the cook had just made for us a mess of hot "scouse," – that is, biscuit pounded fine, salt beef cut into small pieces, and a few potatoes, boiled up together and seasoned with pepper. This was a rare treat…' (Dana 1869: 34). This dating, however, is in need of revision. Belchem reports a slightly earlier use than that given in the *OED* in a volume of correspondence between the Poor Law Commissioners and the Liverpool Poor Law Union in 1837 in which a reference is made to 'Meat Scouse' (Belchem 2000b: 36). But there is clear evidence that the term was in common use considerably earlier – certainly by the last decades of the eighteenth century. For example in Sir Frederic Morton Eden's *The State of the Poor: or, an History of the Labouring Classes in England, From the Conquest to the Present Period* (1797), he cited a parochial report of the early 1790s that listed the expenditure on food per week in the Liverpool poorhouse. It included: 'Beef, 101 lbs. for scouse'; '14 Measures potatoes for scouse' (420 lbs); and 'Onions for ditto' (28 lbs) (Eden 1797: 336). Further evidence for this early use of the abbreviated form is found in an account of conditions in the new prison at Kirkdale in the *Liverpool Mercury* (7 May 1824), which reported that 'the prison diet, though not over-abundant, is wholesome, and, on the whole, appears sufficient to prevent a decay of health. It consists, principally, of oatmeal porridge, scouse, herrings, and bread' (Anon 1824: 358).

It is evident, then, that 'scouse' as a term used to refer to food was current in Liverpool by the last decades of the eighteenth century, and it is certainly clear that the form was in common use by the end of the nineteenth century.[36] One effect of this development was the spread of the both 'lobscouse' and 'scouse' into American English, as evinced by a number of literary maritime references. Thus a short story in *The Southern Literary Messenger* (1843) features a sea captain's reminiscences in which he recalls weather so bad that 'I did not taste a mouthful of food for twenty-four hours—when at last the wind lulled, and down below went I, and such another meal as I made on 'scouse. I remember, too, being once very sick on shore, and I could think of nothing that I fancied but lobscouse' (Milward 1843: 40). Charles Nordhoff's *The Merchant Vessel: A Sailor Boy's Voyages to See the World* (1856) confirms the usage:

> *Lobscouse* is the sea name for a species of hash or stew, made of potatoes, bread, onions, and chopped salt beef. It is a savory mess for hungry tars, and forms a standard dish for breakfast on board all *good* ships. The *scouse*, the beef, and bread, being duly arranged on the forecastle deck, each one helped himself to what he pleased, sitting on his chest, with the pot of coffee, and his tin pan beside him. (Nordhoff 1856: 21)

The appearance of the term in American English is unsurprising. Just as Liverpool's sea trade may have brought 'lobscouse' and 'scouse' to northern Europe, it is probable that Liverpool's maritime connection with the United States was the route by which the words were exported across the Atlantic.

Yet although this account may establish a history of 'scouse' in the sense of the dish, the history of the transferred senses of both 'lobscouse' and 'scouse' is more complicated and difficult to trace. The fifth edition of Eric Partridge's *Dictionary of Slang and Unconventional English* (1961) recorded 'lobscouser' as general for 'sailor' or 'tar' in 1884 (and marked the form as 'known to exist then and presumably some years earlier'). Unfortunately, however, the use was unreferenced, although the term is found in *Marooned*, a novel by William Clark Russell, the popular American writer of the sea: 'The others were plain ginger-haired British lobscousers – one with a beard of stubble that projected from his chin like the thatch of a sou'-wester, both knob-nosed and rugged as the shell of a walnut' (Russell 1889: 80). But 'Scouseland', with the meaning of Liverpool, is given in Partridge's *Dictionary* as 'nautical and (Liverpool) dockers" usage of the late nineteenth and early twentieth century, although again Partridge cites no evidence to sustain the claim. Likewise, there is no reference to buttress Partridge's assertion that the use of 'scouse' or 'scouser' to describe 'a native of Liverpool' dates from the late nineteenth century and early twentieth century. There is, however, some evidence that the term was used as a nickname (or at least a pet-name): a case before the Liverpool Police Court in 1890 for animal cruelty reported that a local man had set a dog on a cat with the shout 'Go on, Scouse, and finish it' (Anon 1890: 8). But a letter to the *Daily Post*, 'Why Scouser?', from a correspondent who was born in Liverpool in 1879 and left to live in the south of England in 1913, appears to date the appearance of 'scouser' as during or after the First World War. It was 'not until years after [1913]', R.H. Bindloss asserted, 'that I heard the unlovely term "Scouser" used, and I feel fairly certain it was a wartime affectionate mark of disrespect that crept into circulation via the Army'.[37] Moreover, he added, 'in my boyhood, and my father used to say it was the same in his youth, a Liverpool man, or boy, was invariably referred to as a "Dicky Sam"' (Bindloss 1957: 6). The editorial response agreed that whenever it was that 'scouser' originated, 'it seems to have crept into general use, in the Scotland Road area of Liverpool after the First World War', a claim that seems to be supported by Garnett's point (cited earlier), referring to the 1920s and 30s, that 'scouse' was 'a generic term applied to Liverpool seamen or members of H.M. forces'.[38] Further evidence for this general dating appears in John Kerr's assertion that 'the word "wacker" was little used until it was popularized with the word "Scouser" on the radio in the late thirties' (Kerr 1966: 6), and in Shaw's claim that 'Scouser' was 'a name not used in my youth [...] when Dicky Sam was the nickname' (Shaw 1971: 20).[39] Yet if the sense of 'scouser' and 'scouse' to refer to Liverpool people is only datable within a rough period, the most striking thing about the use of 'Scouse' to refer to the language of Liverpool is how recently this sense was coined. For as previous chapters have demonstrated, this sense of 'Scouse' is no more than sixty or so years old.[40]

As with 'Liverpolitans', 'Liverpudlians' and 'Dicky Sam', the origin and development of the names 'w(h)acker' and 'scouser' are unclear. Was a 'w(h)acker' the person with whom you shared things – especially illegal spoils? Or did it derive from the name for pea-soup (in some as yet unexplained way)? Was it a term for a big man? A big Irishman? Both perhaps? And was 'scouse' originally lob's course – the dish of a fool or simpleton? Was it an English term used by Nordic seamen and thus lent to their languages? Or was it the imported Nordic (Scowegian perhaps) name for sailors' stew? And how did a term that evidently meant sailors in general – 'lobscousers' – come to mean Liverpool sailors specifically? Moreover, why did the shortened version of the name then come to designate people from the city in general? And why would 'Scouse', if its route did originate in the name of a stew, and then shift to a term for sailors, and afterwards the designation of people from Liverpool, finally come to mean the language/dialect/accent spoken in the city?[41] The answer to these questions is much the same as those examined earlier: it is simply not clear how and why most of these linguistic developments occurred. In other words, we don't know.

Conclusion

This chapter has attempted to outline the narratives that have become attached to the name of Liverpool and to the terms that have been, and still are in some cases, used for the inhabitants of the place. The stories are sometimes strange in their detail and often unreliable, or at least less than wholly convincing, in their conclusions. But perhaps this is beside the point, since it may be that there are simply no reliable answers to questions relating to the origin and development of the specific terms considered above. Instead, what may really matter about the word-stories is the importance that is attached to them, and the sense that they form part of the significant history of Liverpool and its people. The origins of words and names, after all, can often be pretty mundane or prosaic (in the case of 'Liverpool' for example, it may just be that it meant 'muddy pool'). What might in the end be more telling is the fact that people have sought to explain, clarify or even justify the words and names used to refer to Liverpool, its people and certain of its cultural practices. For as noted above, such explanations, clarifications and justifications are necessarily grounded in a confidence that the place, its inhabitants and its culture, are worthy of attention.

Notes

1 Stephan Jack, 'Dialect Expert', *Daily Post*, 6 October 1945.
2 Onomastics, or the study of place names, is a minor field today, but in the nineteenth century in particular it was an important element in linguistic research since the names of specific locations were considered to be significant both in terms of the history of the English language but also in relation to the history of the places themselves.
3 This definition was taken up by Thomas Carlyle. In *Past and Present* (1843), Carlyle imagined the twelfth-century Liverpool scene in characteristic tone: 'The Creek of the Mersey gurgles, twice in the four-and twenty hours, with eddying brine, clangorous with seafowl; and is a *Lither-Pool,* a *lazy* or sullen Pool, no monstrous pitchy City, and Seahaven of the world! The Centuries are big; and the birth-hour is coming, not yet come' (Carlyle 1918: 79).
4 The *Anas clypeata* is now known as the Northern Shoveller; seen from a particular perspective, it looks as much like the Liver bird as most ducks. The Liver bird has been identified as 'a dove, a shoveller duck, an eagle, and a hypothetical bird' (Baines 1836: II, 294), as well as a cormorant and an *Ibis falcinellus* (Glossy Ibis).
5 In his *Liverpool as it was … 1775–1800,* Richard Brooke cited a legal case in 1833 in which 25 variations on the name were listed (Brooke 1853: 15); Edward Baines' *History of the County Palatine and Duchy of Lancaster* (1836) gives 40.
6 Though claims about town charters before that of King John in 1207 persisted throughout the nineteenth century, the text that Troughton cited was a forgery. For a discussion of the fraud, see Brooke 1853: 18–21 and Muir and Platt 1906: 8.
7 In fact the 'ingenious suggestion' had been proposed by Baines' coadjutor, none other than W.R. Whatton; Whatton was responsible for the biographical portions of the work.
8 Baines claimed as supporting evidence the fact that various names of coastal towns included this element – as Lytham and Litherland (Lancashire), Lidford (Devon), Lithermore/Livermore (Suffolk) and Leith (Scotland). He also claims that Dublin's River Liffey had been called the Lith during the reign of King John.
9 The full description of the heraldic device of Liverpool is: 'ARMS: Argent a Cormorant in the beak a Branch of Seaweed called Laver all proper. CREST: On a Wreath of the Colours a Cormorant the wings elevated in the beak a Branch of Laver proper. SUPPORTERS: On the dexter Neptune with his Sea-Green Mantle flowing the waist wreathed with Laver on his head an Eastern Crown Gold in the right hand his Trident Sable the left supporting a Banner of the Arms of Liverpool on the sinister a Triton wreathed as the dexter and blowing his Shell the right hand supporting a Banner thereon a Ship under sail in perspective all proper the Banner Staves Or.' The motto is taken from Virgil: 'Deus nobis haec otia fecit' (God hath granted us this ease). The arms and crest were granted on 22 March 1797; the supporting emblems were granted on 23 March 1797.

10   Picton observes that 'a stuffed bird has from time immemorial been preserved in the town hall, supposed to be a specimen of the genus *liver*'; his somewhat bathetic gloss was that 'it is in reality an immature cormorant, which has not attained its final dark plumage' (Picton 1884: 350).

11   Harrison points out that in the English Dialect Society's glossaries for Lancashire and Cheshire, as well as Picton's account of the South Lancashire dialect, 'lither' is given as 'lazy', 'idle' and 'sluggish'. As noted earlier, 'sluggish' was the derivation given in Baxter's early eighteenth-century account.

12   In 'The Place–Names of North Wales', Richards notes that 'Liverpool' is often rendered 'Lerpwl' in Welsh, though 'Welsh amateur philologists' have called it 'Llynlleifiad' ('llyn' – 'lake' and 'Lleifiad' – 'Liver'). In the nineteenth century, he asserts, 'they evolved the spurious *Lle'rPwll* "Place of the Pool" or "Pit", which often appeared on the title-pages of Welsh books published in Liverpool' (Richards 1953: 248–49). Frank Shaw asked in a speculative and half-serious way whether 'Lyrpol' and its derivatives could have anything to do with Lir – the Irish God of the sea whose children were turned into swans. Shaw argued that 'it would be interesting to prove that Liverpool was half-Irish from its earliest times', but the putative claim is somewhat undermined by the suggestion that this might also be the origin of the name of the district, Old Swan (Shaw 1958b: 14).

13   The late nineteenth-century etymology of 'Viking' gave its derivation from Icelandic *vík* – creek, inlet or bay, with the suffix *ingr* – son of, belonging to – hence 'one who haunted the bays, creeks and fjords', Skeat, *Etymological Dictionary* (Clarendon, 1882) *s.v. viking*. The evidence suggests, however, that it is an earlier formation, in Anglo-Frisian, which may have been based on Old English *wíc* – camp, 'the formation of temporary encampments being a prominent feature of viking raids', *Oxford English Dictionary*, 2nd edn (Oxford, 1989), *s.v. viking*.

14   Ekwall's citation of 'liver-sea' is taken from the *OED*, which gives its use as 'now *hist[orical]*. a sea in which the water is said to be so thick or coagulated as to impede navigation'; *Oxford English Dictionary*, 2nd edn (Oxford, 1989), *s.v. liver* C3. Used by the late sixteenth-century Scottish poet Alexander Montgomerie to refer to the Gulf of Persia, the phrase was probably based on Teutonic precedent (Middle Dutch '*leversee*' or Middle Low German '*lēversē*'). The relevant, dreadful lines from Montgomerie's 'A Cartell of The Thre Ventrous Knights' (written in Scots) are:

> … we saild by syndry shoirs,
> And past the perillous gredy gulfe of Perse,
> And levir sees that syndry shippis devoirs;
> Quhare is no fish, bot monsters fell and feir[se ;]
> Quhais vgly shappis wer tyrsum to reherse (Montgomerie 1887: 213)

15   For a discussion of the election see Revd A. Hume, 'Account of the Liverpool Election 1670' in *Transactions of the Historic Society of Lancashire and Cheshire* (1854); a copy of Sir Gilbert Ireland's letter to the Earl of Derby is reproduced in the Appendix to the same volume, p. 8; Robert Bradshaigh's letter to Ireland is found on pp. 15–16.

16   A letter to the *Daily Post* (23 February 1957) suggested that the proper term for an inhabitant of Liverpool is Liverpudlian or Liverpuddler, on the basis that because of the number of broken pavements in the city there were puddles everywhere.

17   There is another, very modern (and rare) sense of 'Liverpudlian' recorded in the *OED*: 'the dialect or accent of people from Liverpool'. The supporting quotations date from the 1980s on. *Oxford English Dictionary*, 2nd edn (Oxford, 1989), *s.v. Liverpudlian* n 2. 'Liverpudlianese' had been suggested by a feature-writer in the *Liverpool Weekly News* (Anon 1958: 3).

18   See chapter four.

19 As noted in the previous chapter, in his contribution to the debate on the question 'Does Mr Gladstone Speak with a Provincial Accent?' Picton gladly embraced Gladstone as a fellow Dicky Sam (Picton 1888: 211).

20 The sobriquet was used by the owners of racing yachts and a clipper during the century. It was also the name of a coursing dog in the 1830s; 'Dicky Sam' had an un-distinguished if consistent record in the Southport meetings in 1836 and 1837 (ran twice, beaten twice).

21 The letters embossed into the doors of St George's Hall are in fact SPQL – Senatus Populusque Liverpudliensis, the Senate and People of Liverpool.

22 *Sámh* means 'peaceful, tranquil, restful or pleasant' in Irish, while the sense of *sámhaí* is 'easy-going person, sleepy, lazy'; Irish pronunciation rules would give [sa:v] and [sa:vi:]. 'Soft', in the sense of 'more or less foolish, silly, or simple; lacking ordinary intelligence or common-sense; easily imposed upon or deceived' ('soft lad' in contemporary Liverpool English) is given by the *OED* as a seventeenth-century coinage, though the more positive meaning of 'soft' as 'compassionate' or 'gentle' ('soft-hearted') is much earlier. *Oxford English Dictionary*, 2nd edn (Oxford, 1989), *s.v. soft adj 18a, 8a*.

23 In Chandler's *Liverpool*, he also described the Dicky Sam as a 'Liverpolitan born within the sounds of the chimes of St Nicholas's church' (Chandler 1957: 423). R.H. Wynn argued that the term referred to 'one born on Mann Island – West of George's Passage', an area consisting of the salt warehouse, two pubs, ship chandlers and some housing (Wynn 1957: 6). William C. Ford more or less agreed but had an even simpler explanation: a landlord of one of the pubs on Mann Island was called Richard Samuels, and 'sailors home would call for a drink there' (Ford 1957: 6).

24 In the sixteenth century, before 'Cockney' began to refer specifically to Londoners, it was a derogatory term for a townsman (in contrast to the sturdier countryman); *Oxford English Dictionary*, 2nd edn (Oxford, 1989), *s.v. cockney n 3*.

25 'Dicky' or 'dickey' was slang for 'a worn out shirt' (1781) and 'a detached shirt-front' (1811). *Oxford English Dictionary*, 2nd edn (Oxford, 1989), *s.v. dicky/dickey n 5, 6*.

26 The Century Dictionary, the other great American dictionary project, was likewise silent on the term. Belchem may have taken the point from an editorial response in the *Daily Post* in 1957 which commented that 'the modern school of thought con-siders [Dicky Sam] denotes "Imitation American," a sidelight on the city's pioneer links with the U.S.A' (Bindloss 1957: 6).

27 Evidence for the use of 'Dicky Sam' in the twentieth century was elicited by 'Rancid Ronald's' dismissive assertion that 'not one of my Merseyside friends, some of them well into their 80s, have ever heard a Liverpudlian referred to as a "Dicky Sam." Some of them consider it a myth carefully fostered by Mr. Shaw and the "Ekker"' (i.e. the *Liverpool Echo*) ('Rancid Ronald' 1963: 8). This drew a series of letters 'In Defence of Dicky Sam', including one from a correspondent who claimed that 'as for Dicky Sam, when I was a child between the two world wars, this was a common expression' (Butchard 1963: 6). All of the letter-writers confirmed that 'Dicky Sam' was in common use in the early twentieth century; it was also the name of a hard-boiled sweet.

28 Partridge's *Dictionary of Slang and Unconventional English* says that 'sammy' could on occasion be used as an abbreviation of 'Sammy Soft' (or even 'S.S.'), meaning 'fool' – from the 1840s. Partridge *Dictionary of Slang* (New York, 1961) *s.v. Sammy, Sammy Soft*. This sense supports Boult's claim cited earlier.

29 The context makes it clear that the correspondence concerns tips for gambling on horses; the note ends with the slightly enigmatic 'Strange that Dicky Sam should not be aware that a tizzy is the lowest price that will purchase us' (a 'tizzy' was a sixpenny-piece – here it may have been a reference to the cover price).

30   The eighteenth-century reference in the *OED* may well be taken from Fritz Spiegl's
     introduction to the first *Lern Yerself Scouse* volume in 1966, since there is no refer-
     ence to the work that Spiegl cites – Boulton's *The Sailor's Farewell; Or, the Guinea
     Outfit* – in the *OED*'s list of bibliographical sources. Nor is there any reference to
     Spiegl.
31   For an account of both the viciousness of the conditions on the slave ships for crew
     and slaves, and the topic of sexual predation on the slavers, see Marcus Rediker, *The
     Slave Ship. A Human History* (2008), chs. 7–9.
32   'Whacker' or 'wacker' do not feature in Lancashire dialect in the sense referred to
     here. Nodal and Milner's *Glossary of the Lancashire Dialect* (1875) giver 'wacker' as
     a verb meaning 'to shake, tremble, quiver' with citations from the mid eighteenth
     through to the late nineteenth centuries (Nodal and Milner 1875: 276). 'Whacker'
     also meant the equivalent of tall story or lie (compare 'whopper' in contemporary
     usage); *Oxford English Dictionary*, 2nd edn (Oxford, 1989), *s.v. whacker n* 2.
33   In the 'Echoes and Gossip of the Day' section of the *Liverpool Echo* on 11 May 1950,
     a correspondent reported a droll tale. A customer in the local pub, a Swedish sailor,
     was asked 'What did you have for tea tonight?' and answered 'For tea, my friend, I
     have very good "Scouse".' Puzzled by the laughter and the comment that he was 'a
     real Liverpudlian – a scouser in fact', the Swede replied 'Oh! You misunderstand –
     we call the vegetable and meat stew *scouse* all the time in Sweden!' (Anon 1950: 4).
34   In his column 'Over the Mersey Wall', an article by George Harrison (a local
     journalist, not the Beatle) on 'Scouse – The Great Whodunit' contrasted the
     opposing views but ended by citing an entry in a Norwegian encyclopaedia on
     'lobscous' that referred to it as 'a Lancashire dish' (Harrison 1964: 2). One recent
     etymology has challenged this account by asserting the derivation as the Latvian
     phrase 'labs' ('good') 'kauss' (bowl or ladle) – hence 'labs kauss' – 'good bowlful or
     ladleful' (Knobloch 1986: 5–6).
35   Spiegl noted the possibility that 'labskaus' was of German or Norwegian origin but
     concluded simply that 'the origin of Lobscouse is to be found in some ship's galley
     somewhere on the North Sea' (Spiegl 1966: 10). In the 1950s and 60s numerous
     letters were published in the local Liverpool papers, usually from exiles, asking for
     the recipe for 'scouse'. An editorial response in the *Liverpool Echo* (29 January 1958)
     obliged: '1lb of meat pieces (no fat), one or two neck chops, two Spanish onions,
     carrots, 2½ lb potatoes (cut small), pepper and salt. Put them all together in cold
     water, boil and then simmer for an hour or more. The longer the simmering the
     better the flavour. There are numerous variations on this recipe, of course. Blind
     scouse is one without meat' (Reynolds 1958: 6).
36   Other evidence of the spread of the terms into common use is furnished by their
     extension into different senses. Thus a story in the *Knickerbocker* magazine, pub-
     lished in New York in 1839, includes a reference to a table collapsing and 'making
     a fine lobscouse of all sorts of eatables' – the meaning in this case being a mess or
     mixture (*The Knickerbocker* 1839: 39). *Punch*, in an article in 1860 on the portrayal
     of lawyers in contemporary drama, noted the clichéd tendency of sailors to say to
     any lawyer that 'they'll make lobscouse of him' (*Punch* 1860: 2). The contemporary
     term might be 'to make mincemeat' out of someone.
37   In a letter to the *Daily Post*, R.H. Wynn asserted that 'the name Scouser for the
     Liverpool man is modern and I should say was created by the Royal Navy' (Wynn
     1957: 6).
38   The editorial comment is clear in ascribing the use of 'scouser' to 'the widespread
     liking of the citizenry [in the Scotland Road area] for soup reinforced with green
     vegetables, known as "scouse"' (Bindloss 1957: 6).
39   The *OED* record is of little help in this regard: its first attested use of 'scouse' or

'scouser' to describe a native or inhabitant of Liverpool dates from 1945 and is taken from a report of a judge stopping a trial to ask what the word means.

40 As demonstrated in chapter three, John Farrell's essay 'About that Liverpool Accent (or Dialect)' in 1950 is probably the first serious treatment of language in Liverpool, but Frank Shaw was the first to use the phrase 'the "scouse" language' (Shaw 1952: n.p.).

41 In *A Plea for Mersey. Or, The Gentle Art of Insinuendo* (1966), Peter Moloney, one of the workers in the Scouse industry, proposed the most outlandishly jocular derivation of 'Scouse': it was an acronym for 'Saxo-Celtic Oral Uniate Spoken English' – a 'nasal, glottal, plosive dialect unique to Merseyside' (Moloney 1966: 21).

Bibliography

Adams, Michael (ed.) (2009). 'Enregisterment: A Special Issue', *American Speech*, 84.2.

Agha, Asif (2003). 'The Social Life of Cultural Value', *Language and Communication*, 23, 231–71.

— (2005). 'Voice, Footing, Enregisterment', *Journal of Linguistic Anthropology*, 15.1, 38–59.

Aikin, John (1795). *A Description of the Country from Thirty to Forty Miles Round Manchester*, London: Stockdale.

Alford, Henry (1864). *A Plea for the Queen's English: Stray Notes on Speaking and Spelling*, 2nd edn, London.

Andersen, H., and R. Munck (1999). *Neighbourhood Images in Liverpool: 'It's All Down to the People'*, York: Rowntree Foundation.

Anderson, Benedict (1991). *Imagined Communities: Reflections on the Origin and Spread of Nationalism*, rev. edn, London: Verso.

Anon (1765). *The Geography and History of England*, London: Dodsey.

— (1812). *The Stranger in Liverpool; Or, An Historical and Descriptive View of the Town of Liverpool and Its Environs*, 3rd edn, Liverpool: Kaye.

— (1821). 'D.S', *The Kaleidoscope; or, Literary and Scientific Mirror*, 96.

— (1824). 'New County Prison at Kirkdale, Near Liverpool', *Liverpool Mercury*, 7 May, 358.

— [Dicky Sam] (1827). 'A Conundrum', *Liverpool Mercury*, 21 September, 302.

— [A Yorkshireman] (1833). 'A Trip to Paris with Mr. Jorrocks', *New Sporting Magazine*, V.25, 30–41.

— (1841). 'Dicky Sam is Anything but a Sammy', *The Era*, 14 November, n.p.

— [A Liverpudlian] (1845). 'Irregularity of Railway Trains', *Liverpool Mercury*, 1 August, 7.

— [A Dicky Sam] (1854). 'The Amusements at Liverpool', *The Era*, 8 March, 18.

— (1870). 'Liverpool Meeting of the British Association for the Advancement of Science, September, 1870', *Athenaeum*, 2237, 327–30.

— ['Dicky Sam'] (1884). *Liverpool and Slavery: An Historical Account of the Liverpool-African Slave Trade, By a Genuine 'Dicky Sam'*, Liverpool: Bowker.

— (1890). 'Liverpool Police Court', *Liverpool Mercury*, 14 January, 8.

— (1931a). 'Street Names of Liverpool. Interesting Facts about their Origin', *Liverpool Post and Mercury*, 28 October, 5.

— (1931b). 'The Defects of Dialect', *Liverpool Post and Mercury*, 28 November, 4.

— (1950). 'Scouse', *Liverpool Echo*, 11 May, 4.

— [A "Daily Post" London Reporter] (1954a). 'Play Posed Accent Problems But… B.B.C. Found Liverpool as It Is Spoken', *Daily Post*, 5 May, 1.

— (1954b). 'We All Talk Sailors' Slang', *Liverpool Echo*, 9 October, 4.

— [A "Daily Post" Reporter] (1955). 'A Proper Jangle in Scouser Lingo', *Daily Post*, 1 July, 6.

— (1958). 'The First Lesson', *Liverpool Weekly News*, 6 November, 3.

— [A "Daily Post" Reporter] (1961). 'Dese Scousers, Like, Said De Scouse Was Gear', *Daily Post*, 6 June, 3.

Ascott, Diana, Fiona Lewis and Michael Power (2006). *Liverpool 1660–1750: People, Prosperity and Power*, Liverpool: Liverpool University Press.

Austin, T. Jr (1868). 'Dickey Sam', *Notes and Queries*, 4th series, I, 546.

Bailey, W. Ashcroft (1957). 'More About Scouse', *Liverpool Echo*, 7 August, 6.

Baines, Edward (1836). *History of the County Palatine and Duchy of Lancaster by Edward Baines … The Biographical Department by W.R. Whatton*, London: Fisher, Son & Co.

Baines, Thomas (1852). *The History of the Commerce and Town of Liverpool and of the Rise of Manufacturing Industry in the Adjoining Counties*, London: Longman, Brown, Green and Longmans.

Bakhtin, M.M. (1981). *The Dialogic Imagination: Four Essays*, ed. Michael Holquist, Austin: University of Texas Press.

Bamford, Samuel (1850). *Dialect of South Lancashire, Or Tim Bobbin's Tummus and Meary Revised and Corrected*, Manchester: Heywood.

Barrell, John (1983). *English Literature in History 1730–80: An Equal Wide Survey*, London: Hutchinson.

Baxter, William (1719). *Glossarium Antiquitatum Britannicarum, sive Syllabus Etymologicus Antiquitatum Veteris Britanniæ atque Iberniæ Temporibus Romanorum*, London: Bowyer.

Beal, Joan (2009). 'Enregisterment, Commodification, and Historical Context: "Geordie" versus "Sheffieldish"', in Adams 2009: 138–56.

Behrendt, Stephen (2007). 'Human Capital in the British Slave Trade', in Richardson et al. 2007: 66–97.

Belchem, John (1997). '"An accent exceedingly rare": Scouse and the Inflexion of Class', in *Languages of Labour*, ed. John Belchem and Neville Kirk, Aldershot: Ashgate, 99–130.

— (2000a). *Merseypride: Essays in Liverpool Exceptionalism*, Liverpool: Liverpool University Press.

— (2000b). '"An accent exceedingly rare": Scouse and the Inflexion of Class' [revised], in Belchem 2000a: 31–64.

— (ed.) (2006). *Liverpool 800. Culture, Character and History*, Liverpool: Liverpool University Press.

— (2007a). *Irish, Catholic and Scouse: The History of the Liverpool-Irish, 1800–1939*, Liverpool: Liverpool University Press.

— (2007b). 'Liverpool: World City', *History Today*, 57, 48–55.

Belchem, John, and Donald MacRaild (2006). 'Cosmopolitan Liverpool', in Belchem 2006: 311–91.

Bex, Tony, and Richard Watts (1999). *Standard English: The Widening Debate*, London: Routledge.

Bidston, T.J. (1955). untitled letter, *Daily Post*, 19 April, 4.

Bindloss, R.H. (1957). 'Why Scouser?', *Daily Post*, 28 June, 6.

Bobbin, Tim [John Collier] (1748). *A View of the Lancashire Dialect; By Way of Dialogue, between Tummus o'Williams, o'f Margit o'Roafs, an Meary o'Dicks, o'Tummy o'Peggy's. Containing the Adventures & Misfortunes of a Lancashire Clown*, 2nd edn revised, Leeds: Lister.

Boland, Philip (2008). 'The Construction of Images of People and Place: Labelling Liverpool and Stereotyping Scousers', *Cities*, 25, 355–69.

— (2010). 'Sonic Geography, Place and Race in the Formation of Local Identity: Liverpool and Scousers', *Geografiska Annaler: Series B, Human Geography*, 92.1, 1–22.

Boult, Joseph (1871). 'Speculation on the Former Topography of Liverpool and its Neighbourhood', Pt III, *Proceedings of the Liverpool Literary and Philosophical Society*, XXV, 11–38.

Boulton, Thomas (1768). *The Sailor's Farewell; Or, the Guinea Outfit*, Liverpool: printed for the author.

— (1773). *The Voyage, a Poem in Seven Parts*, Boston: printed for the author.

Bourdieu, Pierre (1991). *Language and Symbolic Power*, Cambridge: Polity.

Bright, William (1997). 'Editorial Note', *Language in Society*, 26.3, 469.

Briscoe, Diana (2003). *Wicked Scouse English*, London: Michael O'Mara.

Britain, David (2007). *Language in the British Isles*, Cambridge: Cambridge University Press.

Brocken, Michael (2005). *The British Folk Revival 1944–2002*, Farnham: Ashgate.

— (2010). *Other Voices: Hidden Histories of Liverpool's Popular Music Scenes, 1930s–1970s*, Farnham: Ashgate.

Brontë, Emily (1995). *Wuthering Heights* (1847), Oxford: Oxford University Press.

Brooke, Richard (1853). *Liverpool as it was during the Last Quarter of the Eighteenth Century, 1775–1800*, Liverpool: Mawdsley.

Brophy, John (1934). *Waterfront*, New York: Macmillan.

— (1946). *City of Departures*, London: Collins.

Brown, Jacqueline Nassy (2005). *Dropping Anchor, Setting Sail: Geographies of Race in Black Liverpool*, Princeton: Princeton University Press.

Brown, R., and A. Gilman (1960). 'The Pronouns of Power and Solidarity', in *Style in Language*, ed. T.A. Sebeok, Cambridge: MIT Press, 253–76.

Burke, Thomas (1910). *Catholic History of Liverpool*, Liverpool: Tinling.

Burke, Peter (2004). *Languages and Communities in Early Modern Europe*, Cambridge: Cambridge University Press.

Burton, Sir Robert (1806). *The Anatomy of Melancholy. What It Is, With All the Kindes, Causes, Symptomes, Prognosticks, And Severall Cures of It* (1621), London: Hodson.

Butchard, R. (1963). 'In Defence of Dicky Sam', *Liverpool Echo*, 9 September, 6.

Camden, William (1590). *Britannia siue Florentissimorum Regnorum, Angliae, Scotiae, Hiberniae, et insularum adiacentium ex intima antiquitate chorographica descriptio*, London.

Campbell, George (1776). *The Philosophy of Rhetoric*, 2 vols., London.

Carlyle, Thomas (1918). *Past and Present* (1843), New York: Scribner's.

Cassidy, Daniel (2007). *How the Irish Invented Slang*, Petrolia, CA: Counterpunch.

Chalmers Lyon, J. (1955). 'Liverpool Dialect', *Daily Post*, 18 April, 6.

Chandler, George (1953). *William Roscoe of Liverpool*, London: Batsford.

— (1957). *Liverpool*, London: Batsford.

Chapman, Malcolm (1992). *The Celts: The Construction of a Myth*, Basingstoke: Macmillan.

Cheshire, Jenny (1999). 'Spoken Standard English', in Bex and Watts 1999: 129–48.

Christian, M. (1995). 'Black Struggle for Historical Recognition in Liverpool', *North-West Labour History – Black Presence in the North West*, 20, 58–66.

Clarke, Mrs Richard (1962). 'Let's Have Good Sensible Speech', *Liverpool Echo*, 26 June, 6.

Clough, Arthur Hugh (1888). *Prose Remains of Arthur Hugh Clough. With a Selection from his Letters and a Memoir. Edited by his Wife*, London: Macmillan.

Coles, Gladys Mary (1993). *Both Sides of the River: Merseyside in Poetry and Prose*, West Kirby: Headland.

Colman, J.C. (1950). 'Furly Airly', *Daily Post*, 9 August, 4.

Colvin, Christina (ed.) (1971). *Maria Edgeworth. Letters from England 1813–1844*, Oxford: Clarendon.

Cope, W.H. (1883). *A Glossary of Hampshire Words and Phrases*, London: Trübner and Co. for the English Dialect Society.

Cross, H.J. (1951). *No Language But A Cry*, London: John Murray.

Crowley, Tony (1989). *The Politics of Discourse: The Standard Language Question in British Cultural Debates*, London: Macmillan.

— (1996). *Language in History: Theories and Texts*, London: Routledge.

— (2003). *Standard English and the Politics of Language*, London: Palgrave.

— (2005). *Wars of Words: The Politics of Language in Ireland 1537–2004*, Oxford: Oxford University Press.

Dana, R.H. (1869). *Two Years Before the Mast. A Personal Narrative* (1840), Boston: Fields Osgood.

Daresbury, C.M. (1950). 'Sleeper's Hill – How It Was Named', *Liverpool Echo*, 21 December, 5.

Davie, Donald (2002). *Collected Poems*, Manchester: Carcanet.

Dawson, G.K. (1951). 'Oldsters Will Remember Them. Street Characters of a Bygone Day', *Liverpool Echo*, 5 January, 4.

Defoe, Daniel (2005). *A Tour Through the Whole Island of Great Britain* (1724–26), ed. Pat Rogers, Harmondsworth: Penguin.

de Lyon, H. (1981). 'A Sociolinguistic Study of Aspects of the Liverpool Accent', unpublished MPhil thesis, University of Liverpool.

Dent, Susie (2010). *How to Talk Like a Local: From Cockney to Geordie*, London: Random House.

De Quincey, Thomas (2000). 'Confessions of an English Opium Eater' (1821, 1856), in *The Works of Thomas De Quincey*, ed. Barry Symonds et al., 21 vols., London: Pickering and Chatto, vol. II.

Derrick, Samuel (1767). *Letters Written From Leverpoole, Chester, Corke, The Lake of Killarney, Tunbridge-Wells, and Bath*, 2 vols., Dublin: Faulkner et al.

Dibdin, Mr (1781). 'Nautical Philosophy', in *The Bull-Finch. Being a Choice Collection of the Newest and Most Favourite English Songs*, London: Robinson and Baldwin, 194–95.

Dickens, Charles (1987). *The Uncommercial Traveller and Reprinted Pieces*, Oxford: Oxford University Press.

Dinneen, Patrick (1927). *Foclóir Gaedhilge agus Béarla. An Irish–English Dictionary*, Dublin: Irish Texts Society.

Dolan, T.F. (2004). *A Dictionary of Hiberno-English*, 2nd edn rev., Dublin: Gill and Macmillan.

Duffy, Carol Ann (1994). *Selected Poems*, Harmondsworth: Penguin.

Dunn, Douglas (2008). '*English. A Scottish Essay*', *Archipelago*, 2, 25–34.

Du Noyer, Paul (2007). *Liverpool: Wondrous Place. Music from the Cavern to the Capital of Culture*, London: Virgin Books.

D.W.F.H. (1951). 'Gaelic Words', *Liverpool Echo*, 3 January, 3.

Eagleton, Terry (1995). *Heathcliff and the Great Hunger: Studies in Irish Culture*, London: Verso.

Eden, Sir Frederic Morton (1797). *The State of the Poor: or, an History of the Labouring Classes in England, From the Conquest to the Present Period*, London: Davis.

Edgeworth, Maria and Richard (1802). *Essay on Irish Bulls*, London.

Ekwall, Eilart (1922). *The Place-Names of Lancashire*, Manchester: Manchester University Press.

Ellis, A.J. (1889). *On Early English Pronunciation*, Part V, London: Philological Society.

Enfield, William (1773). *An Essay Towards the History of Leverpool*, Warrington.
— (1774). *The Speaker: or, Miscellaneous Pieces, Selected from the Best English Writers...
    To which is Prefixed an Essay on Elocution*, London: Johnson.
*English Dialect Dictionary, being the complete vocabulary of all dialect words still in use,
    or known to have been in use during the last two hundred years; founded on the pub-
    lications of the English Dialect Society and on a large amount of material never before
    printed*, ed. Joseph Wright, 6 vols., London: Frowde, 1898–1905.
Farrell, John (1950a). 'About that Liverpool Accent (or Dialect)', *Daily Post*, 9 August, 4.
— (1950b). 'A Guide to the Slang of Merseyside. This Half-Secret Tongue of Liverpool',
    Daily Post, 25 August, 4.
Fitzgerald, Edward (1921). *Rubáiyát of Omar Khayyám*, New York: Crowell.
Fleming Prout, Leonard (1950). 'Fleming's Phrase', *Liverpool Echo*, 18 December, 4.
Ford, William C. (1957). 'Who Was Dicky Sam?', *Liverpool Echo*, 21 August, 6.
— (1964). 'They Called Her "Tilly Mint"', *Liverpool Echo*, 31 July, 4.
Frank, Robert (1966). 'That Scouser Accent... It's an Asset Now', *Liverpool Echo*, 2
    March, 8.
Freethy, Ron (2007). *Made Up Wi' Liverpool: A Salute to the Scouse Dialect*, Newbury:
    Countryside Books.
Frost, Diane (2000). 'Ambiguous Identities: Constructing and De-constructing Black
    and White "Scouse" Identities in Twentieth Century Liverpool', in *Northern
    Identities: Historical Interpretations of 'The North' and 'Northernness'*, ed. Neville
    Kirk, Aldershot: Ashgate, 195–217.
Gal, Susan, and Judith T. Irvine (1995). 'The Boundaries of Languages and Disciplines:
    How Ideologies Construct Difference', *Social Research*, 62.4, 967–1001.
Garnett, Ron (1995). *Liverpool in the 1930s and the Blitz*, Preston: Palatine.
Gaskell, Elizabeth (1996). *Mary Barton* (1848), Harmondsworth: Penguin.
Goldrein, Sonia (1962). 'Teach Yourself Wacker', *Liverpool Echo*, 7 November, 10.
Grant, Anthony (2007). 'Looking (Literally) at Liverpool English: Thoughts on the
    Popular (and Less Popular) Documentation of Scouse Lexicon', in Grant and Grey
    2007: 141–63.
Grant, Anthony, and Clive Grey (eds) (2007). *The Mersey Sound. Liverpool's Language,
    People and Places*, Ormskirk: Open House Press.
Grant, Peter (2008). *Talk Like the Scousers*, Liverpool: Trinity Mirror.
Green, Jonathon (2010). *Green's Dictionary of Slang*, 3 vols., London: Chambers.
Grey, Clive (2007). 'Directions of Change in Contemporary Scouse: Reflections on
    Issues of Origin and Empirical Evidence', in Grant and Grey 2007: 189–214.
Grey, Clive, and Anthony Grant (2007). 'Liverpool's English: *Scouse*, or *Liverpudlian*, if
    You Prefer', in Grant and Grey 2007: 1–16.
Griffith, R. (1950). 'Liverpool Slang', *Liverpool Echo*, 14 December, 2.
Griffiths, Niall (2002). *Kelly + Victor*, London: Jonathan Cape.
— (2003). *Stump*, London: Jonathan Cape.
— (2005). *Wreckage*, London: Jonathan Cape.
— (2008). *Real Liverpool*, Bridgend: Seren.
Grindon, Leo (1892). *Lancashire. Brief Historical and Descriptive Notes* (1882), London:
    Seeley.
Grose, Francis (1785). *A Classical Dictionary of the Vulgar Tongue*, London: Hooper.
Gumperz, John J. (2009). 'The Speech Community' (1968), in *Linguistic Anthropology:
    A Reader*, ed. A. Duranti, Oxford: Wiley-Blackwell, 66–73.
Hackwood, R.W. (1889). 'Dicky Sam', *Notes and Queries*, 7th series, VIII, 332.
Haggerty, Sheryllynne (2006). *The British-Atlantic Trading Community, 1760–1810:
    Men, Women, and the Distribution of Goods*, Leiden: Brill.
Haigh, J.L. (1907). *Sir Galahad of the Slums*, Liverpool: Liverpool Booksellers Company.

Hall, Robert (1963). *Idealism in Romance Linguistics*, Ithaca, NY: Cornell University Press.

Hamer, Andrew (2005). 'BBC Voices: Liverpool', http://www.bbc.co.uk/liverpool/content/articles/2005/01/14/voices_linguist_feature.shtml

Harrison, George (1958). 'Our Dockers' Speech on the Air', *Liverpool Evening Express*, 8 January, 5.

— (1964). 'Scouse – The Great Whodunit', *Liverpool Echo*, 29 January, 2.

Harrison, Henry (1898). *The Place-Names of the Liverpool District; Or, the History and Meaning of the Local and River Names of South-West Lancashire and of Wirral*, London: Elliot Stock.

Harrison, Tony (2006). *Selected Poems*, Harmondsworth: Penguin.

Haugen, Einar (1966). 'Dialect, Language, Nation', *American Anthropologist*, 68.4, 922–35.

Harvey, Ted (1950). 'Liverpool Lingo', *Liverpool Echo*, 20 December, 2.

Heaney, Seamus (1984). *Station Island*, London: Faber and Faber.

Heywood, Thomas (1861). 'On the South Lancashire Dialect', *Chetham Miscellanies*, 57, vol. 3, Manchester: Chetham Society, 3–84.

Hickey, R. (2007). *Irish-English. History and Present-Day Forms*, Cambridge: Cambridge University Press.

Hocking, Silas (1966). *Her Benny* (1879), Liverpool: Gallery Press.

Hodgkinson, Kenneth (1960). 'Save Our Scouse – The Dying Language of Liverpool', *Daily Post*, 2 December, 11.

Holbrow, F.G. (1964). 'It's De Gear!', *Liverpool Echo*, 29 January, 6.

Holland, Philémon (1610). *Britain, or A Chorographicall Description of the Most Flourishing Kingdomes, England, Scotland, and Ireland, and the Ilands Adioyning… written first in Latine by William Camden. Translated newly into English by Philémon Holland Doctour in Physick*. London.

Honey, John (1989). *Does Accent Matter?* London: Faber and Faber.

Honeybone, P. (2001). 'Lenition Inhibition in Liverpool English', *English Language and Linguistics*, 5.2, 213–49.

— (2007). 'New Dialect Formation in Nineteenth-Century Liverpool: A Brief History of Scouse', in Grant and Grey 2007: 106–40.

Horton, Steven (2002). *Street Names of the City of Liverpool*, Birkenhead: Countyvise.

Hotten, John Camden (1860). *A Dictionary of Modern Slang, Cant, and Vulgar Words Used at the Present Day in the Streets of London, the Universities of Oxford and Cambridge, the Houses of Parliament, the Dens of St. Giles, and the Palaces of St. James: Preceded by a History of Cant and Vulgar Language: with Glossaries of Two Secret Languages, Spoken by the Wandering Tribes of London, the Costermongers, and the Patterers*, 2nd edn, London: printed by the author.

— (1869). *The Slang Dictionary: or, the Vulgar Words, Street Phrases, and "Fast" Expressions of High and Low Society*, 2nd edn, London: printed by the author.

Hughes, A. and Peter Trudgill (1996). *English Accents and Dialects*, 3rd edn, London: Edward Arnold.

Hughes, Glyn (1963). 'Talking Proper', *Daily Post*, 30 January, 4.

Hume, Revd A. (1854). 'Account of the Liverpool Election 1670', *Transactions of the Historic Society of Lancashire and Cheshire*, 6, 4–17 and Appendix 1–26.

— (1878). 'Remarks on the Irish Dialect of the English Language', *Transactions of the Historic Society of Lancashire and Cheshire*, 30, 93–140.

Hutton, Catherine (1891). *Reminiscences of a Gentlewoman of the Last Century: The Letters of Catherine Hutton*, ed. Catherine Hutton Beale, Birmingham: Cornish Bros.

Isenberg, David (1962). 'A Second Language – Standard English', *Liverpool Echo*, 9 July, 6.

Jespersen, Otto (1925). *Mankind, Nation and the Individual*, Oslo: Aschehoug.

Johnstone, Barbara (2004). 'Place, Globalization and Linguistic Variation', in *Socio-linguistic Variation: Critical Reflections*, ed. Carmen Fought, Oxford: Oxford University Press, 65–83.

Johnstone, Barbara, Jennifer Andrus and Andrew Danielson (2006). 'Mobility, Indexicality and the Enregisterment of "Pittsburghese"', *Journal of English Linguistics*, 34.2, 77–104.

Jones, H. (1955). 'Child's Play Of Old Liverpool', *Daily Post*, 21 April, 5.

Jones, J.W. (1955). 'Liverpool Dialect', *Daily Post*, 19 April, 4.

Jones, T. (1935). 'Liverpool Slang', *Liverpool Post and Mercury*, 15 June, 5

Joseph, John E. (2006). '"The grammatical being called the nation." History and the Construction of Political and Linguistic Nationalism', in *Language and History. Integrationist perspectives*, ed. Nigel Love, London: Routledge, 120–41.

Joyce, James (1992a). *Dubliners* (1914), Harmondsworth: Penguin.

— (1992b). *Portrait of the Artist as a Young Man* (1916), Harmondsworth: Penguin.

— (1992c). *Ulysses* (1922), Harmondsworth: Penguin.

Joyce, P.W. (1991). *English as we Speak it in Ireland* (1910), Dublin: Wolfhound Press.

Kavanagh, Ted (1949). *Tommy Handley*, London: Hodder and Stoughton.

Kelly, Stan (1964). *Liverpool Lullabies – The Stan Kelly Song Book*, London: Sing.

Kerr, John (1966). 'The Origin of Wacker', *Liverpool Echo*, 8 August, 6.

Knickerbocker, The (1839). 'Man Overboard', 13, 35–41.

Knobloch, Johann (1986). 'Labskaus', *Muttersprache*, 96, 5–6.

Knowles, Gerald (1973). 'Scouse: The Urban Dialect of Liverpool', unpublished PhD thesis, University of Leeds.

— (1978). 'The Nature of Phonological Variables in Scouse', in *Sociolinguistic Patterns in British English*, ed. Peter Trudgill, London: Edward Arnold, 80–90.

Labov, William (1972). *Sociolinguistic Patterns*, Philadelphia: University of Pennsylvania Press.

Lane, Tony (1997). *Liverpool: City of the Sea*, Liverpool: Liverpool University Press.

Langton, J., and P. Laxton (1978). 'Parish Registers and Urban Structure; The Example of Eighteenth Century Liverpool', *Urban History Yearbook*, Leicester: Leicester University Press, vol. 5, 74–84.

Lawton, Richard (1953). 'Genesis of Population', in Smith et al. 1953: 120–31.

Laxton, P. (1981). 'Liverpool in 1801: A Manuscript Return for the First National Census of Population', *Transactions of the Historic Society of Lancashire and Cheshire*, 73–103.

Lewis, David (2010). *Liverpool. The Illustrated History of Liverpool's Suburbs*, Derby: Derby Books.

Linacre Lane [pseud.] (1966). *Lern Yerself Scouse. Volume 2: The ABZ of Scouse*, Liverpool: Scouse Press.

Liverpool Record Office (n.d.). Newspaper cuttings relating to dialect and slang, 1931–1972, prepared in Liverpool City Library, Hq 427 CUT.

Lloyd, R.J. (1899). *Northern English: Phonetics, Grammar, Text*, Leipzig: Trübner.

Lloyd-Jones, Thomas (1981). *Liverpool Street Names*, Liverpool: published by the author.

Longmore, Jane (2006). 'Civic Liverpool: 1680–1800', in Belchem 2006: 113–69.

Lovgreen, T.J. (1955) 'Daddy Bunchy', *Liverpool Echo*, 16 March, 6.

Lowry, Malcolm (2000). *Under the Volcano*, Harmondsworth: Penguin.

M (1864). 'Liverpool', *Notes and Queries*, 3rd series, VI, 473.

Macklin, Edward (1963). 'It's a Libel!', *Liverpool Echo*, 4 April, 8.

McCartney, Helen (2005). *Citizen Soldiers: The Liverpool Territorials in the First World War*, Cambridge: Cambridge University Press.

M.G.M. (1874). 'Horrocks, the Astronomer', *Dublin University Magazine*, LXXIII, 709–20.

Mills, David (1976). *The Place Names of Lancashire*, London: Batsford.

Milroy, Lesley (1980). *Language and Social Networks*, Oxford: Blackwell.

Milton, John (1998). *The Complete Poems*, ed. John Leonard, Harmondsworth: Penguin.

Milward, Maria (1843). 'The Winter Night's Club', *The Southern Literary Messenger*, 9, 38–56.

Minard, Brian (1972). *Wersia Sensa Yuma? The Third Volume of the Scouse Press Thesaurus of Merseyside Words and Phrases*, Liverpool: Scouse Press.

Mistrolis (1964). 'About Dem Scuffers', *Liverpool Echo*, 19 October, 8.

Mitchell, Linda (2001). *Grammar Wars: Language as Cultural Battlefield in 17th and 18th Century England*, Aldershot: Ashgate.

Mitford, Nancy (2002). *Noblesse Oblige* (1956), Oxford: Oxford University Press.

Moloney, Peter (1966). *A Plea for Mersey. Or, The Gentle Art of Insinuendo*, Liverpool: Gallery Press.

Montgomerie, Alexander (1887). *The Poems of Alexander Montgomerie*, ed. James Cranstoun, Edinburgh: Blackwoods.

Montgomery, Chris (2007). 'Perceptions of Liverpool English', in Grant and Grey 2007: 164–88.

Morgan, Kenneth (2007) 'Liverpool's Dominance in the British Slave Trade, 1740–1807', in Richardson et al. 2007: 14–42.

Morley, Paul (2007). 'Liverpool Surreal', in *Centre of the Creative Universe: Liverpool and the Avant-garde*, ed. Christoph Grunenberg and Robert Knifton, Liverpool: Liverpool University Press, 42–52.

Moryson, Fynes (1908). *An Itinerary* (1617), vol. III, Glasgow: MacLehose.

Moss, William (1784). *A Familiar Medical Survey of Liverpool*, Liverpool: Hodgson.

— (1796). *The Liverpool Guide*, Liverpool: Crane and Jones.

Mugglestone, Lynda (2003). *Talking Proper: The Rise of Accent as Social Symbol*, 2nd edn, Oxford: Oxford University Press.

Muir, Ramsay, and Edith Mary Platt (1906). *A History of Municipal Government in Liverpool From the Earliest Times to the Municipal Reform Act of 1835*, London: Norgate and Williams for Liverpool University Press.

Mulhearn, Deborah (2007). *Mersey Minis*, 5 vols., Liverpool: Capsica.

Munck, Ronaldo (ed.) (2003). *Reinventing the City: Liverpool in Comparative Perspective*, Liverpool: Liverpool University Press.

Neal, Frank (1998). *Black '47: Britain and the Famine Irish*, Basingstoke: Macmillan.

Nevin, Charles (2006). *Lancashire, Where Women Die of Love*, London: Mainstream.

Newbolt, Sir Henry (1921). *The Teaching of English in England: Being the Report of the Departmental Committee Appointed by the President of the Board of Trade to Enquire into the Position of English in the Educational System of England*, London: HMSO.

Newbrook, Mark (1982). 'Sociolinguistic Reflexes of Dialect Interference in West Wirral', unpublished PhD thesis, University of Reading

— (1986). *Sociolinguistic Reflexes of Dialect Interference in West Wirral*, Frankfurt: Peter Lang.

Nodal, John H., and George Milner (1875–82). *A Glossary of the Lancashire Dialect*, Manchester: Ireland.

Notan, C.H. (1950). 'Liverpool Lilt', *Daily Post*, 9 August, 4.

Nordhoff, Charles (1856). *The Merchant Vessel: A Sailor Boy's Voyages to See the World*, Cincinnati: Moore, Wilstach, Keys.

Oakes Hirst, T. (1951). 'Liverpool Speech: Some Local Pronunciations', *Daily Post*, 29 January, 4.

Ó Dónaill, Niall (2005). *Foclóir Gaeilge-Béarla*, Baile Átha Cliath: An Gúm.

O'Hanri, Hari [an scríob] (1950). 'It's the Irish in Us', *Liverpool Echo*, 13 December, 2.

— [Harry O'Henry] (1955). 'Irish Influence in Speaking Scouse', *Liverpool Echo*, 16 March, 6.
— [—] (1964). 'It's De Gear!', *Liverpool Echo*, 29 January, 6.
O'Henry, Harry, see O'Hanri, Hari.
O'Neill, Michael (1990). *The Stripped Bed*, London: Colins Harvill.
Opie, Iona and Peter (1959). *The Lore and Language of Schoolchildren*, Oxford: Clarendon.
Owen, Alun (1961). *Three TV Plays*, London: Jonathan Cape.
Oxford English Dictionary, prepared by J.A. Simpson and E.S.C. Weiner, 20 vols., Oxford: Clarendon, 2nd edn, 1989.
Partridge, Eric (1961). *Dictionary of Slang and Unconventional English*, New York: Macmillan.
Peyton, V.J. (1771). *The History of the English Language*, London: Hilton.
Phelan, Jim (1948). *The Name's Phelan. The First Part of the Autobiography of Jim Phelan*, London: Sidgwick and Jackson.
Picton, J.A. (1866). 'The South Lancashire Dialect', *Proceedings of the Literary and Philosophical Society of Liverpool* (1864–65), XIX, 17–56.
— (1875). *Memorials of Liverpool. Historical and Topographical*, 2nd edn rev., 2 vols., Liverpool: Walmsley.
— (1884). 'The Bird "Liver"', *Notes and Queries*, 6th series, IX, 350.
— (1888). 'Does Mr. Gladstone speak with a Provincial Accent', *Notes and Queries*, 7th series, VI, 210–11.
Pooley, Colin (2006). 'Living in Liverpool: The Modern City', in Belchem 2006: 171–255.
'Postman' (1931a). 'Nix', *Liverpool Post and Mercury*, 20 October, 5.
— (1931b). 'With Sugar', *Liverpool Post and Mercury*, 26 October, 5.
— (1931c). 'The Artful Dodger', *Liverpool Post and Mercury*, 27 November, 5.
— (1931d). 'The Artful "Dodger"', *Liverpool Post and Mercury*, 28 November, 5.
— (1932a). 'Tatting', *Liverpool Post and Mercury*, 21 January, 5.
— (1932b). 'More about the "Wet Nellie"', *Liverpool Post and Mercury*, 18 February, 5.
— (1933a). Untitled article, *Liverpool Post and Mercury*, 4 April, 7.
— (1933b). 'Moss Nor Sand', *Liverpool Post and Mercury*, 5 April, 7.
— (1936). 'A Merseyside Carol', *Liverpool Post and Mercury*, 17 December, 5.
— (1937a). 'Liverpool Language', *Liverpool Post and Mercury*, 15 March, 6.
— (1945a). 'Easter Custom', *Daily Post*, 5 April, 2.
— (1945b). 'Those "Pace-Eggers"', *Daily Post*, 9 April, 2.
— (1945c). 'Rationed Revels', *Daily Post*, 1 May, 2.
— (1945d). 'Dialect Expert', *Daily Post*, 6 October, 2.
— (1945e). 'Jigger', *Daily Post*, 11 December, 5.
— (1947a). 'Another "Jigger"', *Daily Post*, 24 June, 4.
— (1947b). 'Jowlers', *Daily Post*, 25 June, 6.
— (1950). 'Correct Form', *Daily Post*, 27 September, 4.
— (1955). 'Lazy Talk', *Daily Post*, 4 May, 4.
— (1965a). 'The Rubaiyat's Gone Scouse', *Daily Post*, 16 June, 4.
— (1965b). 'Classic Course', *Daily Post*, 15 July, 4.
— (1966a). 'Lern Yerself Scouse Den', *Daily Post*, 12 July, 6.
— (1966b). 'The Vicar Makes his Point', *Daily Post*, 2 August, 6.
— (1968). 'Paradise Lost', *Daily Post*, 9 June, 4.
Potter, Humphry (1795). *A New Dictionary of all the Cant and Flash Languages, both Ancient and Modern; used by Gipsies, Beggars, Swindlers, Shoplifters, Peterers, Starrers, Footpads, Highwaymen, Sharpers, And every Class of Offenders, from a Lully Prigger to a High Tober Gloak*, London: Mackintosh.
Price, George (1950). 'Liverpool Slang', *Daily Post*, 15 August, 4.
Priestley, J.B. (1934). *An English Journey; Being a Rambling but Truthful Account of What*

One Man Saw and Heard and Felt and Thought during a Journey Through England during the Autumn of the Year 1933, London: Heinemann.

Punch (1860). 'Stage-Lawyers', XXXVIII, 7 January, 2.

— (1864). 'Dickey-Sam Latin', XLVII, 30 April, 186.

'Rancid Ronald' (1963). 'Scouse Not So Exclusive', *Liverpool Echo*, 4 September, 8.

Rao, G. Subba (1954). *Indian Words in English: A Study in Indo-British Cultural and Linguistic Relations*, Oxford: Clarendon.

Ray, John (1674). *A Collection of English Words not Generally Used, with their Significations and Original in Two Alphabetical Catalogues, the One of Such as are Proper to the Northern, the other to the Southern Counties*, London.

Rediker, Marcus (2008). *The Slave Ship. A Human History*, Harmondsworth: Penguin.

Reynolds, Anthony (1958). 'Scouse', *Liverpool Echo*, 29 January, 6.

R.H.W. (1951). 'Parapet', *Liverpool Echo*, 9 January, 2.

Richards, G. Melville (1953). 'The Place-Names of North Wales', in Smith et al. 1953: 242–50.

Richardson, David, Suzanne Schwarz and Anthony Tibbles (eds) (2007). *Liverpool and Transatlantic Slavery*, Liverpool: Liverpool University Press.

Rigby, Barbara (1950). 'In Liverpool "I felt myself in Dublin"', *Liverpool Echo*, 9 August, 4.

Robberds, John (1862). 'History of Toxteth-Park Chapel', *The Christian Reformer; Or, Unitarian Magazine and Review*, new series, XVIII, 343–61.

Roberts, Eleazar (1893). *Owen Rees: A Story of Welsh Life and Thought*, Liverpool: Foulkes.

Roberts, Thomas A. (1986). 'The Welsh Influence on the Building Industry in Victorian Liverpool', in *Building the Industrial City*, ed. Martin Doughty, Leicester: Leicester University Press, 106–49.

Robinson, Peter (ed.) (1996). *Liverpool Accents. Seven Poets and a City*, Liverpool: Liverpool University Press.

Roscoe, William (1853). *The Poetical Works of William Roscoe. Published in Honour of the Centenary of his Birthday*, Liverpool: Young.

Ross, A.S.C. (1954). 'Linguistic Class-Indicators in Present-Day English', *Neuphilologische Mitteilungen* 55, 113–49.

Routledge, F.J. (1914). 'Liverpool and Irish Politics in the Sixteenth Century', in *A Miscellany Presented to John MacDonald Mackay*, ed. Oliver Elton, Liverpool: Liverpool University Press, 142–56.

Rumsey, Alan (1990). 'Wording, Meaning and Linguistic Ideology', *American Anthropologist*, new series, 92.2, 346–61.

Rush, Len (1966). 'Let's Give the Cult a Rest', *Daily Post*, 5 January, 6.

Russell, William Clark (1889). 'Marooned', *Macmillan's Magazine*, LIX, 67–68, 146–77, 264–81, 321–38, 401–25.

Sampson, George (1925). *English for the English. A Chapter on National Education*, Cambridge: Cambridge University Press.

Sampson, Kevin (1998). *Awaydays*, London: Jonathan Cape.

— (2001). *Outlaws*, London: Jonathan Cape.

— (2002). *Clubland*, London: Jonathan Cape.

— (2006). *Stars are Stars*, London: Jonathan Cape.

Sangster, C. (1999). 'A Study of Lenition of /t/ and /d/ in Liverpool English', unpublished MPhil thesis, University of Oxford.

— (2001). 'Lenition of Alveolar Stops in Liverpool English', *Journal of Sociolingustics* 5.3, 401–12.

Saunders Jones, R. (1919). *A Few Interesting Details about Garston and District*, Liverpool: Rockliff.

Saussure, Ferdinand de (1983). *Course in General Linguistics* (1916), trans. Roy Harris, London: Duckworth.

Schuchardt, Hugo (1972). 'On Sound Laws: Against the Neogrammarians' (1885), in *Schuchardt, the Neogrammarians and the Transformational Theory of Phonological Change*, ed. Theo Vennemann and Terence Wilbur, Frankfurt: Athenäum, 39–72.

Scott, Dixon (1907). *Liverpool*, London: Black.

Sexton, Carole (1996). *Confessions of a Judas-burner: A Social History of Judas Burning in the South End of Liverpool*, Little Neston: Cherrybite Publications.

Shannon, Richard (1982). *Gladstone*, vol. I, London: Hamish Hamilton.

Sharples, Joseph (2004). *Pevsner Architectural Guide to Liverpool*, London: Yale University Press.

Shaw, Frank (1950a). 'Liverpool Dialect', *Daily Post*, 18 October, 4.

— (1950b). 'Liverpool's Dialect is his Hobby', *Daily Post*, 1 November, 5.

— (1950c). 'Scouse Lingo – How It All Began', *Liverpool Echo*, 8 December, 4.

— (1951). 'Way of Speech', *Liverpool Echo*, 9 January, 2.

— (1952). *The Scab: a one act play set in Liverpool during the General Strike, 1926. With a Note on the Liverpool Way of Talking*, typescript (author's personal copy), Liverpool Record Office.

— (1955a). 'Do You Want to Speak Scouse?', *Liverpool Echo*, 3 March, 6.

— (1955b). 'Death of a Dialect', *Manchester Guardian*, 20 April, 18.

— (1955c). 'Scouse is the Gear', *The Civil Service Author*, 16.3, 5–11.

— (1956). 'The Liverpool Indicator', *Punch*, 30 May, 8–9.

— (1957a). *Scouse Talks* (text, with translations, of tape sound recordings made in Liverpool City Library), Liverpool Record Office.

— (1957b). 'Scouse Lingo is Preserved for Posterity', *Liverpool Echo*, 16 July, 6.

— (1957c). 'What Songs will be Sung about Speke and Kirkby?', *Liverpool Echo*, 20 August, p. 4.

— (1958a). 'Beware of a "Destroyer" when at the Docks… He may be after a Sub', *Liverpool Weekly News*, 30 January, 3.

— (1958b). 'Dialect of a Seaport I: Dicky Sam, Frisby Dyke, Scouse', *Journal of the Lancashire Dialect Society*, 8, 12–19.

— (1958c). 'There's Poetry in Liverpool', *Liverpool Echo*, 9 October, 6.

— (1958d). 'The Talking Streets of Liverpool', *Liverpool Echo*, 25 October, 6.

— (1958e). 'Malapudlianisms', *Liverpool Echo*, 30 December, 6.

— (1959a). 'Dialect of a Seaport II' [no subtitle], *Journal of the Lancashire Dialect Society*, 9, 32–41.

— (1959b). 'Strange Charm of the Lingo of Liverpool's Dockland', *Liverpool Echo*, 30 July, 6.

— (1960a). 'Dialect of a Seaport III: Rhymes, Games, Pub Names', *Journal of the Lancashire Dialect Society*, 10, 30–42.

— (1960b). 'Ink, Lino and the Lenient Judge', *Liverpool Echo*, 20 June, 5.

— (1962a). 'The Origins of Liverpoolese: Evolution of a Lingo', *Liverpool & Merseyside Illustrated*, January, 9–10.

— (1962b). 'Liverpoolese, Yes, But I Don't Like Scouse', *Liverpool Echo*, 14 June, 8.

— (1962c). 'A Skinful of Words', *Liverpool Echo*, 11 October, 6.

— (1962d). 'Parlez Vous Scouse, La?', *Liverpool Echo*, 14 November, 12.

— (1962e). 'Twenty Scouser Questions – How Well Do You Know Your Liverpoolese?', *Liverpool Echo*, 21 December, 6.

— (1963a). 'Merseyside Should Nurse its Scouse, but Reject Bad English', *Daily Post*, 28 January, 6.

— (1963b). 'In Love with the Pier Head Budgies', *Liverpool Echo*, 7 March, 6.

— (1964). 'It's the Gear! – But How Did the Expression Start?', *Liverpool Echo*, 17 January, 12.

— (1966a). *The Oxtail Book of Verse: 'For Folk's Sake' and Other Liver Lyrics, with Music*, Liverpool: Gear Press.

— (1966b). 'Liverpool Doctors Hear the Strangest Things', *Liverpool Echo*, 2 February, 8.

— (1966c). 'Ollies in the Liverpool Olympics', *Daily Post*, 8 August, 4

— (1966d). 'Diddy Men Man the Boundary', *Daily Post*, 12 August, 6.

—(1966e). 'Buy a Bewk, Ref!', *Times Literary Supplement*, 1 September, 781.

— (1969). *You Know Me Anty Nelly? Liverpool Children's Rhymes. Compiled with Notes on Kids' Games and Liverpool Life*, Liverpool: Gear Press.

— (1970). *You Know Me Anty Nelly? Liverpool Children's Rhymes. Compiled with Notes on Kids' Games and Liverpool Life*, 2nd edn, Foreword by Peter Opie, London: Wolfe.

— (1971). *My Liverpool*, London: Wolfe.

Shaw, Frank, Fritz Spiegl and Stan Kelly (1966). *Lern Yerself Scouse. How to Talk Proper in Liverpool, A Teach-Yourself Phrase Book By Frank Shaw. Edited with Notes and Translations by Fritz Spiegl and a Scouse Poem by Stan Kelly*, Liverpool: Scouse Press.

— (2000). *Lern Yerself Scouse. How to Talk Proper in Liverpool (Millennium Reprint)*, Liverpool: Scouse Press.

Shaw, Frank, and Revd Dick Williams (1967). *The Gospels in Scouse*, Liverpool: Gear Press.

Shaw, George Bernard (1957). *Pygmalion, A Romance in Five Acts* (1912), Harmondsworth: Penguin.

Shaw, H.R. (1950). 'Liverpool Accent', *Daily Post*, 4 August, 2.

Sheridan, R.B. (1975). *Sheridan's Plays*, ed. Cecil Price, Oxford: Oxford University Press.

Sheridan, Thomas (1762). *A Dissertation on the Causes of the Difficulties, which occur, in Learning the English Tongue. With a Scheme for Publishing an English Grammar and Dictionary, upon a Plan Entirely New. The Object of which shall be, to Facilitate the Attainment of the English Tongue, and Establish a Perpetual Standard of Pronunciation*, London: Dodsley.

Silverstein, Michael (1995). 'Shifters, Linguistic Categories and Cultural Description', in *Language, Culture and Society. A Book of Readings*, ed. B. Blount, 2nd edn, Long Grove, Il: Waveland, 187–221.

— (1998). 'Contemporary Transformations of Local Linguistic Communities', *Annual Review of Anthropology*, 27, 401–26.

— (2003). 'Indexical Order and the Dialectics of Sociolinguistic Life', *Language and Communication*, 23 193–229.

— (2004). '"Cultural" Concepts and the Language–Culture Nexus', *Current Anthropology*, 45, 621–52.

Simpson, Matt (1995). *Catching up with History*, Newcastle: Bloodaxe.

Skeat, W.W. (1882). *An Etymological Dictionary of the English Language*, Oxford: Clarendon.

— (1896). 'Liverpool', *Notes and Queries*, 8th series, IX, 173–74.

Smith, Don (1955). 'How the "Scousers" Found their Dialect', *Daily Herald*, 25 February, 5.

Smith, Neville (1971). *Gumshoe*, London: Fontana.

Smith, W., F.J. Monkhouse and H.R. Wilkinson (eds) (1953). *A Scientific Survey of Merseyside*, Liverpool: University Press of Liverpool for the British Association.

Smollett, Tobias (1758). *The Adventures of Peregrine Pickle. In which are included, Memoirs of a Lady of Quality*, vol. I, London: Baldwin and Richardson.

Smyth, William Henry (1867). *The Sailor's Word-Book. An Alphabetical Digest of Nautical Terms*, London: Blackie.

Sorensen, Janet (2000). *The Grammar of Empire in Eighteenth Century British Writing*, Cambridge: Cambridge University Press.

Spear, Jack (1964). 'It's De Gear!', *Liverpool Echo*, 29 January, 6.

Spiegl, Fritz (1962). *Scouser Songs: An Entertaining Evening of Old Liverpool Street Ballads, Sea Shanties and Folk Songs*, programme for concert at Philharmonic Hall, 3 March 1962, Liverpool: n.p.

— (1966a). 'Scouse about the House', *Daily Post*, 12 July, 10.

— (1966b). *Lern Yerself Scouse. Volume 2: The ABZ of Scouse by Linacre Lane, B.Sc. (Bachelor of Scouse)*, Liverpool: Scouse Press.

— (1989). *Lern Yerself Scouse. Volume 4: The Language of Laura Norder*, Liverpool: Scouse Press.

Spiegl, Fritz, Andrée Owen, Hanny Hieger and Masahiro Kurokawa (2000). *Scouse International: The Liverpool Dialect in Five Languages*, Liverpool: Scouse Press.

Stonehouse, James (1869). *The Streets of Liverpool. With Some of their Distinguished Residents, Reminiscences and Curious Information of Bygone Times*, Liverpool: Edward Howell.

Strong, Herbert A. (1896). 'Liverpool', *Notes and Queries*, 8th series, IX, 233.

Sweet, Henry (1908). *The Sounds of English*, Oxford: Clarendon.

Sweet, Rosemary (1997). *The Writing of Urban Histories in Eighteenth Century England*, Oxford: Clarendon.

Swift, Revd J.M. (1937). *The Story of Garston and its Church*, Garston: Proffit.

Syers, Robert (1830). *The History of Everton*, Liverpool: Robinson and Marples.

Taylor, Isaac (1896). 'Liverpool', *Notes and Queries*, 8th series, IX, 233.

Taylor, Joseph (2010). 'Chaucer's Uncanny Regionalism: Rereading the North in *The Reeve's Tale*', *Journal of English and Germanic Philology*, 109.4, 468–89.

Thomas, T.L. (1963). 'Scouse Words', *Daily Post*, 30 January, 4.

Tirebuck, William (1891). *Dorrie: A Novel*, London: Longmans, Green and Co.

Touzeau, J. (1910). *The Rise and Progress of Liverpool from 1551 to 1835*, 2 vols., Liverpool: Liverpool Booksellers Company.

Troughton, Thomas (1810). *History of Liverpool. From the Earliest Authenticated Period Down to the Present Time*, Liverpool: Robinson.

Trudgill, Peter (1984). *Language in the British Isles*, Cambridge: Cambridge University Press.

— (1999). *The Dialects of England*, 2nd edn, Oxford: Blackwell.

Turner, Frank (1954). 'A Curious Custom: The Judas Penny', *Folklore*, 65.1, 47.

Vaux, James Hardy (1819). *New and Comprehensive Vocabulary of the Flash Slang*, in *Memoirs of James Hardy Vaux*, vol. II, London: Clowes.

Wallace, James (1795). *A General and Descriptive History of the Ancient and Present State of the Town of Liverpool*, Liverpool: Phillips.

Wales, Katie (2006). *Northern English. A Social and Cultural History*, Cambridge: Cambridge University Press.

Walsh, Helen (2004). *Brass*, Edinburgh: Canongate.

Ward, Ned (1708). *The Wooden World Dissected*, London: Moore.

Watson, Kevin (2002). 'The Realisation of Final /t/ in Liverpool English', *Durham Working Papers in Linguistics*, 8, 195–205.

— (2006). 'Phonological Resistance and Innovation in the Northwest of England', *English Today*, 22.2, 55–61.

— (2007a). 'The Phonetics and Phonology of Plosive Lenition in Liverpool English', unpublished PhD thesis, Edge Hill College/Lancaster University.

— (2007b). 'Liverpool English', *Journal of the International Phonetics Association*, 37.3, 351–60.

— (2007c). 'Is Scouse getting Scouser? Exploring Phonological Change in Contemporary Liverpool English', in Grant and Grey 2007: 106–40.

Watts, Richard (1999). 'The Social Construction of Standard English: Grammar Writers as a Discourse Community', in Bex and Watts 1999: 40–68.

Wells, J.C. (1982). *Accents of English*, 2 vols., Cambridge: Cambridge University Press.

Welsh, Jack (1964). 'We Owe these Wackers more than We Know', *Liverpool Echo*, 23 March, 8.

Wesley, John (1768). *An Extract of the Rev. Mr. John Wesley's Journal, from February 16, 1755, to June 16, 1758*, Bristol: Pine.

Whatton, W.R. (1817). 'On the Etymology of the Word *Liverpool*', *The Gentleman's Magazine*, LXXXVII, ii, 505–08.

Whittington-Egan, Richard (1955a). 'Liverpool Dialect is Dying Out', *Liverpool Echo*, 14 April, 6.

— (1955b). 'Liverpool Dialect', *Liverpool Echo*, 18 April, 6.

— (1955c). 'Is Liverpool Dialect Dying Out?', in Richard Whittington-Egan, *Liverpool Colonnade*, Liverpool: Philip, Son and Nephew, 216–20.

— (1957). 'Afoot in Allerton', in *Liverpool Roundabout*, Liverpool: Philip, Son and Nephew, 103–08.

— (1972). 'Scouse Isn't What It Used To Be', *Liverpool Echo*, 30 July, 10.

Wilding, C. (1962). 'Model Girls... Until You Hear Them Speak!', *Liverpool Echo*, 12 June, 6.

Willett, John (1966). 'Buy a Bewk, Ref!', *Times Literary Supplement*, 25 August, no. 3365: 763.

— (1967). *Art in a City*, London: Methuen for the Bluecoat Society of Arts.

Williams, Alice (1964). 'She Remembers "Tilly Mint"', *Liverpool Echo*, 6 August, 6.

Williams, Raymond (1965). *The Long Revolution*, Harmondsworth: Penguin.

Williamson, R. (1753). *The Liverpool Memorandum-book; or, Gentleman's, Merchant's and Tradesman's Daily Pocket-Journal, for the Year M,DCC,LIII*, London: Williamson.

Wilson, William [Mrs. Oliphant?] (1852). *The Melvilles*, 3 vols., London: Bentley.

Withers, Philip (1789). *Aristarchus, or the Principles of Composition*, 2nd edn, London: Moore.

Wright, M. (1951). 'Word Explained', *Liverpool Echo*, 1 January, 4.

W.T.M. (1855). 'Dickey Sam', *Notes and Queries*, 1st series, XII, 226.

— (1868a). 'Dickey Sam', *Notes and Queries*, 4th series, I, 493.

— (1868b). 'Dickey Sam', *Notes and Queries*, 4th series, I, 570.

Wyld, H.C. (1907). *The Growth of English*, London: Murray.

— (1909). *Elementary Lessons in English Grammar*, Oxford: Clarendon.

Wyld, H.C., and T. Oakes Hirst (1911). *The Place Names of Lancashire. Their Origin and History*, London: Constable and Co.

Wynn, R.H. (1957). 'Lob-scouse', *Daily Post*, 8 July, 6.

Index

Reynolds, A. 164 n.35
Richards, G.M. 162 n.12
Rigby, B. 47
Robberds, John 139 n.7
Roberts, Eleazar 139 n.8
Roberts, Thomas 139 n.7
Robinson, Peter 125–6, 127, 127–8
Roscoe, William 36 n.5, 69, 117–8, 122,
    125, 136
Rose Hill 82 n.19
Ross, A.S.C. 72, 82 n.22
Rowbotham, Sheila 128
Royal African Company 3
Royal Liverpool Philharmonic Orchestra
    84
rum 4
Rumsey, Alan 112 n.13
Runyon, Damon 64, 80 n.3
rural cultural practices 8, 9, 10, 18
Rush, Len 108, 113 n.30
Russell, William Clark 159

sailors 5, 11, 16, 31, 32–3, 35, 38 n.23, 44,
    46, 57 n.3, 61 n.41, 61 n.48, 127, 147
    n.30, 155, 156, 157, 158, 159, 160, 163
    n.23, 164 n.33, 164 n.36
Saint Edward's College xiii, 128–9, 131
Saint Francis of Assisi (church and
    school) 125
Saint Helens 128–9
Saint Malachy's (church and school) 83
    n.29, 120, 140 n.12
Saint Patrick 119, 120, 139 n.9
Saint Patrick's Chapel 119–20, 139 n.9, 139
    n.10, 140 n.12
salt 1, 2, 50, 124, 163 n.23
salt fish 83 n.31, 108
Sampson, George 104
Sampson, Kevin 129–30, 141 n.20
San Diego 134
Santa Cruz 134
Saunders Jones, R. 43, 124
Saussure, Ferdinand de 93, 112 n.10
Sayle, Alexei 110
scally 79, 108, 137
Schuchardt, Hugo 95
Scotland 2, 24, 28, 31, 101, 161 n.8
Scotland Road 40, 42, 45, 48, 52, 76, 80
    n.3, 81 n.13, 82 n.19, 84 n.35, 108, 109,
    130, 140 n.19, 160, 164 n.38

Scots 46, 48, 60 n.38, 107, 162 n.14
Scott, Dixon 20, 39, 107
Scottish 72, 112 n.10,
Scouse (dish) xiii, 53, 61 n.46, 69, 72, 75,
    107, 156–9, 160, 164 n.33, 164 n.34,
    164 n.35, 164 n.36, 164 n.38
Scouse (language) xi, xii, xiv, xv, xvi n.3,
    15, 16, 18–19, 20, 21–2, 24, 26–9, 36
    n.3, 37 n.6, 37 n.7, 37 n.8, 37 n.9, 37
    n.11, chs. 3–5 passim, 115, 131, 132,
    136–7, 140 n.12, 140 n.20, 141 n.22,
    141 n.23, 141 n.28, 143, 155, 156–9,
    160, 164 n.30, 164 n.33, 164 n.34, 164
    n.35, 164 n.36, 164 n.38, 164 n.39, 165
    n.40, 165 n.41
    as form of cultural capital 131
    Bootle Scouse 79, 141 n.22
    Dingle Scouse 79, 141 n.22
    Scally Scouse 79
    Slummy Scouse 22
Scouse industry xv, 20, 37 n.9, 40, 52, 55,
    63–80, 84 n.36, 155, 165 n.41
Scouse Museum 85 n.39
Scouseness 109
Scouseology 83 n.30
Scouser xi, xiii, xiv, xv, xvi n.3, 53, 55, 61
    n.46, 63, 67, 71, 72, 73, 75, 76, 77, 79,
    80 n.3, 81 n.12, 82 n.15, 83 n.29, 84
    n.34, 108, 111 n.1, 111 n.9, 115, 131, 137,
    140 n.19, 141 n.26, 141 n.29, 143, 155,
    156, 158, 159–60, 164 n.33, 164 n.37,
    164 n.38, 164 n.39
Second World War 44, 56, 75, 82 n.22,
    106, 109, 123, 155
Sectarianism 16, 17, 22, 77, 107, 121
semantic change xiii, xv
Sexton, Carole 58 n.19
Shakespeare, William 132, 134, 148
Shannon, Richard 38 n.16
Sharp, Cecil 64
Sharples, Edward 139 n.10
Shaw, Frank xiv, 20, 22, 35, 36 n.1, 37 n.9,
    44, 47, 48, 49, 50, 55, 58 n.17, 58 n.20,
    59 n.22, 59 n.31, 60 n.35, 60 n.39, 61
    n.40, 63–86, 87, 89, 107, 108, 109, 111
    n.6, 140 n.19, 141 n.21, 151, 154, 160,
    162 n.12, 163 n.27, 165 n.40
    My Liverpool 37, 75, 80 n.4, 83 n.29
    Scouse Talks 67, 78
    The Scab 49, 60 n.39, 67, 78, 81 n.10, 130